2023

For my good friend. Judy Leo,
Thank you for your friendship
for so many years!
Michael

Charlie Brown's Christmas Miracle

The INSPIRING, UNTOLD STORY of
the MAKING of
a HOLIDAY CLASSIC

✦

Charlie Brown's Christmas Miracle

MICHAEL KEANE

CENTER
STREET
New York • Nashville

Center Street
Hachette Book Group
1290 Avenue of the Americas, New York, NY 10104
centerstreet.com
twitter.com/centerstreet

First Edition: October 2023

Center Street is a division of Hachette Book Group, Inc. The Center Street name and logo are trademarks of Hachette Book Group, Inc.

The publisher is not responsible for websites (or their content) that are not owned by the publisher.

Center Street books may be purchased in bulk for business, educational, or promotional use. For information, please contact your local bookseller or the Hachette Book Group Special Markets Department at special.markets@hbgusa.com.

Print book interior design by Bart Dawson

Library of Congress Cataloging-in-Publication Data

Names: Keane, Michael, 1960- author.
Title: Charlie Brown's Christmas miracle : the inspiring, untold story of
    the making of a holiday classic / Michael Keane.
Description: Nashville : Center Street, 2023.
Identifiers: LCCN 2023015279 | ISBN 9781546004905 (hardcover) | ISBN
    9781546004929 (ebook)
Subjects: LCSH: Charlie Brown Christmas (Television program) | Christmas
    television programs--United States--History and criticism. |
    Television--Production and direction--United States.
Classification: LCC PN1992.77.C45 K43 2023 | DDC
    791.45/72--dc23/eng/20230602
LC record available at https://lccn.loc.gov/2023015279

ISBNs: 9781546004905 (hardcover), 9781546004929 (ebook)

Printed in the United States of America

LSC-C

Printing 1, 2023

For all the Hutchinson women—
My grandmother,
Frances (Dee Dee) Kilcoyne Hutchinson;
My mother and aunts,
Margaret (Peggy), Felicia, Attracta,
Ursula, Imelda, Loretta, Marese;
And my sisters and cousins,
Terry, Margee, Loretta Ann, Jeannine, Patricia,
Regina, Ursula Jeanne, Philippa, Nicole, Bethany

And Mary said, "Behold, I am the servant of the Lord; let it be to me according to your word." And the angel departed from her.

—Luke 1:38

CONTENTS

CHARACTERS

The Coca-Cola Company

J. PAUL AUSTIN,
president of the Coca-Cola Company

ROBERT W. WOODRUFF,
chairman and CEO of the Coca-Cola Company

CBS

WILLIAM S. PALEY,
chairman and CEO of CBS

FRANK STANTON,
president of CBS

JAMES T. AUBREY,
president of CBS Network Programming

McCann-Erickson

MARION HARPER Jr.,
chairman and CEO of Interpublic Group of Companies

JOHN ALLEN,
vice president of McCann-Erickson

NEAL GILLIATT,
vice president of McCann-Erickson

NEIL REAGAN,
head of West Coast operations, McCann-Erickson

Time Magazine

RICHARD BURGHEIM,
contributing editor

The Creators

LEE MENDELSON,
producer, Lee Mendelson Film Productions

CHARLES M. SCHULZ,
cartoonist, creator of the *Peanuts* comic strip

BILL MELENDEZ,
animator and director, Bill Melendez Productions

VINCE GUARALDI,
Grammy-winning jazz composer and pianist

Other

BISHOP JAMES PIKE,
Episcopal bishop of California

REV. CHARLES GOMPERTZ,
Episcopal priest, San Francisco

MAX WEISS,
cofounder of Fantasy Records

PREFACE

✦

PREDAWN
TAL AFAR, IRAQ
DECEMBER 2003

Sir, the colonel needs to see you outside." I immediately bolt upright on my cot. From a deep, blackout sleep from exhaustion a moment ago, I'm now fully awake, my mind sharp and racing with worry. The soldier retreats back into the hallway. In the darkness it would be impossible to search his face for any hint of what's happening. But something must be wrong. I don't need to dress, since I sleep fully clothed, with my boots on, so in a moment I'm on my feet.

I scan the hallway left and right, looking for our translator, but he's not here. An Iraqi who apparently spoke little to no English had somehow become our interpreter. Soldiers, who have a wicked gift for nicknames, came to call him Mr. No Problem, because, as we approached any tense situation, he would guide us with the only two phrases in English that he seemed to know: *Problem* and *No problem*. After an initial period of exasperation, we quickly discovered that in a war zone the man's limited vocabulary provided a Zen-like clarity into almost any situation. (Years later I would find myself nostalgic for his succinct guidance when, for example, I was trying to discern the nuance in a text received after an argument, or wondering about the significance of a missed call from a doctor's office after an examination, or when walking down an unfamiliar street at night past impenetrable faces. *Problem* or *No Problem?*)

I follow my messenger outside into the starless night, moving carefully in the inky blackness. For days everything in the sky has been obscured by a cataract of dust, reducing even the sun to an obscure orb, like the pupil of a milky eye. I see the colonel who is standing stiffly in the dark, not far from the complex of buildings housing our brigade. When he sees me there is no greeting, his face emotionless, his hands thrust in his pockets. I halt, waiting for him to break the silence with some news, but there is nothing but awkwardness. He then nods to someone whose presence I hadn't even noticed. My memory of what happens next is oddly both vivid and blurry, like the afterimage following the stun of a flash-bang grenade.

Memories in a war zone are a pastiche of wide-ranging styles and impressions. (*Pastiche* being a word that would have subjected me to endless ribbing if I had ever used it on a patrol. *What? Pasta-teesh? Is that an Italian dish?*) It's a cliché that war is a mash-up of comedic and tragic, sometimes both in the same day, or even the same moment. My own memories are a Bohemian Rhapsody of recollections: a photorealistic mental snapshot of two grieving lieutenants whose beloved sergeant had been gunned down by the enemy; the profane grumbling and annoyed looks of soldiers subsisting for a third day on only cereal with strawberry milk because a promised supply truck had still not appeared; the feeling of isolation from soldiers avoiding standing next to me on a patrol, and the sergeant explaining sheepishly, *Because, well, you look like somebody important* (I wasn't important, but I was older, and, as the soldiers understood, the distinction could be lost through the telescopic sight of a sniper rifle); the pained face of our chaplain delivering a halting benediction before a patrol, overcome with emotion, before stepping back and waving us off with the stern admonition "Just be careful!"; the dull eyes and impassive face of an Iraqi man slowly edging toward me outside our base, throwing open his garment to reveal a mortar shell, and how my heart stopped before I realized that, instead of detonating it, he was surrendering it to me; the warmth in my lap from a steaming hot meal of turkey and mashed potatoes wrapped in tinfoil and delivered on New Year's Eve; our convoy sneaking out of our outpost at night through an adjacent cemetery to avoid the gunfire we would typically receive when we exited from the front gate (and the irony of my terror being greater in the graveyard of tilted tombstones eerily illuminated by moonlight than in the encounter with the enemy).

The colonel nods, and there is a second's pause before the darkness is shattered by a brilliant white floodlight. I follow his eyes, and I see the dramatic focal point of his attention—it's a surreal scene of a majestic evergreen tree, fifteen feet in height, surrounded by a semicircle of soldiers. The tree's rich green color defies adjectives and is further accentuated by the monochromatic setting of endless mud and dirt and paper-bag-brown buildings. A perfectly formed triangle of branches and pine needles, the tree is unadorned with any decorations. Even the most dazzling ornament would have seemed a vulgar affront to the evergreen's dignified and imposing beauty.

The colonel allows me a moment to drink in the scene before he speaks. "Merry Christmas." Until that moment, I had not realized that it was Christmas Day. After a few seconds of stunned silence, I am forced to ask the obvious question. *A tree? In the middle of the desert? How?* The colonel's mischievous eyes pair with a lopsided grin. He nods to my right. "He got it. In Syria." I look over my shoulder, and a disheveled uniform steps forward. A beaming Mr. No Problem. "Christmas tree. No problem." Suddenly I'm overwhelmed with a powerful feeling of déjà vu. And in a flashback it comes to me.

A scene that was imprinted on my memory so many Christmases ago. The singular tree. Encircled by smiling faces in the dark. I blink away tears. But the emotion is too powerful. I close my eyes, and I'm magically transported away. Away from the war. Away from fear. And away from the sorrow that had brought me here.

In my mind I see a small boy desperately fiddling with a tuning knob to horizontally stabilize the flickering images of a tiny black-and-white television perched precariously on a chair. He's anxious because it's only minutes before the broadcast begins, and he doesn't want to miss a second. He can't miss a moment. It's only thirty precious minutes, and then it's over. Until the next year. He struggles to properly position the rabbit-ear antenna, a task made more difficult because one of the ears is broken and a coat hanger has been appropriated to improve the reception. Finally everything is adjusted, if not perfectly, as best it can be. So the boy sits on the floor, his eyes inches away from the screen. He watches the final minutes of the news broadcast and is awed by the televised images of American soldiers fighting in the jungle, in a distant war that he struggles to understand. He sits impatiently through commercials. And then it begins with the strains of a melancholic melody and images of skating cartoon characters, tracing loops and circles on a frozen pond.

I close my eyes. And I'm home. We're all home.

✦ ✦ ✦

When I returned from Iraq, I wanted to write a story that would honor the sacrifices made by the US military members and their families who were separated at Christmastime. After a subsequent posting to Afghanistan, I recalled in my own childhood I had been thrilled by the tracking of Santa Claus on Christmas Eve by the North American Aerospace Defense Command (NORAD).

Building on that military tradition, which dates to 1955, I crafted a story that revolved around Santa Claus being lost in a blizzard while being tracked by NORAD. A military team eventually rescues Santa, but so much time has elapsed by the time he and his team of reindeer are discovered that Santa is unable to deliver all his toys to the world's children before they awaken on Christmas Day. (Spoiler alert: the Army, Navy, Marines, Air Force, and Coast Guard all work together to use their planes, tanks, trucks, submarines, and ships to help deliver Santa's presents on time and save the day!)

In truth I had written the story for the eyes of only one reader, my young niece, Katie, whose two parents were both officers in the military, one of whom was deployed overseas at the time. I wrote the story on Christmas Day and emailed it to her parents. Later that day, when I received a call and heard peals of laughter, it was the best Christmas present an uncle could receive. Emboldened by the positive review from my diminutive critic, I sent the story to a publisher shortly thereafter. I was shocked when, just days later, the president of the publishing house called me saying they loved it and wanted to publish it. (Note to prospective authors: this never happens!) The book was published as *The Night Santa Got Lost: How NORAD Saved Christmas*, and received glowing reviews from readers, military mom blogs, and the *School Library Journal*.

Many of the book's fans told me that they felt the story had a cinematic feel. Noted illustrator Michael Garland had done a phenomenal job with the story's artwork, and the story itself (which in the micro-pitch lingo of Hollywood can be summarized as "Santa with jets!") has a certain *Top Gun* type of flair to it. Fueled by that encouragement, I set out to produce an animated adaptation of the book. That process immersed me in the fascinating world of animation, including script writing, storyboarding, computer animation, casting voice talent, and recording a musical soundtrack. I had become familiar with the process of filmmaking while serving as an executive with Digital Domain, a leading Hollywood digital movie studio, which was founded by famed director James Cameron and notables Scott Ross and Stan Winston. Like any other endeavor, however, there is no substitute for rolling up your sleeves and diving into your own project.

As part of the research for my own production, I began to look more closely at other animated Christmas specials, including *Mr. Magoo's Christmas Carol*, *Rudolph the Red-Nosed Reindeer*, *How the Grinch Stole Christmas*, *Frosty the Snowman*, and, of course, *A Charlie Brown Christmas*. Perhaps because it had been my favorite as a child, I focused on the story of the making of the *Peanuts* special. I was enthralled by the against-all-odds challenges that the program faced with only a six-month production schedule. I learned that Schulz was a combat veteran of World War II, which gave me a newfound appreciation for the cartoonist's annual shout-out to famed Army cartoonist Bill Mauldin in the *Peanuts* comic strip, as well as for Snoopy's aerial engagements with the Red Baron and his adventures behind enemy lines. (In addition to Schulz, all the other principals behind the creation of the special were veterans of the US military, including Lee Mendelson, Bill Melendez, and Vince Guaraldi.)

I thought the story of the making of the special would be an interesting book, providing more context for the millions of fans of the Charlie Brown Christmas special as well as fans of the *Peanuts* comic strip. I felt that my own work producing an animated short film as well as my personal wartime experience could bring an understanding of Charles Schulz's frame of mind in 1965 as he worked on the special. As with any artistic creation, I quickly concluded that the story was impossible to understand without telling the personal stories of those involved in its creation. How can one understand *The Starry Night* without peering through a window into the mind (and soul) of Vincent Van Gogh? No piece of art can truly be understood without studying its creator.

As I dug into the story I discovered conflicting accounts, sometimes given by the same person. Two meetings would be conflated into one meeting. Dates would be moved around. Sometimes writers would confuse the names Melendez and Mendelson. Much of my work was untangling these balls of yarn. Unraveling the mysteries behind many questions surrounding the production from decades ago became a detective story. There would be crushing moments, like discovering that the folder labeled "Charlie Brown special" in the extensive Coca-Cola archives was maddeningly empty, its contents perhaps misplaced, or more likely pilfered. There would be other eureka moments, when I would discover an important missing piece of the special's puzzle and be filled with elation.

I quickly discovered that there were equally important stories of other key characters who played significant roles in the special's greenlighting and broadcast. And as I pulled back the lens to examine these players and the powerful institutions they worked for—CBS, Coca-Cola, *Time* magazine, and McCann-Erickson— I came across a bigger story: America in 1965.

In that critical hinge year of history, the nation was at a crossroads, just healing from the shock of the assassination of President John F. Kennedy but about to lurch into a tragic war in Vietnam. At the same time Americans were wrestling with excising the ugly scar of segregation. The very soundtrack of the country was changing with the British Invasion. Television (now broadcast in color) was transforming how Americans consumed entertainment, but, in many ways, it was also transforming America as well.

So much of America today sadly resembles America then— racial unrest, cultural divisions, rumblings of war. But today, as it did then, one troubled, round-headed cartoon character's probing

question—*Isn't there anyone who knows what Christmas is all about?*—
strikes just as meaningful a chord with children and adults. That
question would be poignantly answered by another small boy speaking with a lisp and clutching a blanket. His inspired response, concluding with "and on earth peace, good will toward men," remains
as simple a remedy to what troubles us today as it did in 1965. And
it is as timeless as it was on that first Christmas Day two thousand
years ago.

Michael Keane
Malibu, California

Charlie Brown's Christmas Miracle

INTRODUCTION

✦

Charles Schulz had a problem. Several, in fact.

The forty-two-year-old cartoonist had lost twenty pounds. He felt unwell. He was anxious, nervous, reluctant to even leave his home. But the physician who examined him in the summer of 1965 found nothing medically wrong with him. Schulz knew he was under stress. He had been suffering from general anxiety disorder for years. Televised images of the escalating Vietnam conflict that were now being broadcast into American living rooms may have triggered PTSD in the World War II combat veteran. The cartoonist also now had the additional stress of a televised Christmas special he was racing to produce. However, when his doctor delicately suggested Schulz see a psychiatrist to treat his anxiety, Schulz demurred.

The creator of the *Peanuts* comics, the most popular comic strip in the country, believed that his worries were the wellspring of his creativity, and he was terrified that if he were ever cured of his disorder he would be stripped of the muse that fueled his imagination. He needed all the creativity he could harness for the new project he was working on—a television Christmas special—his most ambitious (and risky) effort since he launched the *Peanuts* comic strip in 1950. But Schulz wasn't just trying to bring Charlie Brown, Linus, Lucy, and their friends to a new audience in a new medium. He wanted to carry a message he felt was desperately needed in a country on the edge. It was a message of faith that sprang from the gratitude the Army veteran felt toward God every single day for having spared his life amid the horrors of war.

When the production neared completion, Schulz's two partners confronted him (not for the first time) regarding a lingering issue that concerned both of them: the inclusion of a lengthy recitation from Scripture in the program by blanket-clutching Linus, the most thoughtful and mature of all the *Peanuts* characters. Schulz had selected a reading from the book of Luke, chapter 2, verses 8–14, which begins, *And there were in the same country shepherds abiding in the field, keeping watch over their flock by night. And, lo, the angel of the Lord came upon them, and the glory of the Lord shone round about them: and they were sore afraid.*

Mendelson and Melendez argued that the scene might offend both secular audiences, who could see the content as "preachy," as well as devout Christian viewers, who might view recitation of Bible passages by a cartoon character as sacrilegious. Inserting a not-so-subtle religious message into an entertainment product had never been done before. Hanna-Barbera had never done it. It seemed impious that such divine words could come out of the mouths of the likes of Yogi Bear or the Jetsons. Warner Bros. wouldn't do it. It was unthinkable for the likes of Bugs Bunny or Daffy Duck. Neither, Melendez pointed out, would his former boss, the great Walt Disney, ever venture into religious content. It was a dangerous place to go, thought Melendez, who began questioning if he wanted to be involved in the production.

"This is an entertainment show," Mendelson objected. "I don't know if you can animate from the Bible."

Schulz patiently listened to his partners' objections, but the arguments his collaborators made about Disney and Warner Bros.

only seemed to strengthen his resolve. The cartoonist stood firm in wanting the show to communicate the true meaning of Christmas. "If we don't do it," he finally asked, "who will?"

Schulz knew that he was also taking a tremendous risk that if the show disappointed or offended audiences, it could have a crushing effect on how readers viewed the daily *Peanuts* strip, potentially leading to hundreds of newspapers canceling the cartoon. Putting aside what the characters were saying, particularly Linus's religious recitation of Scripture, it was notable that with the exception of a few seconds of some Ford commercials, most *Peanuts* fans had never before heard voices applied to the comic strip characters, other than what they had assigned Charlie Brown and his cartoon colleagues in their own heads. The inevitable mismatch between readers' preconceived notions of the look and sound of the characters and what they would soon witness in the TV special might be jarring. Schulz was gambling fifteen years of hard work in building the *Peanuts* franchise from a handful of newspapers in 1950 to millions of readers in almost a thousand newspapers.

In early December, Lee Mendelson, the special's producer, flew to New York and screened *A Charlie Brown Christmas* for the CBS network's highest programming executives. The two CBS vice presidents were shocked by what they saw. Disappointed in the animation, dismayed by the jazz soundtrack, and nervous about the show's overt religiosity. Mendelson was bluntly told the network would never buy another program from him or Schulz again. Was it possible that the special might be yanked from its broadcast slot the following week? The network executives would bring the matter to the attention of the president of CBS himself.

Charlie Brown would need his own Christmas miracle.

THE MIRACLE

◆

This book tells the inspiring, against-all-odds story of how *A Charlie Brown Christmas* overcame production difficulties, an incredibly tight six-month delivery schedule, and the skepticism of television network executives to become the most popular animated holiday special in history. The ultimately successful making of *A Charlie Brown Christmas*, as well as its enthusiastic embrace by audiences for more than fifty years, was the culmination of an improbable series of events, including:

- The persistence of an inexperienced producer whose previous works consisted of historical documentaries and whose most recent production had been a flop.
- The fortuitous firing of the powerful head of CBS Television.
- The appointment of the president of Coca-Cola to the board of directors of General Electric in 1964, the same year that company sponsored a televised holiday special named *Rudolph the Red-Nosed Reindeer*.
- The selection of the *Peanuts* characters for the cover of an April 1965 issue of *Time* magazine.

- A young Mexican immigrant's chance meeting with the hiring manager at Walt Disney, which launched him on a career in animation.
- The radio broadcast of the song "Cast Your Fate to the Wind," which was heard by the Christmas special's producer as he drove across the Golden Gate Bridge while desperate to find a composer who could craft music to match the quirky *Peanuts* characters.
- The sympathetic collusion of an advertising executive who, fearing the production would be shut down, agreed to provide an upbeat assessment of a rough cut of the special to his colleagues in McCann-Erickson's New York office despite his own serious misgivings about its quality.
- The assignment of a Jewish TV critic at *Time* magazine to write the exclusive pre-broadcast review about the Charlie Brown special.
- Charles Schulz's quiet insistence that the *Peanuts* special answer the question pointedly posed by the program's protagonist, Charlie Brown: "Isn't there anyone who knows what Christmas is all about?"

As Lee Mendelson, the special's producer, told an interviewer years later, "I've never looked up the word in the dictionary, but yes, I believe in serendipity. I had it with *A Charlie Brown Christmas*, and it continued for forty more years. It's happened too often not to believe in it."

This is the story of Charlie Brown's Christmas miracle.

1965

To properly understand the making of *A Charlie Brown Christmas*, it is critically important to understand the cultural landscape of 1965, a hinge year between the optimism of the early 1960s and the seismic rumblings of an emerging counterculture.

The United States made a fateful decision to intervene in Vietnam, sending Marines to Da Nang and commencing Operation Rolling Thunder, the aerial bombardment of North Vietnam. On August 5 CBS News broadcast images of Marines burning huts of villagers with cigarette lighters, which shocked America. An infuriated President Lyndon Johnson would call CBS chief Frank Stanton and demand that the war reporter, Morley Safer, be fired. By the end of the year, the Pentagon was requesting four hundred thousand troops for the war while at the same time tens of thousands of antiwar protesters descended on Washington, DC.

The civil rights of Black Americans were a prominent issue. Congress passed the Voting Rights Act, and Martin Luther King Jr. led thousands of nonviolent protesters on a march in Selma, Alabama. Cassius Clay changed his name to Muhammad Ali and knocked out Sonny Liston in the first round of their rematch bout, and Malcolm X was gunned down in New York City.

At the movie theater audiences were enjoying comedies like *That Darn Cat!*, *The Great Race*, and *What's New Pussycat*, as well as the drama *Doctor Zhivago*. The biggest film of the year, however, was the musical *The Sound of Music*. Best-selling fiction books of the year included *Up the Down Staircase* by Bel Kaufman, *Herzog* by Saul Bellow, *Hotel* by Arthur Hailey, and *The Spy Who Came in from the Cold* by John le Carré. Nonfiction bestsellers included *The Making of the President 1964* by Theodore White, *Is Paris Burning?* by Larry Collins and Dominique Lapierre, *My Shadow Ran Fast* by Bill Sands, and *Kennedy* by Theodore Sorensen.

Leading shows on television included *Bonanza*, *The Lucy Show*, *The Beverly Hillbillies*, *Bewitched*, *The Andy Griffith Show*, and *Gomer Pyle, U.S.M.C.*, as well as two new breakout programs, *Hogan's Heroes* and *Days of Our Lives*—programs many Americans enjoyed while eating frozen TV dinners from aluminum trays on top of tray tables. The color revolution was happening in television broadcasting as NBC announced that almost all of their prime-time programming would now be broadcast in color. Comedian Soupy Sales, who hosted a children's television program in New York City, jokingly encouraged his young viewers to send him money. He was suspended for two weeks.

Top 40 music hits included "Wooly Bully" by Sam the Sham and the Pharaohs, "(I Can't Get No) Satisfaction" by the Rolling Stones, and "Help Me, Rhonda" by the Beach Boys. The Grammy for Best New Artist was awarded to a British group called the Beatles, whose hits in 1965 included "Yesterday," "Ticket to Ride," and "Help!" The Fab Four launched their US tour on August 15 with a concert at Shea Stadium.

Rapid advancements were made in space exploration and technology. NASA launched an unmanned vehicle to the moon that transmitted live televised images. Another probe to Mars sent back the first images of that planet. The world's first commercial satellite, Intelsat I, was also sent into space, while on Earth Sony introduced the first home video tape recorder. PDP-8, the world's first mini-computer with a 12-bit microprocessor, was brought to market by Digital Equipment Corporation.

Americans' eating habits changed with the introduction of Spa-ghettiOs, Apple Jacks, and Honeycomb—all first stocked on gro-cery store shelves in 1965, as were Bounty paper towels. McDonald's nationwide introduced a Filet-O-Fish sandwich and completed its initial public offering. The first Subway sandwich shop opened in August in Bridgeport, Connecticut.

The Los Angeles Dodgers defeated the Minnesota Twins in the World Series, despite losing the first two games. Sandy Koufax did not pitch in game 1 of the series because it fell on Yom Kippur, but he would pitch three of the seven games and win two by shutouts, earning the Series MVP title. The baseball season had been marred by an epic fight between the Dodgers and Giants, who were in a pen-nant race. When Giants pitcher Juan Marichal was at bat, he became furious when the Dodger catcher deliberately buzzed his head when throwing the ball back to the pitcher, and he took revenge by strik-ing the catcher twice in the face with his baseball bat.

The first Super Bowl was still two years away. The AFL champi-ons were the Buffalo Bills and the NFL champions were the Green Bay Packers (although the game shifted from December to January of the following year for the first time, making 1965 the only year without an NFL championship game). CBS broadcast the first color telecast of an NFL game, a Thanksgiving Day contest between the Detroit Lions and the Baltimore Colts.

And also in 1965, fifteen years after its launch in a handful of newspapers, the *Peanuts* cartoon strip was published in seven hun-dred newspapers in the US, reaching tens of millions of readers, and its quirky characters were becoming firmly embedded in pop culture. Five of the *Peanuts* characters—Charlie Brown, Schroeder, Lucy, Linus, and Snoopy—would be featured on the April 9, 1965, cover of *Time* magazine. The sell line on the cover, "The World according to Peanuts," and its accompanying story would be seen by an advertising executive at McCann-Erickson, and it would set off a chain of events that would change television forever.

THE PRODUCER
LEE MENDELSON

✦

Did you happen to see that Willie Mays show?
—Producer Lee Mendelson in his
first call to Charles Schulz

DECEMBER 1964,
BURLINGAME, CALIFORNIA

Lee Mendelson had failed. Spectacularly. And he had done it in the worst possible way a producer could fail: using his own money. And with one of the biggest entertainment brands in the country. *Peanuts.* After over a year of trying to sell a documentary he had made on a day in the life of cartoonist Charles Schulz and his comic strip characters—months of calls and pitch meetings with networks, potential sponsors, advertising agencies—no one was interested.

It had all started so promisingly. Months earlier the thirty-year-old independent producer had suddenly been struck by an idea. After making a well-received documentary called *A Man Named Mays* about the San Francisco Giants' center fielder Willie Mays,

Mendelson was casting around in search of a new project. He had been reading the comics section of his local newspaper. Like almost everyone else in America, Mendelson had become a regular reader of *Peanuts*, which in ten years had become the most popular comic strip in the country. The daily cartoon's four black-and-white panels had an incredible power to make people both wince and chuckle. Charlie Brown was a modern Everyman that seemingly everyone could relate to, identifying with how, despite the lovable loser's daily trials and tribulations, he always kept moving forward.

In that day's comic strip Charlie Brown had lost another base-ball game. And then an idea leapt into Mendelson's mind. Having made a documentary about the best baseball player in the world, why not make one about the worst? Like Mendelson, Charles Schulz lived in the San Francisco Bay area. Could he possibly be listed in the telephone book? Mendelson's fingers flipped through the phone directory and there it was, Charles M. Schulz, on Coffee Lane in Sebastopol, about seventy miles north of the producer's home in Burlingame.

Mendelson inserted his index finger into the rotary dial, dialed the number, the phone rang, and...Schulz answered! Mendelson, an articulate pitchman, introduced himself and his idea for the program. Schulz just as quickly declined. The cartoonist had already had many approaches from Hollywood types, seeking to capitalize on his *Peanuts* characters, and he was just not interested. Mendelson politely said thank you and was about to hang up, but he could not resist one more attempt. "Did you happen to see that Willie Mays show?" he asked. Schulz worshipped professional sports figures, and despite the flailing of his *Peanuts* characters, the cartoonist himself was an excellent athlete and an intense competitor. "Oh sure, he's an idol of mine. I love baseball, and I love Willie Mays," said the cartoonist.

Mendelson seized his opening. "I made that. We have a two-man team, and we just follow you around like that. That's the kind of thing we like to do." There was a pause. A second. Three seconds. Six seconds. "If Willie Mays can trust you with his life, I can certainly trust you with mine."[1]

Leland Maurice Mendelson was born on March 24, 1933, in San Francisco, California. He was a proud third-generation San Franciscan whose grandfather had come during the gold rush in 1851 to sell clothing to the miners. He was the only child of Palmer and Jeanette (Wise) Mendelson. His father was in the produce business, growing and shipping fruits and vegetables to large chain grocery stores around the country. His mother was a housewife who also undertook charity work.

Mendelson believed that his first name was inspired by Leland Stanford, the former governor of California, but he was always a bit amused at the unknown provenance of his middle name. Perhaps his parents merely liked the alliteration that it produced. His boyhood friends typically called him Lee or Mendy. When Walt Disney's animated film *Pinocchio* was released in 1940, seven-year-old Mendy would pick up another nickname, Jiminy Cricket, because of his small stature. For a boy who was obsessed with comic strips—Chester Gould's *Dick Tracy*, Al Capp's *Li'l Abner*, and Hal Foster's *Prince Valiant* were all favorites—it seemed fitting to have a nickname from an animated character.

As a young boy, Lee was fascinated by radio and he was an avid fan of popular radio programs of the time—*Little Orphan Annie, The Jack Benny Program, The George Burns and Gracie Allen Comedy Show,* and *Jack Armstrong: The All-American Boy.* On a family trip to Los Angeles, Palmer and Jeanette would take their son to Hollywood's famous Hollywood and Vine intersection, where Lee was surrounded by the buildings inside which many of his favorite radio shows were recorded. Afterward the family visited Warner Bros. Studios, where they saw a film being shot, *Desert Song*, a 1944 war picture. "[A]s young as I was, I knew that this was what I wanted to do."[2]

After graduating from San Mateo High School,* located half an hour south of San Francisco, Lee attended Stanford University, where he studied English literature. He was thrilled to have professors like Wallace Stegner, a celebrated novelist, as well as Margery Bailey, who had greatly influenced John Steinbeck. "With teachers like Stegner and Bailey, if you couldn't get passionate about writing, then you never could." Mendelson considered embarking on a career in writing, and he even wrote a one-act play that was produced at the university. Like many men of his generation, his career plans were put on hold after graduation when he was drafted into the military, serving three years in the Air Force.

After his honorable discharge in 1957, Mendelson joined his father in the produce business, but he felt a nagging desire to explore a career in the new field of television. In 1950 only 9 percent of the households in America had a television set. By 1955 that number had climbed to almost 65 percent. In 1957, having no background in television production, Mendelson boldly walked into the offices of KPIX-TV, the local CBS affiliate, located in a five-story building in downtown San Francisco, seeking a job. Fortuitously for the ambitious Mendelson, an employee at the station had recently learned she was pregnant and had resigned that very day. The station now desperately needed a production assistant. Mendelson was offered her position with a starting salary of $75 a week. He immediately

---

* San Mateo High School produced a number of entertainers, including television presenter Merv Griffin; actors Kris Kristofferson, Barry Bostwick, and Alicia Silverstone; and jazz musician Cal Tjader.

accepted and was thrilled to be starting a career in broadcasting. He would later also recognize that he was fortunate to be able to start his career in such a large market without having to first toil in a small, distant location. It was the first of many lucky breaks that would mark the fledgling entertainment executive's career.

Mendelson's first day on the job was marked by an embarrassing incident that he would recall in later years with a chuckle. His new employer broadcast *The Marshall J Show*, a locally produced live after-school television program aimed at youngsters. The host, Jay Alexander, was a tall, lean, folksy cowboy who asked kids to "be kind to people and animals." Marshall J also had a sidekick, a dalmatian named Rowdy. On Mendelson's first day on the job, the dog found its way over to the station's newest employee, lifted its leg, and relieved itself on Mendelson. "Welcome to show business," laughed a colleague.

One of Mendelson's first assignments at KPIX-TV was producing local public service spots. The short pieces featured someone like the police chief or the fire chief talking about crime or fire prevention. When the Berlin Wall was constructed in August 1961, fears of a nuclear exchange between the two superpowers spiked and many Americans began constructing bomb shelters. Mendelson, with his military background, was assigned to produce a series on civil defense. The young producer was proud when another segment he created that educated viewers about a pending school bond issuance was instrumental in securing approval for the measure at the ballot box. No education bond measure had passed in the previous twenty years until Mendelson's piece had been broadcast. He had similarly produced a series on the proposed Bay Area Rapid Transit (BART) system, which had also faced stiff opposition from voters. When BART won approval, Mendelson felt that his series deserved some of the credit.

Mendelson next graduated to longer-format documentaries, including a series called *San Francisco Pageant*, which focused on the history of the city. His first program told the story of the monumental construction of San Francisco's Golden Gate Bridge. Mendelson interviewed many of the engineers, riveters, and painters involved in building what was at the time the world's longest and tallest suspension bridge. He planned to stitch together the on-air interviews alongside still photos of the partially built bridge. Ideally he had hoped to locate some film footage of the bridge's construction, but he doubted any existed. Expecting to be disappointed, he made a call to Bethlehem Steel, which had produced the beams and cables for the bridge, and inquired if the company had filmed any of the construction. No was the prompt reply. Three weeks later, Mendelson received a call back from the steel company explaining that because of his inquiry they had checked their offices and discovered a number of boxes of 35mm film in dusty cans. The film footage was shipped out to San Francisco, and it allowed Mendelson's documentary to present a much more vivid tale of the bridge's construction.

More local historical projects followed—a production on the Hearst Castle at San Simeon, one on the 1906 San Francisco earthquake, and another on the San Francisco World's Fair of 1915. Mendelson's work earned him a Peabody Award. He also produced a show called *Baseball's Greatest Dynasty*, for which he was able to interview New York Yankees baseball star Joe DiMaggio, who was from San Francisco. After the interview Mendelson realized that he had forgotten to have DiMaggio sign a release form. He ran after the player and knocked on the window of his car, alarming a passenger inside the vehicle. The ballplayer stepped out of the car and motioned to the car's occupant to indicate that it was okay, he knew the intruder. The car window then rolled down, and Mendelson was stunned to see that the passenger he had alarmed was Marilyn Monroe.

In 1963, emboldened by his Peabody award, confident in his skills, and with a sound body of works produced, Lee Mendelson, not yet thirty, marched into his boss's office and requested a $25 a week raise. His request was declined, and the producer promptly resigned. Joined by a cinematographer named Sheldon Fay from KPIX, Mendelson set up his own shop in Burlingame, next to a hearing aid store, and he began to contemplate life as an independent producer. He had recently read a book by author Charles Einstein about Willie Mays and noticed that the author lived nearby in Mill Valley, north of San Francisco, across the Golden Gate Bridge. Mendelson reached out to Einstein and discussed an idea with him. *Do you think we might be able to follow Mays around for a few days and produce a show?* Einstein said he didn't know, but he introduced Mendelson to the ballplayer. Mendelson pitched his idea to Mays for making a documentary on the star player. Mays's response was that he didn't care what Mendelson did as long as he made the game of baseball look good. Mendelson got exclusive access to the Giants' clubhouse, dugout, and locker room for three months. In addition to Mays, Mendelson shot footage of other Giants players, like Willie McCovey, Juan Marichal, Orlando Cepeda, and the team's manager, Alvin Dark.[3] Mendelson cut the footage down to a half-hour production, flew to New York, and shopped it to the three television networks.

It was only the second visit to New York City for the California-born producer, but he met with success right away. Mendelson's first stop was CBS, where he was immediately offered $20,000 for the production. "Twenty thousand dollars was like a million dollars in those days and I was about to sell it, and I said, well…I'm in

New York, I think before I do, I'll go talk to NBC." Just as Mendelson had hoped, the peacock network was even more interested than CBS. Ed Friendly and George Schlatter told Mendelson if he could turn it into an hour-long program, they would pay him fifty thousand dollars for it. A stunned Mendelson almost fell out of his chair.

Mendelson flew back to San Francisco and reworked his footage into the requested sixty minutes of programming, and *A Man Named Mays* was broadcast on NBC on October 6, 1963. In a smart counterprogramming move, the network put the show up against a program aired by CBS called *Elizabeth Taylor in London*. The Taylor special was shot on location and featured the actress waxing nostalgically about her birthplace. Famous London sites, including Westminster Bridge, the Houses of Parliament, and a church damaged from bombing during World War II, served as backdrops while the famous actress recited poems by William Wordsworth and Elizabeth Barrett Browning. Taylor was reportedly paid $250,000 for her starring role, an astounding sum. Considering that Mendelson's special on Mays had cost one-fifth that amount and drew in a quarter of the television viewing audience, NBC would seem to have gotten a much better return on their investment.

A Man Named Mays had been marred by ugly racism, however. The fact that Mays was African American and was the focus of attention of Mendelson's special generated a lot of hate mail for the producer. At the time it was unusual to make a Black athlete the star of a network documentary. The show had even featured footage from Westfield, Alabama, Mays's birthplace, just outside of Birmingham. But when the show was broadcast, the local NBC affiliate in Birmingham refused to televise it.[4]

✦ ✦ ✦

For his Charlie Brown documentary, Lee Mendelson had his cine-matographer film Charles Schulz at work in his art studio, capturing a typical day in the life of the cartoonist alone with his comic strip creations. The production was not without some technical problems. When Mendelson directed Schulz to sketch important moments from his life on camera, the hot lights from the camera directly over Schulz's shoulder melted the black crayon the artist was sketching with before he could finish the cartoon. Mendelson also enlisted his former subject, Willie Mays, to make an appearance in the Schulz and *Peanuts* documentary. A couple of minutes of animation of *Peanuts* characters were added to the production, some of which was combined with film footage of the baseball star. Schulz considered the best scene in the hour-long program to be a shot of Willie Mays gliding to his left in centerfield, demonstrating to an animated Snoopy how to catch a fly ball. Snoopy attempts to imitate the ballplayer, but when the beagle catches the ball in his mouth, an exasperated Mays exclaims, "If I had to play for that Charlie Brown's team, I'd quit baseball."[5]

Despite the popularity of the *Peanuts* cartoon strip, and what he felt was a quality documentary, Mendelson had failed to find a network interested in broadcasting the program he had titled *A Boy Named Charlie Brown*. He had been thorough in calling on a long list of potential partners, including ad agencies, networks, and prospective sponsors, but no one found the piece to be entertaining enough for a television audience. In true Charlie Brown fashion, it was a flop.

Lee Mendelson never mentioned if he had taken notice of the premier broadcast of a one-hour, stop-motion production by Rankin/Bass featuring a misfit reindeer on December 6, 1964. But the luminous-nosed animal would set in motion a chain of events that would forever change Mendelson's life.

THE SPONSOR
COCA-COLA AND J. PAUL AUSTIN

✦

Things go better with Coca-Cola!
Things go better with Coke!
—Coca-Cola's advertising slogan adopted in 1963

DECEMBER 1964,
ATLANTA, GEORGIA

As soon as he stepped inside the lobby of the Coca-Cola head-quarters in Atlanta, Georgia, J. Paul Austin was immersed into a world of Christmas cheer. From the grandeur of the large evergreen tree sitting between the building's elevators, through the hallways, and into the executive offices, the president of the soft drink company was greeted with holiday displays of sparkling ornaments, white poinsettias, velvet bows, prancing reindeer pulling sleighs, yards of crimson ribbon, and sprigs of holly and berries. Sprinkled amid the array of traditional Yuletide exhibitions were even more imaginative displays incorporating the cola company's own products—iconic, curvy-contoured, logo-embossed thick glass soda bottles (the shape itself trademarked) and sharp, crimped-edge bottle cap crowns—all crafted into holiday decorations. It was a mash-up of commercialism and Christmas befitting a company with the largest advertising budget in America. These holiday creations were an ingenious mix of basic elements, not unlike the soft drink concoction that powered the international company's annual sales of almost a billion dollars.[1]

But on this day in December 1964, the tall, intense president of Coca-Cola was not focused on the upcoming holiday or on the international business that he managed. He had been summoned to an urgent meeting at Ichauway Plantation, the country estate home of Robert Woodruff, Coca-Cola's longtime chairman. Days earlier, on December 10, Martin Luther King Jr., an Atlanta native, had accepted the prestigious Nobel Peace Prize in Oslo, Norway. A public dinner reception was planned to honor King in his hometown. The banquet was scheduled for the following month, on January 27, 1965, and it was hoped that the event would simultaneously honor King while sending a powerful message of racial unity throughout the segregated South, but the Atlanta business community appeared to be boycotting the event. Woodruff was hoping Austin could persuade other Atlanta business leaders to join the dinner.

Austin was well suited for the assignment by temperament, experience, and education. The hard-driving, no-nonsense executive was accustomed to forging consensus by the force of his personality, his overpowering intellect, or his competitive maneuvering. His senior thesis at Harvard had been on the history and influences behind African American spirituals. It was a topic he had once held forth on knowledgeably and without notes for almost an hour, when Woodruff, in a test of his young executive, spontaneously brought up the topic at a bottler's convention in Chicago.[2] Originally from LaGrange, Georgia, Austin was certainly aware of the injustices of the segregated American South, but he had also lived and worked in

South Africa for four years, where he witnessed the grotesque system of apartheid and how it could devastate a society. He was determined to help Atlanta avoid that fate, and he resolved that Coca-Cola would do its part to bend the arc of history in the right direction.[3]

Also attending the meeting at Ichauway was Atlanta's mayor, Ivan Allen Jr. The mayor had been unsuccessful in securing commitments from the city's white business leaders to attend the King dinner, and he now came pleading for help from the head of the city's largest corporation. A letter had been sent out to one hundred business and civic leaders, seeking sponsors for the banquet and noting "This is the second Nobel award that any Southerner has received.* We believe it reflects on the South and, particularly, on our state and city. It is with pride in mind that we join in this undertaking."[4] No one had yet replied.

Ralph McGill, one of the dinner's organizers, grew so discouraged by the lack of response from the city's white community that he considered canceling the event.[5] McGill was the executive editor of the *Atlanta Constitution*, one of the city's two major newspapers, and he had used his columns to voice withering criticisms of segregation.** The editor's stance provoked more than mere threatening letters from angry newspaper readers—crosses were burned into his front lawn, bullets fired into his home's windows, and crude bombs left in his mailbox. When powerful voices called on the newspaper to muzzle McGill, the chairman of Coca-Cola steadied him with a standing offer of employment with the soft drink company, should McGill ever be fired by the *Atlanta Constitution*.[6]

---

* Novelist William Faulkner, who was from Mississippi, won the Nobel Prize in Literature in 1949.

** In his *Letter from Birmingham Jail*, Martin Luther King Jr. singled out by name four white writers who "have written about our struggle in elegant, prophetic, and understanding terms." McGill was the journalist King named first.

Ivan Allen had made two unsuccessful runs for the Georgia's governor's office before successfully campaigning for the job of mayor of Atlanta, handily defeating the segregationist Lester Maddox. Like any white Southern politician of his era, Allen's own record on race issues was imperfect—his two failed gubernatorial campaigns had been run on segregationist platforms. However, Allen's business pragmatism had led him to conclude that racial integration was a prerequisite in order for Atlanta, its businesses, and its citizens to prosper. Even before ascending to the post of mayor, Allen was involved in leading efforts to fully desegregate Atlanta's leading department stores and lunch counters. On his first day in office as mayor, he ordered that all "white" and "colored" signs be removed from City Hall, and he integrated the municipal cafeteria.

In 1963 President John F. Kennedy made a personal appeal to Allen to testify in front of Congress in support of a proposed federal law banishing segregation and mandating public accommodations for Black Americans. Allen wrestled with appearing in Washington, DC, knowing that his testimony would likely ruin his political career and deeply affect his business and personal relationships. Yet on July 26, 1963, Allen appeared before Congress and offered his support for what would become the landmark Civil Rights Act of 1964. He was the only prominent white Southern politician to speak out on behalf of ending segregation. In his remarks, Allen noted that segregation was "slavery's stepchild" and called for legislative action. "We cannot dodge this issue. We cannot look back over our shoulders or turn the clock back to the 1860's. We must take action now to assure a greater future for our citizens and our country."[7]

The testimony brought death threats against Allen and his family, requiring them to have police protection for the next year. Many of his white constituents and business associates shunned him. Yet to Allen it had been a pivotal personal moment. Previously, his attitudes about race relations had been driven by pragmatism reflected in Atlanta's motto, "A City Too Busy to Hate." It simply made good business sense to end segregation, and it was an important step to ensure that Atlanta would evolve into a world-class city. Now his opposition to racial segregation was a deeply held personal conviction.

J. Paul Austin summoned Atlanta's business leaders to a private meeting at the exclusive Piedmont Driving Club, where Austin was a member.[8] His message to the attendees was blunt: "It is embarrassing for Coca-Cola to be located in a city that refuses to honor its Nobel Prize winner. We are an international business. The Coca-Cola Company does not need Atlanta. Atlanta needs the Coca-Cola Company."[9]

The private reluctance of Atlanta's business leaders to embrace their Nobel Prize–winning native son erupted into a national public embarrassment when, on December 29, 1964, the *New York Times* published an article on its front page titled "Tribute to Dr. King Disputed in Atlanta." The article noted that invitations had been "sent to more than 100 leaders in business, education, religion, politics and civic affairs asking them to join as sponsors" of the banquet, but that "most of those receiving the letters have not replied" and that a "few had replied negatively, including one leading banker who strongly stated his objections."[10]

The banquet was scheduled to be held January 27, 1965, at the Dinkler Plaza Hotel. The stately, ten-story hotel had been constructed in 1931 on the corner of Forsyth and James Streets, and over four thousand residents of the city attended its opening to celebrate "one of the most attractive and most modern hotels in America."[*, 11] Yet despite proclaiming itself open to "every Southerner," the doors of the hotel were closed to African Americans. Even at the public library across the street from the hotel, Black people were permitted to read books only in the poorly lit library's basement, and they were not allowed to borrow books until 1959.[12]

The walls of the hotel lobby were adorned with large paintings of Atlanta, both before and after the Civil War. Curiously, in the lobby of the hotel's writing room hung a life-sized portrait of Union Army general William Tecumseh Sherman, the same man who had ordered a swath of Georgia, including a portion of Atlanta, burned to the ground, on his Army's march toward Savannah.[13] The King dinner was notably not the Dinkler Plaza's first encounter with an African American Nobel Prize winner. In 1962 the hotel had turned away Ralph Bunche,[**] refusing to honor his reservation.[14] Bunche had been awarded the Nobel Peace Prize in 1950 for his work as the chief negotiator for the United Nations Special Committee on Palestine in which he mediated an armistice agreement between Israel and the Arab states.[15] The year after being refused his Atlanta hotel room, Bunche was awarded the Presidential Medal of Freedom by President John F. Kennedy.[16] The same year, the Dinkler Plaza and a dozen other hotels in Atlanta agreed to a limited desegregation plan.

On the evening of January 27, 1965, the Dinkler's chandeliered ballroom was packed with an estimated 1,500 people, including representatives of the world's press. Austin's arm-twisting and threat to move Coca-Cola out of Atlanta had worked. While a few diehard segregationists picketed outside, inside the hotel the event proceeded

---

* The hotel was originally called Hotel Ansley. It was sold to the Dinkler hotel chain in 1952 and renamed the Dinkler Ansley and renamed again as the Dinkler Plaza Hotel the following year. The hotel was torn down in 1972.
** In 1965 Ralph Bunche would march alongside Martin Luther King Jr. from Selma to Montgomery, Alabama.

without any problems. The dinner's organizers presented King with a crystal Steuben bowl engraved with a dogwood blossom, the city's symbol. "This marvelous hometown welcome and honor will remain dear to me as long as the cords of memory shall lengthen," King said in his speech. King then called forth the goodwill of millions of Southerners "whose voices are yet unheard, whose course is yet unclear, and whose courageous acts are yet unseen."[17] At the dinner's conclusion, the crowd spontaneously burst into singing the gospel song that had become the protest anthem of the civil rights movement—"We Shall Overcome."[18] To one of the dinner's organizers, one small detail seemed to capture the promising nature of the event. Scouring the banquet room, not one program had been left discarded on a chair or table. Every single one had been taken home as a souvenir, as if all those in attendance recognized that they had partaken in something historic and meaningful.

J. Paul Austin was born on February 14, 1915, in LaGrange Georgia. He attended Culver Military Academy and Phillips Academy in Andover, Massachusetts, before heading to Harvard University, where he graduated in 1937. While in college he competed on the rowing team. He also represented the USA crew team in the 1936 Berlin Olympics. His intensely competitive nature made an impression on his teammates. "If you wanted to beat Paul Austin, you'd have to kill him," said his coach.[19]

Austin went on to study at Harvard Law School, graduating in 1940. During World War II he served in naval intelligence and was assigned to a PT squadron in the Pacific. He achieved the rank of lieutenant commander and was awarded the Legion of Merit. The highly intelligent Austin exhibited a facility with languages and in addition to his native English he could speak French, Japanese, and

Spanish, and he had some familiarity with Italian. During his days traveling with Coca-Cola, he could always be seen carrying a language book to learn at least a few phrases that would be helpful in the country he was heading toward.

Robert Woodruff had plucked Austin from his job at the New York law firm of Larkin, Rathbone & Perry, but not before he had a private background check done on the man. Austin joined Coca-Cola in 1949 and he first went to work in a bottling plant. The Harvard-trained lawyer spent five months mastering almost every job in the building. The competitive new employee bet the fastest case-filling operator in the plant that he could best the man's speed. The two men made a wager of a penny a bottle. Austin won.

When he became president of Coca-Cola in 1962, Austin instituted management courses for his executives as well as for the company's bottlers. The classes employed the same case study method as found in the Harvard Business School and utilized some of the same instructors. The highly educated executive frequently employed erudite references in his speeches and talks, references that were sometimes lost on some of his more blue-collar managers, but Austin was always pushing his colleagues to keep learning. "Growth is essential. We must grow as individuals, as a company, as a nation."[20]

While Austin could be professorial when introducing modern business practices to Coca-Cola, he was cunning when it came to corporate infighting and outflanking his rivals for the CEO position. One man who fell into Austin's crosshairs was Benjamin H. Oehlert Jr. When Austin had been promoted to president of the company, Oehlert remarked that Austin had to be Woodruff's bastard son.[21] Like Austin, Oehlert was an Ivy League–educated lawyer— a graduate of Wharton and the University of Pennsylvania School of Law. He had excelled at every managerial challenge that Woodruff had assigned to him, beginning with the outbreak of World War II when he successfully navigated around the War Production Board's rationing of sugar. Aided by a company executive who had been slipped into a job with the board, Oehlert had ensured that the rules included one very large loophole—an exemption for sales of Coca-Cola to the US military.

As the war progressed and American soldiers headed overseas, Woodruff, chomping on his cigar, reputedly barked out an order to his executives: "See that every man in uniform gets a bottle of Coca-Cola for five cents, wherever he is, and whatever it costs." When the crushing logistical realities of delivering on Woodruff's demand became clear—transporting sugar, CO_2 gas, cola syrup, and glass bottles to battlefronts around the globe—executives began to question the chairman's mandate. Oehlert fought back against the doubters, successfully rescuing the plan from being shelved. In a lengthy memo, the young executive argued that Coca-Cola "must be an inseparable part of the war effort." Oehlert correctly foresaw that if the company could supply the young, homesick GIs with a sugary, refreshing bottle of civilian-life normalcy, Coca-Cola would be securing consumers for generations to come. The strategic opportunity demanded that the company "strain every resource to get and keep all of this Army business while it possibly can regardless of cost."[22]

After the war Oehlert successfully fended off the FDA's efforts to enact regulations implementing a law requiring ingredient labeling before heading to Orlando to manage Minute Maid, a company Coca-Cola purchased in 1960. He returned to Atlanta in 1965 as a senior vice president and immediately began to clash with Paul Austin. Being in Austin's proximity triggered an uncontrollable disdain in Oehlert, something that he had previously been able to manage when he was working in Florida. Oehlert's contempt for his superior manifested itself in a blizzard of memos that raised objections to every one of Austin's initiatives.

The clash between the two headstrong executives was an open secret at the company's headquarters and became a source of concern within the company's ranks. Austin ingeniously resolved the rivalry with assistance from President Johnson, who offered Oehlert the position of ambassador to Pakistan. When the executive expressed some reluctance about accepting the position, Woodruff encouraged Oehlert to take the assignment. Austin had almost certainly already secured the Coca-Cola chairman's cooperation in the transition of his rival not merely out of the company but also out of the country. With Oehlert shipped off to Islamabad, Austin's path to CEO was secured. For his part, Oehlert never forgave Austin for the betrayal, even one that bestowed him with the title of ambassador for the rest of his life. If he could, Oehlert would tell his family, he would kill the man.[23]

By the early 1960s Coca-Cola had transcended its status as an American consumer staple into an international brand. The company's Spencerian scripted logo and its fluted glass bottle were now achieving an even loftier status—as a pop culture icon. This mash-up of commerce and culture was captured perfectly by artist Andy Warhol in works like his famous *Campbell's Soup Cans* in 1961 and 1962. At the same time Warhol created similar works involving Coke bottles titled *Coca-Cola (3)*, *Coca-Cola (4)*, and *Green Coca-Cola Bottles*. These works established Warhol as a founder of the Pop Art movement. "A Coke is a Coke, and no amount of money can get you a better Coke than the one the bum on the corner is drinking,"

noted Warhol, a concise commentary on the egalitarian nature of mass-produced consumer products generally.[*],[24]

In the summer of 1964, Austin was elected to the board of directors of the General Electric Company. It was a notable achievement, elevating Austin to the highest ranks of another of the world's most prestigious companies, one that had been a component member of the Dow Jones Industrial Average since the composite was formed in 1896. Notably Austin no longer felt obligated to seek Woodruff's permission to accept GE's invitation. Only a few years earlier, when S&H Green Stamps had approached Austin about joining its board, the Coca-Cola executive had sought the permission of his company's chairman and CEO, and his request had been denied. It was Woodruff's subtle reminder to Austin who was the boss. In 1964, however, Austin was confident and secure enough about his position within the soft drink company to move decisively on his own. Similarly, when the International Advertising Association named Austin their Man of the Year, the executive flew to West Berlin to accept the honor. He did not ask Woodruff if he could attend.[25]

When Austin joined the board of directors of General Electric in 1964, the company was already a year into production on a stop-motion animation program that was scheduled for broadcast in December of that year. GE had commissioned the program to hawk its wares around the critical holiday season. Commercials featuring characters from the special would appear during the show's broadcast, marketing an abundance of GE home appliances, including a cordless knife, an electric blanket, a coffeemaker, and an automatic toothbrush.

---

[*] Over his career Warhol created fifteen works involving Coca-Cola. In 2013 his painting *Coca-Cola (3)* was sold at a Christie's auction for more than $57 million.

Austin had experience with Hollywood productions. Four years earlier, he had been tasked with deciding whether or not to approve Coca-Cola's cooperation with the producers of the movie *One, Two, Three*. The film was a political comedy, satirizing Cold War tensions and American domestic politics. Billy Wilder was set to direct the film, and James Cagney was set to star in the lead role as a Coca-Cola manager working in West Berlin attempting to open up new markets for his company's soft drink product behind the Iron Curtain. Although he ultimately green-lit Coca-Cola's support, the movie caused Austin more anxiety than any of his other corporate responsibilities. Such a high-profile undertaking had the potential to tarnish the company's closely guarded brand, and, if it went badly, it could derail the executive's career just as he was closing in on securing the role of president of the company. The film was of immense interest and concern to Woodruff, who followed anything involving the company's image closely, and the chairman's focus only heightened Austin's worries. When the film was privately screened in Atlanta for Coca-Cola executives, only days before its general release, a nervous Austin sat beside the chairman thinking he had made a mistake to ever support the project. The executive was greatly relieved when the lights came up at the film's conclusion and he saw a big smile on Woodruff's face. To Austin, having successfully navigated the company's brand through the shoals of a Hollywood film and secured the chairman's congratulations meant he had finally "made it" at Coca-Cola.[26]

GE's holiday special was adapted from a booklet released by the Montgomery Ward department store in 1939 titled *Rudolph the Red-Nosed Reindeer*. The story was written by one of the retailer's admen, Robert L. Mays, and over two million copies were printed for free distribution to the store's customers throughout the country. The book was written in the same style of rhyming couplets as

Clement Clarke Moore's 1823 classic poem *A Visit from St. Nicholas*, more commonly known as *'Twas the Night Before Christmas*. Mays's uplifting tale of the bullied, ruby-nosed misfit who overcomes outcast status to lead Santa's sleigh skyrocketed to even greater popularity when country music star Gene Autry recorded a song based on the book. The tune's lyrics were written by Mays's brother-in-law Johnny Marks, and the song reached number one on the US chart the week of Christmas 1949.

On December 6, 1964, NBC broadcast the stop-motion animated special based on Mays's book and Marks's song. The show was made by Rankin/Bass Productions and was narrated by Burl Ives. *Rudolph the Red-Nosed Reindeer* aired under the programming umbrella billed as the General Electric Fantasy Hour. The hour-long animated musical became an instant holiday classic, elevating Rudolph to iconic status alongside Santa Claus himself as part of the secular Christmas mythology. The special also redefined how families celebrated the holiday season. Parents and children would now gather to watch a televised holiday program as a new Christmas tradition, alongside exchanging gifts, picking out a fir tree, and baking cookies.

The exact provenance of the original inspiration behind Coca-Cola seeking out its own Christmas special is uncertain, but it had to have originated either at Coca-Cola's headquarters or at the offices of the company's advertising agency, McCann-Erickson. Given J. Paul Austin's position on the board of the sponsor of the hit show *Rudolph* and the soft drink executive's successful experience with a major film production, it is most likely that it was Austin who reached out to McCann and instructed the ad agency to think about ideas for a Coca-Cola Christmas special.

The ad agency would still have a number of obstacles to overcome to kick off a holiday special. The biggest initial challenge for

McCann-Erickson would be finding an existing entertainment brand, à la *Rudolph*, that could be adapted for television. It would have to have broad recognition and be a brand that was family friendly. Perhaps Disney would cooperate on a project, but the Burbank-based entertainment company had recently worked with Pepsi, which had sponsored Disney's "It's a Small World" exhibit at the 1964 New York World's Fair. Perhaps Warner Bros. would be amenable, but could their wise-cracking characters—Bugs Bunny, Daffy Duck, Porky Pig—really transfer to a heartwarming Christmas special? Coca-Cola was demanding to get something out this year. That left a production schedule of maybe only six months, precious little time to write a script, prepare storyboards, and undertake casting, production, and postproduction. Rankin/Bass had taken eighteen months to produce *Rudolph the Red-Nosed Reindeer*. The ad agency would also need to find a network willing to broadcast the program. The whole undertaking so late in the year was madness, really. It would take, well, a miracle.

THE AGENCY
McCann-Erickson and Marion Harper Jr.

✦

Truth Well Told.
—McCann-Erickson slogan

NEW YORK CITY,
AUGUST 1955

When Marion Harper Jr., the CEO of McCann-Erickson, entered the lobby of the Art Deco–styled DuMont Building at 515 Madison Avenue in Midtown Manhattan, it was for the most important meeting of his career. Indeed, this was not just the most important meeting of Harper's career; it was the most important meeting in the history of the ad agency he oversaw, and perhaps the most important meeting in the history of Madison Avenue. The advertising work of Coca-Cola was under review, and every agency sought to capture what was one of the most coveted accounts in the world, not merely for the $15 million in annual billings it provided but for the incredible prestige that the account would bring, for the other large accounts that it could draw, and for the advertising talent that having the account would attract. And for Marion Harper, the accolades from winning the Coca-Cola account would provide, at least temporarily, the personal validation that he so desperately craved. To Harper, it wasn't just business; it was personal—deeply personal.

Coca-Cola's advertising business had been handled for forty-nine years by the D'Arcy Advertising Company, a St. Louis agency that was headed by Archibald Lee.[1] One of the agency's other large accounts was Anheuser-Busch, and in the 1940s the agency had created the slogan "This Bud's for you," which became a successful marketing campaign for Budweiser beer. Archie Lee and illustrator Haddon Sundblom had also created the iconic Coca-Cola Santa Claus ads, which were a perennial holiday seasonal classic. The omnipresent ads at Christmastime defined the enduring modern image of Santa Claus as a jovial, well-nourished old man with a white beard and wearing a red suit. In fact, the decades-long campaign would be so impactful that it would give birth to an urban myth that the soft drink company had actually invented Santa Claus and that his suit was red because red was the color of Coca-Cola's logo.[2]

But D'Arcy's recent ad campaign for the Atlanta company—"The Pause That Refreshes"—had fallen flat. Coke's bottlers were disenchanted and were pressuring the company for change. The recent death of Archie Lee, who had been a friend of Coca-Cola president Robert Woodruff, seemed to present an opportunity to revisit the ad agency's relationship with the company. No ad executive at D'Arcy had emerged who approached Lee's creative talents.[3] When the company unveiled its ad campaign for 1955, Madison Avenue had mocked its resemblance to that of Coke's archrival, Pepsi, to which it was now shockingly losing domestic market share.[4] Perhaps the most noteworthy element of Coca-Cola's ads for the early 1950s was the inclusion of African Americans in marketing materials, including the Harlem Globetrotters as well as Olympic gold medalists Jesse Owens and Alice Coachman.[5] In 1955 Coca-Cola also featured its first female African American model, a young Clark College student named Mary Alexander.[6]

Coca-Cola had narrowed the field down to two finalists, McCann-Erickson and Young & Rubicam. McCann's final competitor was in its prime, with an excellent client list and a reputation for producing fresh, compelling, and effective advertising. McCann, however, had two strategic assets. The first was an unmatched global presence, which was critically important to the global soft drink company. In fact, McCann had done work for Coca-Cola in Brazil since 1941.[7] The second essential asset that McCann had that neither Young & Rubicam nor any other advertising firm on Madison Avenue could match was Marion Harper.

On a sweltering August day in Manhattan, Harper and his team entered awaiting limousines for the ten-minute drive from McCann's offices at 50 Rockefeller Plaza to Coca-Cola's New York offices at 515 Madison Avenue, less than a mile away. The McCann colleagues observed a strict silence during the car ride, in accordance with the long-standing understanding that their boss wanted to collect his thoughts. Harper was like a professional athlete observing a pregame ritual. The silence could be broken only by Harper himself, should he decide to ask a last-minute question. But the CEO rarely gave any indication that he would hear the answer. As they pulled up to Coke's offices, Harper leaned back to stretch out the long legs of his six-foot, two-inch frame, tossed the reading material that he had taken one last look at to an aide, and said, "I guess we're here." His McCann colleagues, clutching presentation materials—charts, graphs, slide carousels, and speculative ads in finished form, as well as supporting binders full of data and statistics—tumbled out of their limousines and walked into the lobby of the DuMont Building. A McCann executive noted that Harper himself always confidently entered a client's building as if he did it every day of his life.[8]

The CEO's path from the building lobby to the meeting room had ritual observances followed with a liturgical-like predictability. As Russ Johnston, a longtime McCann executive and close friend of Harper's, recalled, "[Harper] would comment on the décor of the lobby, have a kind word for the elevator boy, ask the receptionist if she would please tell Mr. Big that Mr. Harper and Mr. X from McCann-Erickson were here—remarking favorably on the young woman's coiffure, her dress or a vase of flowers on her desk. Then he would walk around idly about the reception room, inspecting the photographs or paintings on the walls, pausing occasionally to comment on some detail that would have escaped most people."[9]

Months in advance of the meeting, Marion Harper had assembled a working group for the Coca-Cola pitch. Harper himself met with the group twice a week to go through the reams of data they had collected. Even before Coca-Cola had announced the competition, Harper, always keenly aware of the market, had anticipated the opportunity and launched a worldwide survey of consumer drinking habits, including profiles of typical consumers, as well as a psychological analysis of their needs. Understanding the critical role that bottlers played in Coca-Cola's distribution, Harper had a trusted aide conduct a survey of bottlers to gain important insights into their attitudes and operations. Luckily, one of the McCann executives, Neal Gilliatt, an account group head in the ad agency's Chicago office, had a bottler friend in Indiana, where the ad executive was from. Weeks of work were invested into the bottling survey alone, and when it was completed, the team at McCann-Erickson knew more about the global company's distribution operations than any other ad agency on Madison Avenue, and possibly more than even those inside Coca-Cola itself.[10] Once the group's findings had been finalized, a team of artists and copywriters worked around the clock to finish the final pitch materials before they were rushed out to a twenty-four-hour print shop for production. It was not uncommon for some of McCann's glossy presentations to have production costs of $50,000 to $75,000 (a staggering sum, equal to a cost of $550,000 to $825,000 today).

Harper's team for the presentation included key McCann executives. One of Harper's management strengths was recruiting the best and the brightest to join his vision for the advertising behemoth. Another was being able to assemble the right mix of that talent for each client presentation. The McCann talent in the Coca-Cola boardroom that day included Robert Healy, who would manage the account if it were to be awarded to the agency. Healy had been born in Brooklyn and had sold Hoover vacuum cleaners door to door as a teenager. He had joined McCann three years earlier from Colgate-Palmolive, where he had headed advertising. Also present was John Tinker, the agency's creative director who would shortly go on to head up McCann's internal think tank, and Herta Herzog, an Austrian psychologist. Herzog had done a groundbreaking study of housewives and what motivated them to consume soap operas.[11] She had survived a crippling case of polio as a student, from which her right arm had never fully recovered.[12] Other highly paid McCann executives had been enlisted to attend the meeting to act as stagehands, crouching behind a large screen and operating a battery of slide and film projectors.[13]

It was Harper's typical practice to let his executives undertake the presentations while he acted almost as an independent adviser to the client. It was not uncommon, after the McCann executives had concluded their pitch, for the client to turn to Harper, who had remained silent throughout, and ask, "Mr. Harper you've heard what's been said. What do you think we should do?" Sometimes some of the toughest questioning of the McCann team came from Harper himself. On one occasion, after a McCann presentation, the targeted company asked the ad agency executives to leave the room so the executives could discuss the just-delivered pitch in confidence. Harper, however, remained behind with the client, Delphi-like, as if his opinion on the marketing advice that had just been dispensed was not from the firm that he oversaw as its chief executive officer. If Harper's presence in the closed session troubled any of the client's executives, no one seemed to notice.

For the Coca-Cola pitch, however, Harper took center stage. With the sounds of Madison Avenue traffic and the wail of police sirens filtering in through the windows, Harper began to speak over the calming hum emanating from the fans cooling the incandescent bulbs of the multiple 35mm slide projectors in the room. Dressed in a Brooks Brothers suit and a French-cuffed shirt with cufflinks, accompanied with a muted tie and suspenders, Harper always clad himself professionally but was never sartorially elegant to the point where it would overpower the real message, which was the advertising brilliance and wisdom of Marion Harper. His height and muscular build gave him an imposing physical presence to accompany his intimidating intellect. Balding since young adulthood, his round face was accentuated by black-framed eyeglasses, and the combination had always given Harper the appearance of a man ten years older than he was.

Harper began the pitch dramatically, showing a slide with the line "Coca-Cola puts you at your sparkling best" before announcing, "That, gentlemen, is your next advertisement for Coca-Cola."

The marketing guru presented consumer research that revealed that Coke's main appeal was "refreshment," supporting his central argument that the Atlanta company was not in the Coca-Cola business but was in the *refreshment* business. Once the company understood this, Harper argued, it would open up new products, new flavors, and new packaging. He also impressed upon the assembled executives the importance of pursuing the youth market, reinforcing his argument with substantial data. With their major competitor, Pepsi, gaining market share by targeting this specific group, the point was an important one for the Coke managers.

Harper's proposal also included a detailed chart of the international organization that he would put in place to support the Coca-Cola account, including the creation of a task force, similar to marketing teams McCann had deployed for existing clients, such as Westinghouse, Esso, and Swift & Co. The diagram also included the creation of a Bottler Service Group. In total there would be 121 full-time McCann employees, across all functions in the ad agency, who would be servicing the Coca-Cola account. The three team leaders would be Robert Healy, the firm's executive vice president; George Giese, the international president; and Marion Harper himself.[14]

Accounts vary on whether the meeting lasted a marathon six hours (according to McCann-Erickson's official company history) or a still formidable four hours (according to one of Harper's colleagues not present at the meeting). A third account is that after presenting for the two hours that had been allotted for the meeting, Harper concluded by bemoaning the fact that the limited time required him to leave out many ideas and potential solutions that the McCann executives felt were relevant to Coca-Cola's pressing problems. If this was a ploy by Harper to entice Coca-Cola to ask him to return for a second session, it worked, and so, according to this version, Harper and his team came back days later and dispensed more wisdom to the soft drink company's executives. Regardless of which account is true, the fact is that just weeks later, McCann was handed a client with annual billings of $15 million—the largest advertising account that had ever switched from one agency to another.* Rumors of the impending change abounded in Madison Avenue circles almost immediately, but a formal announcement of the change was not made until October 13, 1955, in Los Angeles, with Coca-Cola president William E. Robinson noting that the change was driven by rising international sales of the company's products and a desire to further integrate international and domestic advertising. "McCann-Erickson has offices throughout the world and can effect this integration of effort with a minimum of difficulty," said Robinson while the deflated head of D'Arcy, the agency that McCann had just displaced, stood beside him.[15] For many executives on Madison Avenue this might have been the crowning achievement of their career, but for Marion Harper, only

---

* One of the early copywriters assigned to the Coca-Cola account was James Dickey, who was hired by McCann in April 1956. Dickey was a veteran of World War II and the Korean War. He grew up in Atlanta's upscale Buckhead neighborhood, where he had learned bow hunting in his youth. A talented poet and aspiring novelist, Dickey undertook an advertising career to support his creative writing ambitions. "I was selling my soul to the devil all day...and trying to buy it back at night," he would later explain. McCann would eventually fire Dickey for shirking his work duties to focus on his personal writing while in the office. Dickey would achieve commercial success and popular recognition with the publication of his novel *Deliverance* in 1970. The powerful tale of four Atlanta city dwellers (one of whom was a soft drink executive; another worked in advertising) struggling for survival in the Georgia backwoods would be made into a movie two years later starring Jon Voight and Burt Reynolds. A *New York Times* reviewer described Dickey as "the closest thing the South had to a deep-fried Norman Mailer."

thirty-nine years old and whose meteoric rise had already made him legendary in advertising, this was merely a stepping stone.

Marion Harper Jr. was born on May 14, 1916, in Oklahoma City, Oklahoma, where his father was the advertising director for the daily *Oklahoman* newspaper. Marion's parents separated when the boy was five years old, and the wound left by Marion Harper Sr.'s departure would follow the young boy like a long strip of Route 66 stretching through the flat, treeless landscape of Oklahoma. He was raised for the next ten years by a strong-willed mother, who instilled in her son a respect for the Bible, a strong work ethic, and the importance of being able to communicate well.

The young boy lived up to his mother's expectations, becoming president of his Sunday school class at their Methodist church, selling newspapers and soda pop, and, at the age of ten, making a public speech at a gathering of the United Daughters of the Confederacy.[16] The topic the young speaker chose was a weighty one: "The Time Is Here for the North and South to Forget Their Differences and Pull Together."[17] As her boy rose to the podium, Lotus Harper could not conceal her pride in the son she had raised alone for the past five years. The confident young boy accepted his introduction without a hint of childhood innocence, instead carrying himself with the presence and air of a fully grown adult. "It's been more than fifty years since our nation emerged from the most destructive civil war in history, and yet many of the pressures and attitudes which brought about this war still remain. The time has come to bind our wounds, forget the past, and pull together," he began. Young Harper spoke for another ten minutes without notes. He had memorized the speech that he had written himself. When he finished he was rewarded with polite applause, which he acknowledged with a slight bow before returning to his seat.[18]

At the age of fifteen, Harper's father reentered his life. The teenager stopped off in New York City, where his father worked as a vice president of General Foods, before heading off to prep school at Phillips Academy in Andover, Massachusetts. On his final night in Manhattan, his father took him to dinner at Original Joe's, a restaurant on the city's East Side. While at dinner the father schooled the boy on what he should expect to encounter at Andover, outlining the rules and rituals of an East Coast elite education. One of those rituals was card playing. When the elder Harper learned that his son was ignorant of any card games (not surprising for an Oklahoma Methodist), he insisted that his son learn to play blackjack as soon as they returned to his apartment.

Taking out a deck of cards, the father had his son withdraw all the cash that he had in his billfold. Marion Sr. patiently explained the numerical value of each card and the rules and objectives of the game, including the strategy involved in understanding when to hit and when to stay. Yet despite his father's guidance, the boy lost every hand, until he had finally run out of money. The father then returned only enough of the winnings he had taken from his son to allow the boy to pay for his bus fare to Andover. "Well, at least you know how to play blackjack," the father said, sending his son off to school broke. The emotional scar left by his father's misguided attempt to prepare him for the world's cruelties would shape Marion Harper forever.[19]

After graduating from Andover with honors in Bible, Harper went off to Yale, where he graduated in the top 10 percent of his class, winning top honors in math, psychology, and economics. After college Harper briefly worked as a door-to-door salesman of housewares and silk stockings[20] in order to test and observe the reaction of customers (almost always housewives at the time) to various sales pitches.[21] From the earliest Harper was interested in bringing a more scientific, research-driven approach to a field that was just beginning to undertake a more analytical approach to consumer behavior.

In 1939 Harper went to work in Manhattan for the McCann-Erickson advertising agency, starting off, as all new trainees did, in the mailroom, but every evening he would stay late in the agency's research library, reviewing market reports, trade papers, and journals to continue his education. Harper quickly captured the attention of the senior ad executives when he decided to conduct a personal experiment with their water consumption. One of Harper's tasks as a trainee was to refill the tall brown water bottles that sat on the executives' desks before the managers arrived at work. One morning an early rising senior vice president named Chet Posey noticed Harper refilling the bottles with a paper cup, carefully counting the number of cups required, before making notations in a notebook. Curious, Posey asked the young trainee what was going on. Harper matter-of-factly responded that he was conducting a "private experiment." Now even more curious, Posey pressed the matter, pointing out that since he would be drinking the water, he was entitled to know more. The ad executive lit up a cigarette as Harper responded. "It's an experiment in consumption. I've noticed that you gentlemen really don't use these water containers very much, and I found out why by tasting the water." Harper explained he had washed out the insides of the bottles and started with fresh water, noting that since that time consumption had increased by almost 25 percent, concluding that the water's taste was impacting how much of it was being drunk. Posey, a serious man not easily humored, erupted with peals of laughter that startled the secretaries sitting at their desks outside his office. "And who is the leader in this consumption test?" he asked. "You are," Harper replied, eagerly pulling forth his notebook to share the data. "The bottles were very dirty and the water was stale." Posey's encounter with Harper quickly circulated in the executive offices at McCann, and the study marked Harper as a young man who would go places within the ad agency.[22]

Shortly after Harper's water experiment, he approached Posey with another idea, seeking to enlist his support. Harper proposed to conduct a massive market study analyzing what made a successful ad. He wanted to take existing observation and readership figures for ads in four categories—food, drugs, industrial products, and hard goods—and rank them from top to bottom. He then proposed to identify all the key distinguishing features of each ad such as type font, type size, location of a photo versus the text, colors, length of headline, size of illustration, and amount of text. Harper hoped to identify the common distinguishing features behind ads that worked and ads that flopped. It was a massive undertaking that he planned to reduce in scope by analyzing just the top 25 percent or best performing ads and the lowest 25 percent or worst performing ads. Harper's theory, simply put, was that he could create a formula designed to produce ads that would get a high rating from consumers. "The creation of an ad can never be a mechanical function," Harper conceded to Posey. "That's where true creativity comes in. But I believe it's possible to establish some guidelines, so that creative people will know the odds. If they want to violate them and strike out on their own, that's their decision."

Harper then illustrated the bottom line impact of his research, if it were to work. Pointing out that a full color page ad in *Life* magazine cost $12,000, and that *Life*'s readership was about 6 million, designing an ad read by, say, 10 percent more people meant an additional 600,000 more prospective buyers. A 20 percent bump meant more than 1 million at no extra cost. Intrigued, Posey asked the young trainee what he would need to perform the study. Harper pleaded that to conduct his research he would need to be relieved of his mailroom duties and apprenticed to the research department. Posey arranged for Harper to present his proposal to Stan Biggs, who was senior vice president in charge of all creative work. Two days after the pitch, Posey phoned Young Marion, as Harper was now being referred to at the firm, and told him the good news. "You've made a sale, young man. Congratulations." Harper expressed his sincere gratitude to Posey for his assistance before Posey interrupted him. "You made the sale, not me. Spend some time in research and get to know the people. You'll need their help. They're a good bunch, and they've already been wondering what's going on. Don't be a loner."[23]

Harper reported to the research department, and after months of toiling he presented his work, which he clinically titled "Continuing Study of Magazine Readership." The report was bound and disseminated to McCann clients. Many old-school marketing managers were skeptical and resisted the new quantitative approach, including some of the admen at McCann. Yet Young Marion made enough converts with his research that many began to implement his findings. (One of the early adopters was John Tinker, who would become a legendary adman, and who would be making the pitch to Coca-Cola with Harper.) There was a long gestation period between when an ad was designed and when it was completed and published. During that time the indefatigable Harper continued to refine his analysis and to widen his research to include black-and-white advertisements as well as newspaper ads.

When the new ads hit the market, Harper's work was vindicated. Slowly McCann's ads moved to the top of the ratings. Harper had even made predictions of the success of each ad placed by the agency. Each layout was analyzed, and a rating score was calculated. When Clarks, the third-party rating service, issued its reports measuring reader reaction to the ads, Harper's forecast was proven to be remarkably accurate. Madison Avenue was abuzz with talk about the new system of producing ads based on the qualitative research that McCann had introduced. Jealous detractors began to refer to the agency and its formulaic approach as "Mechanical Erickson," but Harper had established himself and McCann as a forward-thinking agency that would get quantifiable results for its clients and their ad dollars by applying proprietary analytical research.[24]

While working in the research department Harper met a young woman named Virginia Epes, who had been hired by McCann shortly after Harper had joined as a trainee. Harper was immediately captivated by the tall, attractive woman, and the two began dating. Not surprisingly, many initial dates involved eating sandwiches while reviewing a stack of research reports. After two years, Harper invited Epes to Oklahoma, where she met his mother and sister. The second night in Oklahoma City Harper proposed, and Epes accepted. They were married in New Haven on April 4, 1942, by the Yale chaplain.[25]

Four years earlier Harper had been in the mailroom. He was now twenty-six years old. In six more years, at the age of thirty-two, he would be appointed as the agency's president. Madison Avenue, an industry used to superlatives, would not have enough adjectives to describe the dizzying climb of young Marion Harper to the top of one of the biggest ad agencies in the country.

◆ ◆ ◆

Harrison K. McCann founded his ad agency after a meeting with his founding partners on November 13, 1911, at the Mansfield Hotel in New York City. To McCann the number 13 would forever be a lucky number. He had begun his first job on October 13. He had opened his agency across the street from Standard Oil at 26 Broadway (twice 13), and the company's second headquarters was in the

Adams Building, which had thirteen letters in its name. The name "H. K. McCann Co." also had thirteen letters, as did the company's motto, "Truth Well Told." Whenever the company relocated, Harry McCann always insisted that the company's headquarters be located on the thirteenth floor. Before moving into 50 Rockefeller Plaza, McCann insisted that the building's floors be renumbered to include a thirteenth floor (the only building in all of Rockefeller Center with the number). And when the company moved again to 750 Third Avenue, by tradition one of the floors occupied by the ad agency was number 13.[26]

Harry McCann was a man of genteel manners. Unlike other executives, he would never bark orders to his secretary, Kitty Kelly, demanding, "Tell Mr. Smith to come up to my office." Even if he was terminating an employee he would politely say, "Miss Kelly, would you ask Mr. Smith if he could spare a few minutes?" Similarly, McCann had a patrician attitude toward attracting new business to his advertising agency. He was perfectly content to rely on his existing clients, grow as their business grew, and let word of mouth bring new clients to his door. He was quite happy to accept new business, and was grateful and eager for the work, but he was not eager to compete for it, and he would never deign to steal an account from another agency. This approach was anathema to an ambitious, highly competitive executive like Marion Harper, who was eager to market his hard-earned, research-driven insights showing ways he could improve companies' advertising results. It occasionally resulted in an elaborate dance, where, in order to appease Harry McCann, a client (or the agent who represented them) would have to first quit their existing agency, technically becoming a free agent, unentangled by any agreement with a McCann competitor, before the company (or agent who represented them) could be taken on by McCann.

Harper had no such illusions about the highly competitive nature of the advertising agency or of the business world in general.* "Stealing" clients was a long tradition on Madison Avenue, celebrated when your agency stole a client from another ad firm, and a crushing blow when it happened to yours. Once he was put in charge of the agency, Harper would abandon McCann's approach and adopt aggressive competitive tactics. A colleague noted that Harper's philosophy was to look for a weakness in the competing agency: "Get a foot in the door. Foster discontent. Tactfully illuminate errors in the other agency's service; meet people; hire disgruntled former employees of other firms and use their knowledge."[27]

Harper was a natural in pitch meetings with prospective clients. He had forged his speaking skills since childhood, and his raw intellect, fueled with data, never failed to impress people. If Harper had a weakness, it was that perhaps, for some clients, his brilliance shone too brightly. Knowing so much about a client's business could embarrass the assembled senior executives of a prospect in front of their own CEO, who, understandably, might question why a Madison Avenue executive knew so much or, more bluntly, why his own executives knew so little. Harper's brilliance and extensive knowledge could generate resentment, conscious or subconscious.[28] During at least one McCann presentation, a red-faced CEO exploded at his own management team, angry at the lack of understanding that his own executives had of the business compared with Harper's ad agency.

Harper's basic philosophy for client pitches was to make its focus about the *client*—its problems, its operations, and its future—not

---

* "The day you sign a client is the day you start losing them," noted character Don Draper in the fictional television drama series *Mad Men*, a series replete with references to the Harper era in advertising, including to the McCann agency itself and to its prestigious Coca-Cola account.

the ad agency, the opposite approach of most Madison Avenue firms, and Harper's distinctive approach usually resulted in new business for McCann. "If you've been given an hour, talk for forty-five minutes about [the client], ten minutes about the agency, and leave five minutes for questions. If they want to go longer than that, it'll be up to them."[29]

Harper's preferred medium to work from in a pitch was large three-by-four-foot cards containing charts or phrases that Harper used to reinforce major ideas and themes in his presentation. He disliked using slide projectors because when the room was darkened for the projector, he would lose eye contact with his audience and couldn't tell if they were following along. It was not unheard of for a client to fall asleep in a darkened room listening to the hum of the projector and the recitation of innumerable facts and figures.* Charts provided Harper with the flexibility his mind required to change the order of his ideas or to eliminate a point altogether. He would often return to a central theme printed on a card and display it again and again to drive home his argument.[30] Harper wielded his charts like a general deploying troops on a battlefield to reinforce a faltering division or provide overwhelming force at a decisive point.

Harper had, in fact, studied military strategy, a knowledge he once used in an attempt to rescue an account. In the mid-1950s McCann-Erickson received a termination notice from Brunswick,

---

* When he was made head of research, Harper proudly boasted that no client could fall asleep during one of his presentations. Russ Johnston, another McCann executive, took that as a challenge and chose his moment to strike. At a presentation with a notoriously narcoleptic client, who had just consumed a steak and three martinis at a lunch at 21, Johnston mischievously inserted a slide of a nude woman in the second carousel of slides, certain that the client would have nodded off. When the slide appeared, the client was sound asleep, and a stunned Harper faltered for a moment but then continued his presentation (Russ Johnston, *Marion Harper: An Unauthorized Biography* [Crain Books, 1982], 52).

a long-standing company based in Illinois that manufactured sporting goods, including bowling machines. McCann's Chicago office had somehow fumbled the account and likely would lose it to a strong Chicago-based competitor like Leo Burnett or Needham, Harper & Steers. Even with McCann's business growing rapidly, Harper would not take defeat easily. He requested and received an audience with the company's five-man executive committee, including its president. Rather than defensively trying to argue that McCann's performance had in fact been admirable and advocating for the agency's reinstatement, Harper brilliantly sidestepped that issue entirely and went on the offensive, not on behalf of the ad agency but on behalf of Brunswick. "I won't keep you long," Harper said. "I want to thank you for granting me this opportunity to talk to you. I'm not going to discuss whether we deserve to be fired or not, or what we may have done wrong, or what we did right. But if you would like to become the General Motors of recreation, I'm going to tell you how to do it."

For more than an hour, speaking entirely without notes, Harper held forth on a dazzling vision of what the future could look like for Brunswick—a company growing by acquisition, targeting new segments in recreation, leveraging a common management infrastructure for support. Harper concluded with a sneak preview tease calculated to heighten Brunswick's interest enough to make them forget about whatever their past troubles had been with the agency's Chicago office. "We in New York have made a comprehensive study of the opportunities for a single company, such as yours, to emerge as the General Motors of Recreation. If you'd like to work with us, I will assign a group of the finest minds in our business to prepare a blueprint showing you how to make it possible. McCann-Erickson has had a long association with Brunswick. We hope to have an even longer and more profitable one." Harper departed the room to await the committee's decision. Five minutes later Harper was informed that Brunswick wanted to continue to work with McCann to implement the plan that the head of the agency had just outlined to them. When Harper returned to New York, a colleague congratulated him on having saved the account. "I didn't even talk about the account. I merely changed the battlefield," Harper said. "You what?" asked his puzzled colleague. "It's all spelled out in Clausewitz's *On War*," Harper said. "If you decide you can't win the battle, change the battlefield."[31]

In a business world of monstrous egos, not everyone was susceptible to Marion Harper's brilliance. In February 1961 *Fortune* magazine printed an article titled "What Is Marion Harper Saying?"—the piece ran an incredible nine pages, an almost unheard of length for a profile on a single individual. It garnered the attention of Leonard Lavin, the blunt-spoken head of Alberto-Culver, a Chicago-based cosmetics firm, who was notoriously difficult to gain a meeting with. His company's VO5 product, through savvy television marketing, had recently gained respectable market share against much larger competitors. Intrigued by, and perhaps a bit jealous of, the laudatory *Fortune* piece, Lavin agreed to an ill-fated meeting with Harper. Following a brief presentation by McCann executives, Lavin dismissed everyone but Harper and one other McCann executive and then brought both men into his private office. Closing the door, Lavin, using a strong tone that had an insulting edge to it, told Harper, "I hear you're a pretty big shot." Harper tried to deflect the comment and responded in kind, "I hear you're a pretty big shot yourself." Lavin continued to press the attack. "At least people can understand me," he said, a clear jibe at Harper's reputation for speaking and writing in academic-type jargon. "Tell me, Mr. Harper, why you want my business." Harper stiffened his posture and responded, steely-eyed, "I'm not sure I do." Lavin refused to back down. "Then why waste your time and mine coming to Chicago?" Harper rose from his seat, signaling he considered the meeting concluded. "I was curious about you," the ad agency head replied. "My curiosity has been satisfied. Thank you for seeing us." Harper then turned and left the office.[32]

There were rumors, inevitably for someone of Harper's ambitions and success, that the advertising executive harbored political ambitions, that perhaps he would return to Oklahoma and run for governor or the United States Senate. He would not be the first head of a Madison Avenue firm to seek elected office. There had been Chester Bowles, cofounder of Benton and Bowles. The former adman had served as governor of Connecticut and then been elected to Congress. A liberal icon, Bowles had been assiduously cultivated by John F. Kennedy when the young senator was seeking his party's nomination for the presidency. A Cold War hawk, Kennedy desperately needed protection from left-wing challengers like Adlai Stevenson and Hubert Humphrey, and Bowles had provided it.

Harper and Bowles were both Yale men, and both were progressive on civil rights. It was Bowles's aide Harris Wofford who, during the 1960 campaign, with the election just days away, had persuaded Kennedy to make a phone call to Coretta Scott King, the wife of Martin Luther King Jr., when King was imprisoned in the Georgia state prison.[*][33] However, Harper and Bowles differed in one important respect: advertising was not the true love of Chester

---

[*] Historians credit Kennedy's phone call to King's wife, expressing concern for the jailed civil rights leader's safety, as well as Robert Kennedy's work behind-the-scenes to help secure King's release, as critical to Kennedy's success in the 1960 presidential election over Richard Nixon.

Bowles. It merely provided him with the financial resources to pursue his true passion, which was politics. But for Harper advertising was not merely a career; it defined him. Even when discussing his political ambitions, he could not resist slipping into an adman's pitch about how proper marketing could improve the republic. "I believe we can get politics up on to a whole different level," Harper told a reporter shortly after Kennedy's narrow presidential victory. "Do you think so many people would stay home on election day if the product they were offered were a little more stimulating? We've got to update the bosses, and teach the parties to find out what people really want. We've got to release the candidates from the traditions of the party system and show them how to achieve real success." Warming to his subject Harper began gesturing excitedly with his dark-framed eyeglasses. "The point is simply to apply modern concepts to marketing!"[34]

Harper's only true ambition, however, was to run the largest ad agency in the world. By 1953, after only five years running McCann, he had already doubled the firm's billings to $106 million. The one obstacle that stood in his way of growing the firm as rapidly as he wanted was that, because of perceived conflicts, advertising agencies were only permitted by their clients to serve one company in each business category. Because the conflicts were broadly defined, the situation was even worse. As Harper himself lamented to a colleague in 1954: "If we had General Foods' Jell-O, for example, we couldn't take a major coffee account like Hills Brothers, because General Foods owns Maxwell House. We couldn't take a competing coffee account even if we were not the Maxwell House agency. We'll never become number one in this business unless we break those restrictions!" When a client bought a business that competed with another client of the firm, the ad agency would be expected to resign one of the accounts. This frustrated a client that may have been perfectly happy with the agency but was now forced to find advertising services elsewhere if their current provider resigned, and it was maddening to the agency that lost the business.

Harper provided a solution to the dilemma: create a holding company to own more than one agency and thereby be able to serve competing accounts. The agencies would be operated completely independently, and even maintain physical separation, to ensure that no confidential data would be shared between competing accounts. But Harper's proposed solution challenged the most bedrock precept on Madison Avenue and would require a revolutionary change in how clients understood their agency relationship. For the rest of the 1950s Harper wrestled with the issue until he formed the Interpublic Group in 1960. Its headquarters were set up in the new Time-Life Building in New York, and Marion Harper became the company's chairman, chief executive officer, and president. The concept was replicating the same model as General Motors, which owned Buick, Oldsmobile, Chevrolet, and Cadillac, all of which competed against one another. By the end of 1961 Interpublic had acquired ten businesses. Harper's concept had detractors, including Norman Strouse, the CEO of J. Walter Thompson, the number one agency, which Harper had fixed his sights on toppling from its perch. "We thought Marion's idea of owning several agencies to service competing accounts was wrong and wouldn't work. We felt that clients would never stand for it. But looking back, we were wrong."[35]

✦ ✦ ✦

Don Johnston, an executive at McCann, who was close personally with Harper, also spent time with Harper's father when occasionally the McCann chief and Johnston would be traveling for business and Harper would stop by to visit his father's small dairy farm in Bucks County, Pennsylvania. Johnston was struck by the fact that the two men never discussed advertising, or the son's meteoric rise at McCann, or his stunning success in driving the firm to ever increasing heights by winning new accounts.[36] To Johnston it seemed as if the elder Harper had not followed his son's career at all. The two men seemed locked in an undeniable contest with the father not acknowledging the son's success, withholding the validation that his offspring naturally craved, while the son simmered with resentment at having been abandoned as a child by a father who would later remarry and start a new family.

In January 1960 Harper was unanimously selected to receive the Charles Coolidge Parlin Award, a prestigious industry award that was considered to be the highest honor in American marketing. Harper was the first advertising executive to be so honored by the American Marketing Association.[37] Harper invited Johnston to attend the black-tie award ceremony with him, and the two men departed in a limousine from Manhattan for the two-hour ride to Philadelphia, where the dinner was being held. On the drive, Harper asked his colleague to keep an eye out for his father, who would also be attending the dinner, driving from his Bucks County farm. "See that he gets a good seat, and if he gets there in time, bring him in to the predinner reception." Two more times along the drive, Harper made the same request of Johnston, that he wanted to make sure his father would be well taken care of, which Johnston assured him he would be.

The senior Harper arrived before the private reception and was met by Johnston in the hotel lobby. Johnston escorted him into the small guest room where Harper was being congratulated by the marketing association's distinguished guests. To Johnston's surprise, Harper merely acknowledged his father's presence with a slight nod while continuing the conversation he was engaged in. Since it appeared that Harper was not going to speak with his father, Johnston guided him to the bar. When the event's proceedings began, Johnston steered the elder Harper to a large table in front of the speaker's podium, where he had already reserved two seats.

After dinner, Harper proceeded to the podium, accepted his award, and spoke eloquently about the coming Information Revolution, the need for better information for government decisions, and he called for the creation of a new corporate position, a vice president of information. When he concluded there was enthusiastic applause. Johnston thought Marion Sr. seemed pleased as the pair exited the ballroom. He then excused himself to go to the men's room, where he met Harper coming out. Harper said, "Let's get out of here. The car is waiting outside." A surprised Johnston asked, "What about your dad?" Harper abruptly responded, "He saw and heard it. He'll find his way okay. Let's go!"[38]

Harper's father would pass away two years later, at the age of seventy-three, on November 5, 1962.[39] The following year Harper would complete the acquisition of another advertising agency, his company's fifth merger since 1961. The purchase of Erwin, Wasey, Ruthrauff & Ryan lifted Interpublic's billings to $500 million, well ahead of J. Walter Thompson's $420 million, and in the process making Interpublic the world's biggest advertising agency.[40] Marion Harper had finally achieved the goal he had set for himself since starting in the mailroom of McCann-Erickson earning $14 a week twenty-four years earlier.

Achieving his lifelong ambition of running the number one advertising agency now did not seem enough. Harper set out a new goal for himself and his firm: $1 billion in billings by 1970.[41]

Long-term colleagues of Harper, some of whom had known him since he had been referred to as Young Marion, would bemoan the changes in his character and management style. To them the 1960s Harper was starkly different from the 1950s Harper. His smiles, never frequent, became rare or nonexistent. He seemed more ruthless and much quicker to eliminate those who did not serve his purpose. Ad executive Emerson Foote wistfully recalled an earlier Marion Harper who had taken a risk by hiring him after Foote had suffered a nervous breakdown. In an era when any whiff of mental illness held a crushing stigma, no other agency would even consider hiring the talented adman. It was a kindness that Foote never forgot.[42]

Harper eliminated the company's executive committee and ruled his global advertising empire like, well, an emperor. He tolerated no dissent and could snap at anyone bold enough to question his decisions. He reported only to a hand-picked board of directors, all of whom were insiders beholden to him. Associates would relish any flashes of the humanity of the earlier Harper, but they became increasingly rare.

In pursuit of his never-ending quest for a bigger and bigger firm, Harper became increasingly reckless about business matters. Any focus on the firm's profitability was almost nonexistent, to the growing alarm of Interpublic's other shareholders as well as to its bankers. Harper's spending became increasingly profligate and indulgent. The company's aircraft, which in an earlier time had been an accommodation to efficiency, ensuring no executive time was wasted, now had grown to a fleet of aircraft, each one luxuriously appointed. Business decisions seemed increasingly about ego and indulgence. As Harper would tell a *Time* magazine reporter in 1962, "Man is captured by what he chases." And Marion Harper was captured by an obsession to lead the biggest ad agency in the world.

In 1963, three and a half years after divorcing his first wife, Harper married Valerie Feit, a charming, beautiful twenty-eight-year-old woman (nineteen years younger than Harper) who had been raised in both Paris and New York. She was a graduate of the Dalton School in New York and of both Science Politiques in Paris and Smith College, and she worked for a highly respected fashion agency owned by Interpublic. On their first wedding anniversary, Harper publicly vowed that he would never spend a night away from his wife, and, even when the couple had a child two and a half years later, Harper was accompanied on his business trips by his wife, their baby, and an entourage consisting of a nurse, a valet, and other attendants.[43] By all accounts Harper was a devoted husband, and the couple frequently arrived at business meetings holding hands, with Valerie carrying a rose her husband had presumably just presented to her. Occasionally, after too many drinks at a business function, Harper would weepily describe how lucky he had been to find love with a woman who was so devoted to his happiness.[44] The marriage, however, did not seem to otherwise soften Harper's business persona, which only seemed to get harsher.

A McCann executive who had known Harper since his days in the research office sought him out, seeking to perhaps reignite a glimmer of the old Harper. The two men had been through countless pitches together, their wives had become close, and there had been visits to each other's ranches. Meeting with Harper—privately, of course—he reminded the head of the world's largest advertising agency of a time, years ago now, when the two men had been in Los Angeles on business. With their work responsibilities concluded, they had made plans the next day to go out on the executive's Harley Davidson 61-cubic-inch motorcycle, a monster of a bike known by enthusiasts as the Knucklehead. With Harper holding on for dear life in the back, the two men cruised past the upscale mansions of Beverly Hills before heading out onto the winding roads of Pacific Palisades and then tackling the harrowing switchback firebreaks of the scenic Santa Monica Mountains beside Malibu. It had been an exhilarating experience in an earlier, more carefree time. The colleague looked to Harper for some flicker of a nostalgic smile, a glimpse of the younger Harper, but he was only met with a stony silence. Harper acted as if the joyful excursion the two men had once shared had never happened.[45]

Soon after McCann-Erickson was awarded the prestigious Coca-Cola account, Neal Gilliatt was selected by Harper to oversee the soft drink company's account. The round-faced, balding adman bore something of a passing resemblance to the McCann CEO. Gilliatt had established a solid reputation managing the marketing affairs of Swift & Co., the country's largest beef processor, from McCann's Chicago office. With his elevation to managing Coca-Cola's advertising, the adman relocated his wife and two sons to Greenwich, Connecticut, from where he would make the daily commute to McCann's Manhattan offices. Gilliatt was a Midwesterner, born in the small town of Washington in southern Indiana, where his father owned and operated a tomato cannery. He graduated from Indiana University, where he was a member of the Sigma Alpha Epsilon fraternity, before earning an MBA at Northwestern University. He became an instructor at Indiana University for two years before joining the Office of Price Administration, overseeing food prices during World War II. When the war ended Gilliatt entered the advertising field, joining McCann's Chicago office. He was active in his church's affairs, where he helped establish a counseling center. He was also engaged in philanthropic activities, fundraising for the Epilepsy Foundation of America and serving on the board of directors of the New York Philharmonic.

Gilliatt would shortly come to know J. Paul Austin, when that Coca-Cola executive returned from a four-year assignment to South Africa. Shortly after his return to Atlanta, Austin was given overall responsibility for Coca-Cola's massive advertising budget, where he would come to work closely with Gilliatt and McCann. The Hoosier and the Harvard grad quickly bonded over more than just business, having shared interests in community and civic affairs. The two men developed a strong friendship, and their families would even vacation together.[46]

It seems likely Austin's imagination had been sparked at Christmas of 1964 by *Rudolph the Red-Nosed Reindeer*, which was sponsored by General Electric, whose board of directors the Coca-Cola president had joined earlier that year. Austin would have then logically turned to his close friend Neal Gilliatt at McCann to explore the idea of a Christmas special for Coca-Cola, perhaps during an annual Christmas season trek that Gilliatt made every holiday season to Atlanta, to visit his friend, frequently with Harper and his wife, Valerie. Gilliatt, whose birthday was on Christmas Eve, would have in turn discussed the concept within McCann to generate potential ideas.[47]

Just as critically, the show would need a television network to preempt its regularly scheduled programming slot to broadcast a special. NBC would certainly be repeating the *Rudolph* special and that left only Leonard Goldenson at ABC and Frank Stanton at CBS. Harper was very close to the CBS president. The two men had both come up in the research side of their respective businesses. In fact, Harper had hired Herta Herzog, a psychologist and market researcher who was the wife of Stanton's business partner, Paul Lazarsfeld, in manufacturing the Radio Program Analyzer, a product Harper had exclusively licensed for McCann. However, CBS's programming head, James T. Aubrey, had a well-known policy against broadcasting specials. That would be an obstacle.

THE NETWORK
CBS AND FRANK STANTON

✦

Jim, you've got to be out of your mind.
—Frank Stanton, president of CBS,
to James Aubrey, head of CBS Television

FEBRUARY 1965
CBS HEADQUARTERS, NEW YORK CITY

Frank Stanton, the president of CBS, had just finished working late, past ten p.m., at the company's newly opened headquarters at 51 West 52nd Street in Manhattan. As he prepared to exit the office, he saw James T. Aubrey, the head of CBS Television, who was also about to retire for the evening and return home. The two men exited the building together, and Aubrey, who lived near Stanton on the Upper East Side, asked his boss how he was heading home. Stanton responded that he had not arranged for his car and driver that night, and that he intended to just hail a cab. "Would you like to walk?" asked Aubrey. It was a surprising suggestion to walk the forty-six blocks late on a winter night, but Stanton agreed, perhaps sensing that his restive executive had something on his mind. He had, after all, noticed that Aubrey had recently become increasingly testy and arrogant with his colleagues. Like many others, Stanton felt that the calm demeanor that Aubrey projected disguised some type of inner turmoil.

The two men engaged in polite conversation for nine blocks as they walked up Fifth Avenue, and as they neared the Pierre Hotel, opposite Central Park, Aubrey made another odd suggestion. "Would you like a nightcap?" Stanton replied that what he would really like to do is get some food. Aubrey mentioned that the two men could get some food inside the hotel. The two men entered, found a table inside the bar, and ordered drinks and sandwiches. When they finished eating, they departed the hotel, and resumed walking up Fifth Avenue. Aubrey then said he had something important he would like to discuss with Stanton.

The two television executives could not have been more different. Stanton, fifty-six, was a product of the Midwest and had the detached, academic manner befitting a man who held a doctorate from Ohio State University in psychology. The Midwesterner's even temperament made him a natural choice to smooth over delicate issues with sensitive celebrity talent as well as with prickly government regulators and preening politicians. Princeton-educated Aubrey, forty-six, was a man who seemed to take sadistic enjoyment in his blunt, heavy-handed treatment of celebrities and his fellow colleagues at CBS. Lucille Ball detested the man.* Nicknamed "Jungle Jim" and "the Smiling Cobra," Aubrey himself enjoyed telling the

---

* When CBS decided that Lucille Ball's popular show had to be rescheduled to a different time slot, the performer resisted the change and, as the star of one of the network's highest rated programs, expected to be accommodated. Jim Aubrey personally flew out to Los Angeles to deliver the news that she would not be. As soon as he left, Ball phoned Frank Stanton to tell him "I can't live with this man" (Lewis J. Paper, *Empire: William S. Paley and the Making of CBS* [St. Martin's Press, 1987], 235).

story of when he fired an executive who was in the middle of making a presentation. "You're through," Aubrey said, interrupting the man. The executive explained that he had a few more minutes of things to discuss. "No," Aubrey interrupted again. "*You* are through." Stanton had married his childhood sweetheart, Ruth Stephenson, whom he had met at a church party when both were freshmen in high school. He had never dated another girl, and the married couple seemed to enjoy a cloistered private life, rarely availing themselves of the entertainment opportunities in Manhattan. Aubrey's marriage to Hollywood actress Phyllis Thaxter had broken up in 1962, and he was frequently seen out on the town with a revolving door of young beauties on his arm.

Stanton feared that Aubrey was about to tell him that he was resigning from CBS. Aubrey was a highly sought-after executive. He had been brought into CBS in December 1959, when the network's net annual profits were $25.2 million. Two years later earnings had more than doubled.[1] Aubrey had proven that he had a gift for programming that captured audiences and delivered advertising dollars. In the 1963–1964 programming season, all twelve of the top daytime programs and fourteen of the top fifteen prime-time shows were on CBS. (*Bonanza* on NBC was the lone exception to Aubrey's dominance.) The programs were decidedly lowbrow, typically comedies like *Petticoat Junction* and *The Beverly Hillbillies*. Aubrey's programming choices may have embarrassed CBS's founder, William S. Paley, in the elite salons of New York City, but Paley was more than well compensated for his shame with ratings success, revenues, the network's stock price performance, and a dramatic rise in his personal fortune.

Aubrey's bottom-line focus would bring him into conflict with the powerful head of CBS News, Fred Friendly, whose focus was on preserving the network's status as a prestigious news organization building upon the legacy of legendary journalist Edward R. Murrow. "All I'm trying to do is save the company some money," Aubrey explained in a tense management meeting. "All I'm trying to do is save the company," was Friendly's tart rejoinder. "Look, Fred," Aubrey told the newsman, "I have regard for what Murrow and you have accomplished, but in this adversary system you and I are always going to be at each other's throats. They say to me, 'Take your soiled little hands, get the ratings, and make as much money as you can'; they say to you, 'Take your lily-white hands, do your best, and bring us prestige.'"[2]

Just a month before Aubrey and Stanton's late-night stroll down Fifth Avenue, Stanton refereed a battle between Fred Friendly and Aubrey over whether or not to interrupt the network's regularly scheduled programming to broadcast the funeral of Winston Churchill. Friendly urged all-day coverage for the state funeral, made possible by the Telstar satellite. On a phone call with Aubrey and Stanton, Friendly acidly commented that if CBS was showing cartoons while NBC was broadcasting the funeral cortege of one of the great leaders of the twentieth century, they would all regret it for the rest of their lives. Friendly would win that round of the continuous tug-of-war between profits and the "unscheduled news" that Aubrey so thoroughly resented.[3]

Instead of tendering his resignation, however, Aubrey shocked Stanton by introducing him to a plot that Aubrey had been organizing. The brash head of CBS Television explained to his boss that he had put together a group of investors to buy out Paley, the network president and chairman. Aubrey sought to enlist Stanton's support in his corporate mutiny. In Aubrey's designs, Paley would be pushed out, Stanton would be elevated to chairman, and Aubrey would become the network president. Stanton was stunned to learn that some of the investors Aubrey identified were men who were purportedly close friends of Paley. "Jim, you've got to be out of your mind," said Stanton. While he conceded that the plan was not impossible, Stanton refused to be a party to it. Aubrey told his boss that he was a fool for not seizing the opportunity, and that neither of them needed Paley to run the network.

Frank Nicholas Stanton was born on March 20, 1908, in Muskegon, Michigan. When he was three months old, the family returned to Dayton, Ohio, where his parents had previously lived. As early as grade school, the future president of CBS displayed an industrious nature, by securing a part-time job at the Metropolitan, one of Dayton's large clothing stores. His first duties were wrapping packages and running errands, but the boy's curiosity would send him exploring into every corner of the store, where his fresh-faced earnestness made an impression on his older colleagues. Every day after his last class, young Stanton raced downtown on his bicycle and scurried throughout the store looking for any way in which he could be useful—greeting customers, organizing clothing racks, straightening inventory, arranging a window display, or making a sale. His employer was so impressed by the boy's work ethic that he was even invited to sit in on a meeting of the store's board of directors.

After high school, Stanton went on to college at Ohio Wesleyan University and then to Ohio State, where he earned a PhD in psychology in 1935. That same year, the ambitious Midwesterner, having set his sights on the big city, sent monographs of his work on radio research to CBS suggesting politely that he might be a useful man to have around. CBS agreed, and the same young boy who had made himself indispensable at the Metropolitan clothing store in Dayton, Ohio, now worked assiduously to make himself just as useful at CBS in New York City. He worked seventy- to eighty-hour weeks and was quickly promoted to research director. During World War II Stanton took on additional duties at the Office of War Information and the War Department, commuting between Washington, DC, and New York, spending Tuesday, Friday, Saturday, and Sunday in Washington and the remaining days working at CBS in Manhattan.

While working at CBS Stanton also took on an outside research project with sociologist Paul Lazarsfeld of the University of Vienna. The two men had developed what they called a Program Analyzer, a machine used to test audience reactions to radio programs. Listeners were seated in a chair with two push buttons, a green one for the right hand and a red one for the left. The buttons were connected by wires to a machine that looked like a cross between a typewriter and a cash register. Pens were attached to slow-moving rolls of paper, and the ink from the pens would record a listener's reactions. When hearing something they enjoyed they would press the green button, and when hearing something they disliked they would press the red button. A discussion was held with psychologists afterward to probe the listeners for more feedback to understand their responses. Marion Harper of McCann-Erickson was fascinated by the machines, and he had his ad agency sign a licensing agreement with Stanton and Lazarsfeld for the exclusive use of their machine. (Lazarsfeld's wife, psychologist Herta Herzog, would also go to work for Harper in the research department at McCann.)

Stanton's diligence brought him to the attention of William Paley, the network's cofounder and chairman. After only ten years at CBS, in his first one-on-one meeting with Paley, Stanton was astonished when he was offered the job of president of the company. He asked for time to think about the proposal. When three months passed by without Paley reaching back to him for his answer,

Stanton assumed that the chairman had reconsidered his offer. On Christmas Eve the two men ran into each other outside Paley's office's reception area on the twentieth floor of the CBS offices at 485 Madison Avenue. Stanton awkwardly suggested that perhaps he could visit with Paley sometime in the next couple of weeks, if the chairman had time. "Let's do it right now," suggested Paley. Stanton said, "It's clear from the fact that you've made no effort to follow up on our conversation that you've had second thoughts." A surprised Paley responded, "Oh no, I was just waiting for you to announce it." He then sought to confirm that Stanton did indeed want the job. "I would like to do it," was Stanton's reply. "Whenever you want to do it, go ahead and announce it," said Paley. There was no discussion of money, titles, or offices.

For years, Stanton was the leading advocate for holding a series of televised debates between the two leading parties' presidential candidates. In 1952 he broached the idea with Dwight Eisenhower, suggesting that the Republican nominee debate Adlai Stevenson, the Democratic candidate. Eisenhower, who typically delegated decisions to his staff with relevant expertise, asked Stanton if he had run the idea past Ben Duffy of BBD&O, the ad agency that served as the candidate's media adviser. Stanton replied that yes, he had. "And what did he say?" asked the candidate. "No," said Stanton. "Well, that's my answer," said Eisenhower.[4]

Stanton finally succeeded eight years later in the 1960 presidential election between Democratic senator John F. Kennedy and Vice President Richard Nixon. William Paley and Frank Stanton both flew to Chicago, where the first debate was being staged at CBS station WBBM-TV. The producer for the debate was CBS executive Don Hewitt. When Nixon stepped out of his dressing room, minutes before the faceoff was to begin, Hewitt was shocked by the candidate's appearance. Nixon had lost over twenty pounds from a staph infection resulting from a knee injury, and the candidate had just reinjured the same knee on a car door on the way to the television station. His face had a grayish tone, the same color as his suit, which Hewitt immediately knew would look washed out on viewers' black-and-white television screens. If Nixon looks terrible, thought Hewitt, the show will look terrible. The network executive approached Nixon's television adviser, Ted Rogers, and asked him if he was satisfied with his candidate's appearance. Rogers shared Hewitt's concerns over Nixon's haggard appearance, but he also knew it was too late to do anything about it. Fearing a charge that CBS had somehow set up the Republican to look bad, Hewitt went to see his two bosses, Sig Mickelson, head of CBS News, and Frank Stanton, the network president. He told the two men that he thought they had a real problem with Nixon, and they better take a look at him. Stanton looked over Nixon, and, sharing Hewitt's concerns, he also approached Rogers and asked him if he was sure that Nixon looked all right. For a second time Rogers said yes.

The broadcast was a disaster for Nixon, whose pallid appearance was accentuated by the unforgiving camera lens. Kennedy, by contrast, looked confident, and his tan and his tailored dark suit looked striking on television. "That night the entire nation watched, and presidential politics came into living rooms in an intensely personal way. All feel, all senses," wrote historian David Halberstam. Stanton thought Kennedy had performed terrifically. "The first debate elected him," he said years later. As soon as the debate ended Stanton left the control room and headed for the stage to express thanks to each candidate for taking the time to participate in an event that the CBS president had worked for years to achieve. When he arrived at the stage he saw Nixon's briefcase and his topcoat, but not the candidate himself. When he inquired where Nixon was, he was told that the vice president had just gotten up and left. Stanton then approached Kennedy. The two men shook hands, and Kennedy invited Stanton to the office that each candidate had been provided at the station. Once inside his private room Kennedy took a personal call, and when it was over, he turned to Stanton and introduced him to Richard Daley, the mayor of Chicago. Before the debate, Daley had shunned Kennedy. "I'm changing my mind," Daley told Stanton. "I'm gonna tell my boys I'm gonna support him." Daley's support was critical to delivering Illinois's electoral support to John Kennedy and, as a result, likely the presidency itself.

Stanton's closest relationship with a politician was with one of the men Kennedy had held off to earn his party's nomination, Lyndon B. Johnson. The Texan had first come to CBS's offices in 1938 as a young congressman. Bill Paley's secretary announced to the company chairman that there was a very tall Texan wearing boots and a big hat waiting out in the reception area to see him. "Mister Paley, I have this here ticket for a two-hundred-and-fifty-watt station in Austin, and I'd like to join CBS as an affiliate," said Johnson. Paley explained that, unfortunately, that was a small station and, well, the radio network already had two perfectly good stations nearby, one in Dallas and one in San Antonio. Nonetheless, Paley sent his visitor to see Frank Stanton, then a young man in the CBS research department. This was the kind of sensitive situation that Stanton would prove adept at handling throughout his career. He didn't need to look at a map to understand the importance of cultivating a political relationship in Washington, DC, for the regulated network. Stanton made the station owned by Lyndon and his wife, Lady Bird, a CBS affiliate, and as it prospered it enriched the Johnsons. It was a favor that the Texas couple never forgot. There was a sense that large companies pushed an inordinate amount of advertising dollars at the small station, a disproportionate spend for the relatively small Austin market. When he was vice president, people on Johnson's staff, as well as occasionally Lady Bird herself, would call advertising agencies to harangue them to increase their spending on the station. Even as president, Johnson carried with him a piece of paper showing him the station's ad sales for the week.[5]

Beginning in 1965, the relationship between Johnson and Stanton would be tested by CBS News's reporting on the escalating war in Vietnam. Stanton's home had a direct line from the network's switchboard, and the phone would frequently ring at seven thirty p.m., precisely at the conclusion of the CBS News nightly broadcast. "For God's sake, don't take the call," Stanton's wife, Ruth, would say, knowing that on the other end of the call would be the irate resident of the White House upset about that night's coverage. Frequently the Texan's tirade would not be exhausted until after nine p.m.

In September 1964 Stanton visited Vietnam on a fact-finding mission for the US Information Agency, where he was an adviser. When he returned the network executive gave a bleak report to both President Johnson and secretary of defense Robert McNamara. Two months later, after securing his election to the presidency in a landslide, the president invited Stanton to a secret meeting at the Johnson ranch in Texas. Johnson took his friend on a walk, and he offered him two posts in his administration, undersecretary of state and secretary of health, education, and welfare. Stanton declined both. He anticipated that Bill Paley would resign in 1966, and he hoped that, after years as president of CBS, he would finally accede to the top job of chief executive officer.[6]

In the summer of 1965, CBS dispatched a thirty-five-year-old reporter named Morley Safer to Vietnam. A tested war correspondent, Safer had reported from conflict zones in the Middle East,

Cyprus, and Algeria. The reporter suspected that he wasn't chosen for this new assignment merely for his experience, however. He thought that, just perhaps, his status of being single and a Canadian made him expendable in the eyes of his superiors in New York, should the worst befall their reporter. Safer decided, somewhat randomly, to visit Da Nang in central Vietnam, where he would report on the US Marines who were operating from a staging area there. When he arrived, an officer told him of an operation his troops planned to conduct the following day, and he invited Safer to come along. The officer told the reporter that his troops were going to conduct a "search and destroy" operation in a village complex called Cam Ne.

The next day the CBS correspondent and his Vietnamese cameraman, Hà Thúc Cần, set out with the Marines in amphibious carriers. As they approached their target, the Marines dismounted and in a single line began firing at the huts. (The Marines claimed they had taken fire from the village. Safer believes that the troops had actually mistakenly shot at each other.) The troops then descended on the villages and began setting dozens of buildings on fire with Zippo lighters and flamethrowers, while the residents wept and protested the destruction of their homes. Safer's cameraman, who spoke both Vietnamese and English, interceded with a group of Marines, begging and screaming at them to stop, and thereby saving a group of cowering women and children from being torched by an American about to fire a flamethrower into a deep hole where they had taken refuge.[7]

When CBS News broadcast Safer's report, the televised images rocked the nation. Viewers were furious at the network, incredulous that such acts could have been committed by American troops, as well as horrified by what they had witnessed, the violence of war now being transmitted directly into their living rooms. The next morning Frank Stanton was awakened at home by a phone call. As soon as he lifted the receiver the caller unleashed a profane explosion into the CBS president's ear. "Who is this?" asked a still groggy Stanton. "Frank, this is your president," said Lyndon Johnson before continuing his obscenities-laced rant. Stanton was summoned to the White House, where Johnson demanded that the network head fire Morley Safer, accusing the reporter of being a communist. Stanton defended his reporter, explaining that, no, he wasn't a communist; he was a Canadian. "Well, I knew he wasn't an American," responded Johnson.

The incident was another powerful indicator of the growing influence of television. If television could make presidents by bringing the candidates into voters' living rooms and making politics personal, as in the Kennedy-Nixon debates, then it could also break presidents by broadcasting the ugly reality of their policies into the homes of voters as well. Television was not just shaping American pop culture by feeding viewers a steady diet of sitcoms and game shows and dramas; it was shaping America itself.

Shortly after his late-night conversation with James Aubrey, Frank Stanton phoned CBS chairman William Paley and told him that the time had come to part with Aubrey. "Are you sure?" Paley asked. Stanton told him there was no other course. He did not share the details of the corporate coup that Aubrey had outlined to him outside the Pierre Hotel. The CBS president did not wish to have any involvement in damaging Paley's relationships with his network of friends, some of whom, according to Aubrey, were involved in funding the prospective deal.

Before terminating such a key executive, Stanton knew he had to make immediate arrangements for a successor. On Friday, February 26, 1965, Stanton phoned Jack Schneider, who was functioning as manager of CBS's New York station, having previously run stations in Chicago and Philadelphia, and summoned him to his office. Schneider had been in his role in New York for only five months. Stanton told Schneider that he intended to fire Aubrey and that Schneider would replace him in the role as head of CBS Television. Schneider had to be shocked by the news of Aubrey's pending termination as well as by his own elevation to head of the entire network's non-news operations. Stanton instructed him to tell no one else of the news except his wife, and then he ordered him to take the rest of the day off.[8]

That same day, Michael Dann, a CBS vice president for programming and one of Aubrey's immediate subordinates, got a sense that something was afoot with Aubrey when Bill Paley reached out to him directly and began discussing programming. Dann, an animated elfin-like man with a high-pitched voice, was referred to by the executive assistants as "the Screamer." Paley had not spoken with him in months, but now the chairman was oddly peppering him with questions about the new fall lineup. A half hour after their initial phone conversation, Paley called Dann back and ordered him to buy a program they had discussed.[9] Paley was clearly reasserting his authority, thought Dann, and the executive could not be more thrilled. He considered Aubrey to be "committable" and would refer to working for the man as "his own personal Vietnam." Dann lamented that CBS had lost out on buying the program *Bewitched* from Screen Gems because Aubrey insisted that the show, which came with Ralston Purina as a sponsor, be sold to CBS clean without any obligations. When Screen Gems refused Aubrey's demand, he threatened the production company, saying that they would never do business with CBS again. The show would be purchased the following day by ABC, where it would go on to become a ratings success.

Having secured his replacement, Stanton reached out to Jim Aubrey himself, who was in Miami, Florida, for a weekend celebration of Jackie Gleason's forty-ninth birthday. Aubrey was staying at the residence of Jack Smith, a close friend of Aubrey's who worked at CBS in advertising sales. Stanton told Smith to convey a message to Aubrey that he needed to speak with him and that he wanted him to return to New York City. The request alarmed Smith, who blurted out, "You're going to fire him." Stanton replied, "I didn't say that." Smith warned Stanton that he would have a lot of trouble if he tried to fire the executive, a bold warning from the sales manager to the network president. At some point that day Stanton and Aubrey connected by phone. Stanton requested that the executive return to New York the following day to meet. Aubrey was told that if he couldn't book a commercial flight, a private plane would be sent to retrieve him.

Aubrey caught a flight at ten the following morning and met with Stanton in his office at CBS early that afternoon. The CBS president told Aubrey that after careful consideration he and Paley had both decided it was best for the network and Aubrey to part ways, and he asked for the executive's resignation. Aubrey did not resist. Stanton asked, "How shall we handle this?" Aubrey responded, "Nothing can be gained by dragging it out. There will be no graceful exit, no world cruise for me. I'll just clean out my desk and not be here on Monday." He asked for a meeting with Paley, and Stanton arranged for the two men to meet at the Regency Hotel, where Paley was living while his apartment was being refurbished. Aubrey then departed for his meeting with Paley.

An hour after Aubrey had exited Stanton's office, Paley called Stanton, informing him that Aubrey had never arrived. The Regency Hotel was just a five-minute walk away, so Aubrey's absence was troubling. Stanton began to panic. He called down to the security men in the lobby, who reported that they had not seen Aubrey depart. Stanton ordered the men to search the building for the missing executive. He rushed to Aubrey's office but found it empty. He began to fear that the network head, distraught at having just been fired, may have committed suicide. After thirty minutes Stanton's phone rang again. It was Aubrey, who was calling to explain that he had taken a walk in Central Park to clear his head. He was now heading over to see Paley.

Bill Paley, the CBS chairman, and Jim Aubrey had an awkward relationship. To other executives it appeared that Aubrey treated Paley with a mix of condescension and contempt, which seemed to worsen with the executive's programming success. Aubrey's tone of voice when interrupting Paley in a meeting had an edge of impatience and insult. If Paley called when Aubrey was visiting with a friend, he would wink and tell his secretary, "Tell the chairman I'll call him back." But on this Saturday afternoon Aubrey was full of contrition. "I know I've made a mess of things. I want to ask you for another chance and tell you that I would never let these things happen again, but I know you won't do it; I know I don't deserve another chance. And I want you to know that I understand your actions and will never say or do anything to hurt the company." Paley wished his former executive well, and James T. Aubrey, the man whom the founder of CBS had once seen as in line to become his successor, departed gracefully.

The departure of the imperious Aubrey, who had complete authority over CBS's programming, opened up the potential for the network to broadcast specials. Just as he opposed the intrusion of "unscheduled news" programs into his programming lineup, Aubrey had a strict policy against broadcasting specials, which he believed ruptured the established viewing habits of the network's loyal viewers, sending them to competing channels. The few exceptions that Aubrey allowed, such as the network's annual broadcast of *The Wizard of Oz* and the Miss America pageant, were proven ratings winners.

Aubrey's position against specials, also known as "spectaculars" to distinguish them from the network's regular programs, was conventional programming wisdom in television. As *Broadcasting* magazine noted in 1965, "Networks acknowledge that only in rare instances can specials triumph in the ratings race."[10] Legendary advertising executive David Ogilvy, founder of Ogilvy and Mather, wrote in his book *Confessions of an Advertising Man*, published in 1963: "We have never produced a television spectacular. I have a phobia for these extravaganzas; with rare exceptions they cost too much in relation of the size of the audience that they deliver."[11] NBC, a perennial ratings loser, was also known as "the specials network" and aired more of these nonrecurring type programs than ABC and CBS combined.[12] However, the peacock network's airing of specials seemed more of a concession to the failure of their scheduled lineup than a viable programming strategy.

Aubrey's firing would be fortuitous to the ad agency McCann-Erickson, however, when two months after the executive's firing they began to search for a network time slot for their client, Coca-Cola. The soft drink company had planned to broadcast an animated special on ABC that year—a modern adaptation of the 1865 Lewis Carroll novel *Alice's Adventures in Wonderland*. The production had the lengthy title *Alice in Wonderland (or What's a Nice Kid like You Doing in a Place like This?)*. Hanna-Barbera, the creators of *The Jetsons*, *The Flintstones*, and *The Yogi Bear Show*, was producing the special, and it was tentatively scheduled to be broadcast during the holiday season between Thanksgiving and Christmas in 1965.[13] The one-hour special was delayed, however, most likely due to production problems, and it would not be broadcast until March 30, 1966.

Coca-Cola was still interested in sponsoring a special for the coming Christmas, however. It is likely that the impatient president of Coca-Cola, J. Paul Austin, was not happy to learn that the holiday special he had commissioned for the soft drink company would not be ready in time. McCann-Erickson would need to seek out another Christmas special.

On April 9, 1965, *Time* magazine featured the *Peanuts* characters on its cover with a story titled "The World According to Peanuts." That magazine cover was seen by a McCann executive named John Allen. Allen recalled seeing a documentary by a San Francisco–based producer named Lee Mendelson. The production had been well done, but did not, in the adman's opinion, have any commercial marketability. The documentary had been about Charles Schulz, the creator of the highly successful *Peanuts* comic strip. Would Mendelson and Schulz possibly be able to produce a Christmas special?

THE CARTOONIST
PEANUTS AND CHARLES M. SCHULZ

✦

Happiness does not create humor.
There's nothing funny about being happy.
Sadness creates humor.
—Charles M. Schulz[1]

MAY 5, 1965
SAN FRANCISCO BAY AREA

A stunned Lee Mendelson put down the handset of his phone and stared at it for a minute before picking it up off the cradle, placing his index finger into the rotary dial and dialing the seven digits of Charles Schulz's phone number. When Schulz answered, Mendelson excitedly gave him the news. "I think I just sold a Charlie Brown Christmas special." Schulz was confused, knowing the two men had never discussed such a program. "Oh yeah? What in the world is that?" asked the cartoonist. "Something you're going to write tomorrow," Mendelson shot back. The producer then explained the call he had just received from John Allen of McCann-Erickson and Coca-Cola's interest in possibly sponsoring a *Peanuts* Christmas special.

Allen had inquired if Mendelson and Schulz had ever considered making a Christmas special. Mendelson fibbed, replying, "Of course." The McCann executive explained that his firm's client Coca-Cola was looking for a Christmas special. "The bad news," Allen had explained, "is that today is Wednesday and they'll need an outline in Atlanta by Monday."

Schulz had historically brushed aside all overtures from Hollywood. Fans of the *Peanuts* comic strip, however, had increasingly expressed an interest in seeing their beloved round-headed characters on television and/or film, but whenever children would write to the strip's creator to beseech him with the idea, he would consistently write back the same terse reply: "There are some greater things in the world than TV animated cartoons." Despite his prior skepticism, however, and notwithstanding Mendelson's recent failure to sell the *Peanuts* documentary, Schulz was intrigued. Possibly because of Coca-Cola's involvement and the potential association of *Peanuts* with such a premier brand, he seemed immediately captivated by the opportunity and inclined to move forward. The two men agreed to meet up the following day at Schulz's Sebastopol home to sketch out their ideas for a Christmas special.

The next morning Mendelson made the ninety-minute drive from his Burlingame home to Schulz's twenty-eight-acre property in Sonoma County, north of San Francisco, situated midway between the Pacific Ocean to the west and Napa Valley to the east. Referred to as Coffee Grounds by Schulz and his wife, Joyce, because of the home's location on a street named Coffee Lane, the property had had two homes, horse stables, a corral, and a work studio when they had purchased it seven years earlier. Joyce had also overseen an ambitious "parks and recreation" construction project, including building lighted tennis courts, a baseball diamond, a four-hole golf course, and a heated swimming pool—all to occupy her active, athletic husband and their five rambunctious children: Meredith, Monte, Amy, Jill, and Craig. Roaming the extensive property were an assortment of animals and pets, including ducks, turtles, dogs, cats, horses, cows, a rabbit, and a pet mouse. The property also had an aviary full of an assortment of birds. The rural home sat in an area known for its apple orchards, and the heavily wooded property included many tall pine trees and redwoods. The couple had purchased the property for $70,000 in 1958.[2] Schulz enjoyed taking visitors on tours of his property, leaving guests with the feeling that the cartoonist was just as astonished at his wondrous lifestyle as they were.[3]

When Mendelson arrived at Schulz's studio, the cartoonist interrupted his daily ritual of working on the *Peanuts* comic strip—he could usually produce one day's comic strip in one hour, and when focused and productive, could produce up to six per day. Unlike many successful cartoonists, Schulz insisted on doing all the artwork and lettering himself and would not even contemplate using an assistant to ink any of his *Peanuts* panels. He managed to stay weeks ahead of his production deadline, even though every day he would also take phone calls, and sometimes had up to one hundred letters[*] a day to answer.[4] The conscientious cartoonist personally responded to every inquiry and piece of fan mail, oftentimes including a hand-drawn sketch. His daily responsibilities also included driving his five children to school in the morning. When they returned

---

[*] The number of letters arriving at the Schulzes' home varied with what was going on in the strip or, later with the airing of a *Peanuts* special. When "A Charlie Brown Valentine" aired, viewers responded to the sad plight of Charlie Brown not receiving any valentines at his school party by inundating Schulz's office with valentines (Charles M. Schulz, *My Life with Charlie Brown* [University Press of Mississippi, 2010], 97).

home, the devoted father would often stop working and engage his children in a game of touch football or some other play. One of his daughters would later comment that she never knew her father even had a job until she was a teenager.

The producer and the cartoonist quickly got down to business as soon as Mendelson arrived. Schulz began eagerly rattling off ideas, themes, and possible scenes, having obviously spent time thinking about the project after the prior day's call. Mendelson just as quickly jotted down the cartoonist's thoughts. "If it's to be a Christmas special, I want it to certainly deal with the true meaning of Christmas," he said. "And I'd like to do a lot of scenes in the snow and with skating." Before moving to California, Schulz and his wife had both grown up in Minnesota, and so they had experienced wintry holiday weather and enjoyed winter recreational activities. They had gone skating on their first date, and when Joyce slipped and fell on a candy wrapper, Schulz, an excellent skater, scooped her up.[*]

Schulz also suggested including a scene involving a Christmas play, something that had a special provenance in his own childhood. One particular play had always stuck in Charles Schulz's mind. The cartoonist collected childhood humiliations the way other people might collect stamps or seashells. When he was six years old Schulz's family had moved from Minnesota to Needles, a remote desert town in California where summer temperatures can reach 120 degrees.[**] The family spent only two years in the rugged, desolate area before

---

[*] Schulz's first date with Donna Johnson, the red-haired young woman who became the inspiration for the little red-haired girl in the *Peanuts* comic strip, was also to an ice skating rink, to watch an Ice Capades show (Darryn King, "Charlie Brown Never Found His Little Red-Haired Girl, but We Did," *Vanity Fair*, November 6, 2015).

[**] Devoted *Peanuts* fans will recognize Needles as the hometown of Spike, one of Snoopy's brothers.

returning to St. Paul, but while there young Schulz had attended second grade in the newly constructed D Street School, where he was one of only two students in his class to make the honor roll. Sparky,* as the boy was called, lined up onstage with thirteen of the school's other students, from various grades, each holding out a letter spelling out M-E-R-R-Y C-H-R-I-S-T-M-A-S. As part of the performance, each child was expected to stand forward in turn and sing out a rehearsed sentence that had been crafted to spotlight the letter they were holding. Sparky who was holding the letter "A" stood ready with his memorized line: *"A" stands for all of us—all of us! "A" stands for all of us!* When the performance began, however, the first couple of youngsters got stage fright, whispering their lines and shyly hiding behind the oversized letters. In an attempt to bolster her students' confidence, their teacher stepped forward and motioned with her arms for the remaining students to sing louder, but to no avail. Sparky vowed to himself that, when his turn came, he would not falter, and he projected his voice loudly and clearly so that everyone in the assembled crowd, which included his mother, Dena, easily heard him. The crowd burst out in spontaneous laughter, chuckling at Schulz's robust enunciation, but the young boy was stung by the response. Even years later he would recall how he felt. "It kind of hurt my feelings because, after all, I'm doing it right. Those other dumb kids, they didn't speak it loud enough."[5]

Schulz's recounting of the incident is more telling than the incident itself. The cartoonist carried the slights of childhood, real or imagined, like they had a handle. There was no heartbreak,

---

* Schulz was nicknamed by his uncle after a comic strip horse named Spark Plug found in Billy DeBeck's *Barney Google and Snuffy Smith*, a leading cartoon at the time of Schulz's birth (Charles M. Schulz, *Conversations* [University Press of Mississippi, 2020], xiii).

humiliation, or indignity from his earliest years that he could not recount years later with a stunning clarity and, with its recounting, revisit the emotional wound, revealing it to be still as raw as the day the injustice was inflicted. This was precisely Schulz's genius, however, and why he was able to become the chronicler of childhood cruelties. He had, after all, created a cartoon that was populated with children, who, more often than not, were surprisingly callous and unaware. The comedy for readers of *Peanuts* would often be accompanied with a wince of recognition of hurts long ago brushed aside or suppressed now suddenly erupting to the surface, but the reader's pain was always salved with an ironic punchline delivered in the fourth and final panel of the comic strip.

Schulz also gave Mendelson guidance for the special's soundtrack. "And maybe we can do something with a Christmas play and mix some of that jazz music with traditional music." Schulz was not a fan of jazz music; he was a classical music aficionado and had a huge collection of recordings of all the great composers (Brahms, not Beethoven, was his favorite[6]),* but the cartoonist had been quite impressed with the songs that had been composed by San Francisco jazz composer Vince Guaraldi for the unaired documentary Mendelson had made about Schulz. The two men worked through other ideas, which Mendelson was quickly able to collect and process into a workable one-page outline. Never one to waste time, the producer submitted the proposal to Coca-Cola's Atlanta

---

* Why didn't Schulz make Brahms the favorite composer of Schroeder? He simply thought Beethoven sounded funnier. "There are certain words and names that work better than others. I don't believe it would be half as funny if Schroeder admired Brahms," said Schulz. When the cartoonist showed musical notes in the comic strip, he took care to authentically recreate the actual notes from a Beethoven composition (Charles M. Schulz, *My Life with Charlie Brown* [University Press of Mississippi, 2010], 155).

office that same day. And then began the nerve-racking process of awaiting a response.

❖ ❖ ❖

ST. PAUL, MINNESOTA, NOVEMBER 1942

Charles "Sparky" Schulz received his draft notice just days after his twentieth birthday on November 26, 1942. He was given orders to report to the induction center at Fort Snelling, Minnesota, across the Mississippi River from his nearby home at 170 North Stelling in the Highland Park section of St. Paul. He was furloughed for Christmas, but an air of doom hung over the Schulzes' small two-bedroom apartment. Sparky was about to be sent off to fight in a war that America had just entered a year earlier, while a more immediate tragedy was unfolding right inside the family's home. Dena Halverson Schulz, Sparky's forty-nine-year-old mother, was lying in bed, dying of cervical cancer.

It had been four years since the onset of the disease, and a hysterectomy had perhaps slowed its progress, but now the only thing that eased the woman's cries of pain were the regular injections of morphine administered during visits from the nearby druggist. "She suffered terribly. I used to wake up at night and hear her down the hall crying in pain. It was a terrible time."[7] One night Sparky visited his mother in her room, and she confronted her son with a painful question: "Why can't they help me? Can't they do anything?" Her sensitive twenty-year-old only child stood speechless, unable to even form a response. Sparky then headed angrily into the kitchen, where he approached his father and his aunt Marion, who had temporarily moved into the apartment to provide assistance. "Why don't they do something?" he demanded. "What is wrong?" His aunt turned to him. "Sparky, your mother has cancer." It was the first time he learned of his mother's diagnosis, and he suddenly fully appreciated what the inevitable outcome would be.

Soon after, Sparky had another conversation with his mother, where, in a glimmer of optimism, she allowed herself the indulgence of considering a future, one where they would get a new dog, and she had even assigned it a name. The family already had a dog named Spike. Although neighbors thought it was the meanest dog on the block, Sparky adored the animal, which appeared to be very bright. The boy could order Spike to go into another room and retrieve a potato, and the animal would dutifully obey.* For a woman with just days to live, talking about what she wanted to name the family's next dog seemed fantastical, perhaps enabled by the administration of morphine.

On Sunday, February 28, with his furlough over, Sparky entered his mother's room for a final visit. He was due to report to Fort Snelling within the hour. Streetcars rattled by outside the apartment building, and the neon light from the liquor store on the building's ground floor glowed through the dying woman's windows. "I guess it's time to say goodnight," said Sparky. Dena struggled to turn to face her son, while lying in bed. "Yes. I suppose we should say goodbye," she responded. She fixed her gaze on her boy. "Well," she said. "Goodbye, Sparky. We'll probably never see each other again." Her son departed, and Dena Schulz died the next day, Monday, March 1, 1943, at 3:32 p.m.

Nine years earlier, Dena Schulz had been struggling to find a way she could help her son pursue his passion for comics and drawing. She knew the boy had a gift, but she understood nothing of the

---

* The dog had even been featured in *Ripley's Believe It or Not* publication after a fourteen-year-old Sparky had submitted a profile on his pet: "A hunting dog that eats pins, tacks, screws and razor blades is owned by C.F. Schulz, St. Paul, Minn." A sketch of the dog in profile noted as "drawn by Sparky" appeared next to the writeup.

craft of cartooning. Her husband at least enjoyed poring over the Sunday comics with their son, but the art form had no appeal to Dena. Then one Monday evening in February 1934 she noticed an announcement in the newspaper that an exhibition of comic strip art would be opening at the St. Paul Public Library. Dena insisted that her husband, Carl, close up his barber shop the next day so that the whole family could attend.

The following morning eleven-year-old Sparky Schulz, flanked by his two parents, walked wide-eyed past the original framed work of the leading comic strips of the time: *Skippy, Joe Palooka, The Katzenjammer Kids, Dave's Delicatessen, Wash Tubbs,* and *Count Screwloose.* Previously exposed only to the sanitized final product in a Sunday newspaper, he now saw the intricate process of how the messy creative process came together, from initial pen line sketches, to revisions and alterations, to margin instructions from editors. There was magic in being able to see the original drawing and lettering made by each cartoonist's own hands.

After he had taken in every cartoon in the exhibit on the third floor of the library, Sparky and his parents returned home, where the boy was eager to review his own work. He laid out all his own drawings and was immediately disappointed with what he saw. With his artistic sensibilities now sharpened by the professional work he had just seen, he instantly appreciated how far he had yet to go in his own artistic development. Not in a pique of anger, but with a determined resolve, he tore up all his work. "I knew that I had to start over again."[8]

Dena Schulz would never live to see her son's first comic strip published in a newspaper, but, years later, she would have an impact on her son's career, and on all *Peanuts* fans, beyond having steered her boy into the library exhibit of cartoons that wintry day in 1934.

✦ ✦ ✦

Devastated by the tragic loss of his mother, Schulz now had to endure both being torn away from the world he had known since birth and tossed into the harsh, impersonal discipline imposed on the thousands of draftees being prepared for war. The loneliness and shock of basic training is bracing for any recruit, but for the bereaved Schulz it was soul crushing. His first night in the barracks, desperately afraid that someone might hear him, he sobbed. The innocent young man from the Midwest had never sworn, had never consumed alcohol, and had been chaste, but now he was exposed to the profanities and vulgarities of multitudes of men much rougher than him. Camp Campbell (now known as Fort Campbell), where Schulz was stationed, had just been constructed the prior year to train American troops for World War II. Now it processed as many as twenty-four thousand soldiers, preparing them for the harsh realities of combat by indoctrinating them in the ways of professional soldiering.

One day Private Schulz offered himself up for sign painting duty to Bravo Company's master sergeant, pointing out, perhaps too proudly, his artist's credentials and proficiency in lettering. The sergeant looked him over with distaste before barking, "What we need in this outfit are riflemen, not artists." For the rest of the war, except for the occasional sketch of his fellow soldiers, Schulz kept his artist's pad and pencils stowed away and focused on learning his new deadly profession. He would never abandon his career ambition, though. Like almost all soldiers, however, he would develop an incredible admiration for the work of Bill Mauldin, a US Army soldier who drew cartoons for *Stars and Stripes*. Mauldin's two famous characters were Willie and Joe, a pair of exhausted but dutiful Army infantrymen who faced the hardships of soldiers fighting in World War II.*

---

* Schulz would pay tribute to Mauldin in an annual Veterans Day cartoon where Snoopy would toast Mauldin or head over to his home to drink root beers. The two cartoonists would eventually strike up a friendship.

Schulz would eventually make friends with a fellow soldier named Elmer Roy Hagemeyer. Elmer, a married policeman from St. Louis, was ten years older than the twenty-one-year-old Schulz. He noticed Schulz's desperate loneliness and provided a big-brother type of companionship that the younger soldier desperately needed. Elmer invited Sparky to his home in St. Louis, where he introduced him to his wife, Margaret, and the three would go out on the town for an evening of dinner and dancing. Sparky often provided comical illustrations for letters Hagemeyer sent home to his wife from Camp Campbell. Schulz never forgot the older man's thoughtful intervention into his life at a moment when he greatly needed it, and the two men remained friends for the rest of their lives.

Once he adjusted to barracks life and to the rougher personalities of his fellow conscripts, Schulz took to soldiering and found that his intelligence, facility with weapons, and self-discipline not only made him a good soldier but also made him a good leader. He gained twenty-five pounds of muscle from his military exercise regimen, and he was promoted to corporal in the fall of 1943. He was selected to train troops, so instead of shipping out with his cohort, many of whom would be destined to storm the beaches of Normandy, Schulz focused on furthering his studying of soldiering. He subscribed to *Infantry Journal*, consumed Army manuals, and even read *Infantry Attacks* by German general Erwin Rommel.

On February 5, 1945, Sparky's outfit, the 20th Armored Division, departed Boston and landed at Le Havre, France, on February 18. Schulz, now a staff sergeant, and his squad of men were billeted for the entire month of March at Chateau du Mal Voisin (the Castle of the Bad Neighbor). On Easter Sunday, April 1, Schulz and his eleven men moved out in their ten-ton mechanized halftrack, which the men had notably named "Sparky" after their sergeant, a gesture that reflected the high regard that his soldiers had for him. Their convoy moved across Belgium and then into the Netherlands before heading into Germany.

On April 29, while driving through the town of Rossbach, Sparky's unit first took fire from the enemy. Bullets slammed into Schulz's halftrack, destroying a bazooka. In retaliation, the Americans burned the village down, in accordance with their rules of engagement. The image of a hysterical German woman standing in her yard watching while her house burned would be forever seared into Schulz's memory.

That same day, the US Seventh Army's 45th Infantry Division liberated the Dachau concentration camp, bursting the main gates open and discovering the monstrous horrors it contained. At dawn the following day, Schulz's convoy skirted the camp, passing by its guard tower, fencing, and wooden buildings. His platoon was ordered to keep moving and leave the camp to be secured by infantry units. Before they moved out, a few members of the platoon ventured past the gates and were shocked by what they saw. As the task force departed, emaciated survivors stumbled alongside the convoy, stopping occasionally to hug the sides of the American vehicles.

On May 1, 1945, Schulz's convoy, now outside of Munich, came under rifle fire from a concealed enemy position. One of the troopers in halftrack *Sparky* returned fire but missed his target. Schulz jumped to the vehicle's heavy machine gun, wheeled it around to face the enemy, and pulled the trigger, but the weapon failed to fire. In the heat of the moment, he had forgotten to rack the sliding mechanism on the .50-caliber *twice*, not just once, to engage the weapon. The slight delay gave the two Germans hiding in a foxhole time to raise their hands and surrender.

On May 4, Schulz's men stopped in a village to administer first aid to a wounded German soldier. The enemy fighter had apparently been left behind by his comrades when his unit withdrew. Schulz took it upon himself to scout out the village and was surprised to find a set of stairs descending into what he thought might be an underground barracks. The entryway of the structure was painted completely black. Schulz grabbed a concussion grenade and was prepared to toss it inside to wipe out any German resisters who might be lurking inside. Just then a small white dog trotted down the stairs and disappeared inside the building. Schulz couldn't contemplate harming the dog, so he decided to return to his troops at the halftrack.

On May 5, just three days before V-E Day but with the war's outcome inevitable, the convoy entered Salzburg, Austria, where Sparky began rummaging through a German military warehouse in search of a war trophy to pilfer. An American Army officer at first scolded him but then permitted Schulz to take one pistol. Later Schulz was sitting on a house porch, admiring his new possession. Assuming the weapon was not loaded, he took aim at an American Army medic (identifiable by his distinctive red circle and white cross helmet). Pulling the trigger slowly, Schulz was shocked when the gun discharged, firing the live round that had been in the pistol's chamber. The bullet grazed the medic's cheek, but he was otherwise unharmed. After expressing his obvious displeasure at Schulz, the medic departed, leaving a stunned Schulz to wonder, for the rest of his life, how his own life would have been altered if the bullet's trajectory had struck the medic.[9]

Returning home from the war, Sparky resumed his life, living with his father in the same apartment where they had lost Dena, and he began searching for work. The veteran quickly found a job working as a teacher at Art Instruction, an art correspondence school, where he graded the assignments completed by students. Schulz greatly enjoyed working at the school. He and his colleagues had a shared interest in drawing, and everyone seemed to have a good sense of humor.* It was the same school from which a door-to-door salesman had signed young Sparky up for art lessons after he graduated from high school. The cost for the school had been $170, with a payment plan of $10 per month. His father had made the payments, despite the meager family budget, and not infrequently Sparky would notice dunning letters from the school's accounting office in the family's daily mail.

After returning home from Europe, Schulz also became a devoted Christian. He was sincerely grateful to God for his having survived the war when so many others had not. "I felt that God had protected and helped me and gave me the strength to survive because I could have gone off in all sorts of wrong directions. I always felt that I was helped to live through those three years and come home, because I never got shot or anything."[10] Seeking mooring and a community of friends who shared his values, Schulz joined the nondenominational Church of God and was baptized in Lake Phalen on the northern edge of St. Paul. (It had been a Church of God pastor, a client of Carl's, who had ministered to Dena in her dying days. Carl had invited the man when their Lutheran pastor had failed to appear as promised.) In the middle of July, barefoot and wearing street clothes, Sparky waded in up to his chest, and under the gaze of his congregation he was submerged by Brother Marvin Forbes.

---

* The *Peanuts* character Charlie Brown would take his name from one of Schulz's work colleagues at Art Instruction. Schulz asked the man's permission to use his name and the man consented. Thereafter the man would claim to also be the inspiration for the character himself, a claim Schulz denied.

Sparky wrote of his conversion to one of his former Army friends: "I wasn't a steady churchgoer when you knew me, but I did believe in God. My lack of formal religion was due merely to not knowing better. Now, however, I am right where I belong. I am a firm believer in Jesus Christ."[11]

The aspiring cartoonist also put a portfolio together of artwork drawings and of a potential comic strip, and he began to peddle his work to various newspapers and syndicates. Schulz was a man riddled with self-doubt in so many other undertakings, but no amount of rejection could dampen his self-confidence that he was destined to one day ink his own comic strip. Years later, rereading letters that he had written to his army buddies where he had discussed his career ambitions, even Schulz would be struck by his optimism and his certainty that he would one day succeed at his objective.[12]

In pursuit of his career ambitions, Sparky made regular trips to Chicago on the train, where he made the rounds of syndicates and newspapers. He practiced his social skills on the train ride, attempting to strike up conversations with complete strangers, a newly learned skill for the reticent Midwesterner. Once in the city he would show up, often without an appointment, and try to present his portfolio of work to editors. Years later Schulz could recall the names of anyone who had indulged him an audience or shared an encouraging word, as well as those who had been rude or abrupt: "I was making regular trips to Chicago to try to sell a comic feature and was always gratified to talk with Mr. John Dille, Jr., at his National Newspaper Syndicate, for he was invariably kind and patient with me. This was not always true at some of the other syndicates. I dropped into the Chicago *Sun* one day and showed my work to Walt Ditzen, who was then their comic editor, and he was very impressed with what he saw. I recall him exclaiming, 'I certainly cannot say no to this. We'll have to take it in to the president.' We went into the man's office; he barely looked at the work and abruptly said, 'No.'"[13] Schulz never became discouraged, however. With each rejection, he knew he was only getting closer and closer to succeeding.[14]

Success finally came in the summer of 1950. He received a letter from United Feature in New York City stating that they were interested in a two-tier panel feature, and they extended an invitation to Sparky to visit them in Manhattan. Sparky left Sunday, June 11, by rail and checked into the Roosevelt Hotel. The next day he arrived at the syndicate's offices in the Daily News Building at 220 East 42nd Street, but the eager aspiring cartoonist arrived so early that the only person at work was the switchboard operator. The woman kindly offered to hold the visitor's samples while he went out for breakfast. When Sparky returned to the office he was surprised to see that not only had the syndicate executives arrived at work, but they were intently poring over his samples, which they had opened and were now passing around the room. Initially interested only in a single-panel cartoon, they were now inquiring about a strip, having been impressed by the work they had discovered in his portfolio. "We think we'd rather have a strip, if you think you could draw a strip." Schulz was thrilled. It was his life's dream to draw a comic strip, which he greatly preferred to one- or two-panel gag comics.

On Wednesday, June 14, Larry Rutman, vice president and general manager of United Feature, offered Schulz their standard five-year contract—the syndicate would own the copyright on the strip's characters and would split the profits fifty-fifty with the cartoonist. Schulz promptly had his signature notarized and returned the contract, and then boarded a westbound train home. He celebrated by treating himself to a steak dinner in the dining car.

Two issues quickly erupted before the publication of Charles Schulz's new comic strip, both involving copyright. The first was regarding the name of the cartoon. Schulz had proposed *Little Folks*, but the name was too similar to other comics at the time, so the syndicate unilaterally decided to call the strip *Peanuts*. Schulz felt that the name lacked the dignity he had wanted for his creation, but he was forced to accept the syndicate's decision. The name would rankle the cartoonist for the rest of his life. Second, he had named the black and white dog in his cartoon Sniffy, but a recent comic book featuring a dog with that very same name had just been published. Schulz had to come up with a name quickly. He dreaded the forced creativity imposed by the pressure of time. While walking, he suddenly remembered one of his final conversations with his dying mother while she painfully wasted away from cancer. There was a brief moment when she had incredibly imagined a future where she would still be alive and the family would pick out a new dog. Schulz suddenly remembered the name his mother had suggested: Snoopy.*

Sparky returned triumphantly from New York on June 15, 1950. Around ten thirty that same night, a Thursday, he appeared at the home of a twenty-one-year-old coworker named Donna Mae Johnson, not only to tell her the news but also to propose to her. The couple had had their first date only three and a half months prior, on March 2, which she had noted in her calendar "CS. Ice Capades! NICE!!" Donna had been employed in Art Instruction's accounting department since graduating from high school two years earlier. The young woman was slender, attractive, vibrant, and seven years his junior, but her most distinguishing physical characteristic would leave an indelible mark on the history of *Peanuts*: her violent red hair.

Sparky had coached the women on the company softball team. Donna was not a talented athlete, but she had joined the team just to see more of the tall coach with a shy smile. Sparky would drive

---

* Schulz's mother was Norwegian and Snupi is a Norwegian term of affection.

some of the team members home in his car after practice, and somehow he always arranged to drop Donna off last. On only their third date, Sparky told her, "I wish I had a diamond ring in my pocket to give you right now." But the new cartoonist faced competition for his newfound love interest. Donna was also romantically involved with a handsome young Navy veteran and fireman named Al Wold. Al lived next door to Donna's church, Holy Trinity Lutheran. The two had known each other since elementary school, where they both stood out because of their red hair, and the two had dated, on and off, for more than two years. Dating in the 1950s was far more demure and innocent than it is today, and certain rituals of courtship were observed. Sparky knew there was another suitor pursuing Donna, and he accepted the challenge.

Every workday Donna delivered an apple to the third-floor desk of her favorite instructor at the art school, braving the knowing looks of her coworkers. Sparky would drop by her second-floor desk, and if she was away he would jot a note on her desk calendar, letting her know he had been there. The couple had a number of other outings during those spring months—picnics, walks, a Lakers basketball game,* card playing, and movies at the local theater. On their dates Sparky frequently wore his favorite shirt, which had a distinctive black zigzag design around it. There were also gifts, including two items that he had purchased at the Roosevelt Hotel in Manhattan during the consequential trip where he had signed his cartoonist contract: a tiny silver hope chest charm meant to be affixed to a bracelet, and a gilded box decorated with rhinestones designed to contain lipstick, perfume, candies, and, of course, cartoons he had

---

* The Lakers basketball team played in Minneapolis from 1947 until 1960, when they moved to Los Angeles. The name Lakers reflected Minnesota's nickname, Land of 10,000 Lakes, and the name curiously was not changed when the team moved to the drier environs of Southern California.

drawn for her as well. One gift had momentous meaning, though. When he returned from New York, Sparky presented Donna with a small toy, a whiskered white cat that was curled up asleep with its tail around its body. The cat came with instructions: when Donna was ready to get married, she was to put the cat on his desk at work. Donna carefully kept the cat in a desk drawer, as she considered her growing love for Sparky but was torn because of her deep affection for Al.

Donna met Sparky's father, and Sparky became well acquainted with Donna's family. Her father was skeptical and seemed unimpressed since the cartoonist had not played football. Her one sister adored Sparky, however, telling her sister that he was the only boyfriend she had had who had been nice to her. Sparky had impressed her mother well enough that she would make him pancakes for lunch, one of his favorite meals. In an impulsive moment, Donna had asked him to elope with her, but Sparky, who took pride in conducting himself as a gentleman and doing things the proper way, said he could not do that to Donna's mother. It was a decision he would come to regret.

On Saturday, June 24, the couple spent a long day together. It began with a romantic picnic at Taylor Falls near Minneapolis that included swimming in the St. Croix River. Donna surprised Sparky by bringing pancake batter her mother had prepared, which the couple fried in a skillet over a fire. That evening they went to see a movie. The film was, appropriately perhaps, a romantic drama, *My Foolish Heart* starring Dana Andrews and Susan Hayward. The couple sat in the back row of the theater, more interested in each other's company and some stolen moments of affection than in the happenings on the distant screen. When Donna told him she was cold, it successfully prompted her shy date to put his arm around her. After the movie the couple sat in Sparky's car talking some more, until finally returning home late in the evening. When she entered the front door after her day-long absence, Donna's mother expressed her surprise—she had begun to think that her daughter and Sparky had run off and gotten married, and she seemed amazed that they hadn't.

One week later, on July 1, 1950, Al Wold proposed to Donna. It is likely that Sparky Schulz's interest in the auburn-haired beauty had spurred the fireman to action. The twenty-one-year-old woman now had a decision to make. She was genuinely in love with and cared deeply for both men. Sparky expressed his feelings for Donna's predicament by typing a note on his typewriter at work: "I am so sorry for the sadness that I have caused you. It's because you are so good that you feel all these things so deeply, which is another reason why I love you..."

Two weeks later, Donna made her choice. She summoned Sparky to her home. When he arrived, she was ironing clothing in the kitchen. The young couple went out on the home's back stairs to talk. Sparky asked Donna to marry him in a proper wedding ceremony. They would live happily ever after, he told her, especially now that he had his own cartoon strip. Donna responded that she had decided to marry Al. Sparky then drove away, while Donna went inside and cried. After thirty minutes, the front door bell rang. Donna, her eyes red from her tears, went to the door. Sparky had returned. "I thought maybe you had changed your mind," he said.[15]

Donna Johnson and Al Wold were married at the Holy Trinity Lutheran Church they both attended on October 21, 1950. The *Peanuts* cartoon strip was nineteen days old. Donna left her job at Art Instruction, because she knew it would be too awkward and painful for her to see her former suitor at work. Sparky was crushed by the rejection. "I can think of no more emotionally damaging loss than to be turned down by someone whom you love very much," he would later say. "A person who not only turns you down, but almost immediately will marry the victor. What a bitter blow that is. It is a blow to everything that you are. Your appearance. Your personality."[16] The unrequited love of Donna Mae Johnson gave birth to the unattainable little red-haired girl perpetually pursued by Charlie Brown in the *Peanuts* comic strip.* But, as Schulz noted years later, the day his affections were spurned by the woman he loved was the day that forged the character of Charlie Brown.

Six years later, Charles Schulz was a married man and a father, and his *Peanuts* comic strip was on its upward trajectory, bringing him fame and financial success. He had arranged to sign autographs at a downtown Minneapolis bookstore. A number of fans and well-wishers lined up for Schulz's signature. One woman exclaimed, "I'm your biggest fan!" The next woman Schulz instantly recognized. It was Donna, now pregnant with her second child. Schulz signed her book, but the inscription was generic. "For Donna, with sincere best wishes." The words stung the woman—the perfunctory notation, lacking warmth, without any recognition or romantic nostalgia for the wonderful times the couple had shared. Even years later, it bothered her. *With sincere best wishes.*

Schulz devoured literature throughout the whole course of his adult life. Although he was self-conscious about his lack of a formal education, he was always quick to point out that he was more well read than many, if not all, of his far better-educated friends. The cartoonist's favorite writer was F. Scott Fitzgerald, who was also, like Schulz, from Minnesota and a US Army war veteran. His favorite

---

* In the *Peanuts* comic strip on November 19, 1961, Charlie Brown sits down to lunch, glimpses a new student in the schoolyard, and says, "I'd give anything in the world if that little girl with red hair would come over, and sit with me" (Darryn King, "Charlie Brown Never Found His Little Red-Haired Girl, but We Did," *Vanity Fair*, November 6, 2015).

novel, perhaps predictably, was *The Great Gatsby*,* the story of a veteran of a world war, obsessed with Daisy, a woman who had married another man. In many ways the perpetually pursued, but always out of reach and off-screen, red-haired girl was to Schulz like the green light that burns all night at the end of the dock across the bay from Gatsby's estate. Donna Johnson was Schulz's Daisy. Unlike Gatsby, though, for Schulz, "his count of enchanted objects" would never diminish. Not even by one. They would only accumulate. The traumas endured by the sensitive cartoonist—the painful death of his mother, the agony of war, the wound of romantic rejection—these would become for Schulz, like the famous last line of *The Great Gatsby*, his "boats against the current, borne back ceaselessly into the past."**

In 1965, just as Coca-Cola began to contemplate a Christmas special, Charles Schulz had reached the zenith of success for a cartoonist. His *Peanuts* comic strip reached 60 million people and was published by seven hundred newspapers in the US and Canada and another seventy-one internationally.[17] It was being translated into a dozen languages. The *Peanuts* characters were featured on the cover of *Time*

---

* Schulz first read *The Great Gatsby* riding the trolley car going to work at Art Instruction. The US military had provided free paperback versions of the book (and others) to American troops at the end of World War II, and it is likely one of these copies that Schulz had read. It is believed that this massive free distribution saved the book from obscurity.

** A bow-tied Snoopy alter ego named Scott Fitzgerald Hero was introduced to the *Peanuts* comic strip on May 21, 1998. He appears at the school's spring dance, where Charlie Brown hopes he will be able to dance with the little red-haired girl. In a subsequent strip Snoopy refers to himself as Gatsby and calls others "Old Sport," just as Gatsby did in the F. Scott Fitzgerald novel. Snoopy dances with the little red-haired girl, imagining her to be Daisy Buchanan, but he has to be rescued by Charlie Brown and carried home after consuming too much punch.

magazine on April 9, 1965. His book *Happiness Is a Warm Puppy* had become an instant *New York Times* bestseller. Licensing opportunities were piling up and so was Schulz's commercial success. Revenues for the *Peanuts* brand were skyrocketing and in less than two years would reach $20 million, before more than doubling again two years later. In April 1965 the National Cartoonists Society announced that Schulz had once again been awarded the coveted Reuben Award for Outstanding Cartoonist of the Year, which was to be presented to Schulz on April 20 at the society's annual dinner at the luxury Plaza Hotel next to Central Park in New York City. It was the second time the award had been made to Schulz, an unprecedented recognition that the cartoonist from Minnesota had reached the pinnacle of his profession and received the critical recognition of his peers. But in 1965 Charles Schulz had become a very troubled man.

Schulz suffered an attack of agoraphobia and would not fly to New York to attend the Reuben Award ceremony. He became increasingly reluctant to leave home. At times Schulz's wife took him to the airport to drop him off for a flight for a speaking engagement or a business meeting but the panic-stricken cartoonist would simply catch a cab and arrive back home—once even arriving home before his wife had returned herself. "I drew a strip where Charlie Brown's little sister, Sally, said that she didn't mind going on any kind of a trip as long as she could be home by noon. I think I know how she feels."[18]

Throughout his adulthood, the cartoonist had always seemed to have some symptoms of anxiety and depression. He had frequently injected these topics into his cartoon strip—Lucy first began dispensing "psychiatric help" from her makeshift booth* to

---

* Lucy originally dispensed psychiatric counseling from a simple table. The booth would not appear until May 4, 1961, and it would have a sign noting if the doctor was "IN" or "OUT."

Charlie Brown ("I have feelings of depression") on March 27, 1959, unhelpfully advising "Snap out of it!" before demanding her nickel payment.* Schulz had even popularized the anxiety-calming term "security blanket." Topics of mental health were frequent in the *Peanuts* comic strip, and in an increasingly frenetic postwar world full of anxious adults where psychotherapy first gained a foothold in both healthcare and popular culture, Schulz's comic takes on the topic resonated with his readers. Many may have just thought that Schulz was mining the topic for laughs, but it is more likely that Schulz was working out his own issues in the black-lined boxes of his cartoon panel, and it may even have been a hidden-in-plain-sight cry for help.

Schulz's anxiety also began to manifest itself physically. In 1965 he lost twenty pounds from his already lean frame in two months, prompting a visit to a doctor. His stomach bothered him constantly. His physician at first suspected an ulcer, but neither X-rays nor other tests supported that diagnosis.[19] The prior year, the Schulzes had taken a rare family vacation—a luxury cruise ship, with multiple stateroom accommodations, to Honolulu, Hawaii. However, as soon as they arrived at their destination, the Hilton Hawaiian Village on Oahu, Schulz began to feel anxious. When he visited the hotel doctor, he was given a complete examination and pronounced medically fit.[20]

---

* Lucy's standard fee for psychiatric care was five cents, but there were two strips where she raised her rates to seven cents for "seasonal rates," and on one occasion her fee was a quarter. During the inflation of the early 1980s, she raised her price to ten cents, and then to thirty-four cents and even fifty cents, before reducing it once again to a nickel. Snoopy at one point set up a competing booth offering "Friendly Advice" and undercutting Lucy's pricing, charging only two cents. Another time the beagle charged only a penny to "Hug a Warm Puppy."

✦ ✦ ✦

After submitting the one-page outline for a Christmas special to Coca-Cola's Atlanta headquarters, Lee Mendelson began the process of nervously awaiting a response. A week passed without any news. Then two weeks. Mendelson decided to make a phone call inquiry to John Allen's New York office seeking any update, only to learn that the adman was in Europe. Mendelson had no other contact at the agency to reach out to for any feedback.

Around the same time that Lee Mendelson was nervously awaiting a call back from McCann-Erickson on the outline that he had submitted, Schulz decided to play a practical joke on his friend. He would make the producer's phone ring. And not just ring once. But over and over again. In an epic prank, the cartoonist decided to put Mendelson's phone number in a Sunday *Peanuts* comic strip— Sunday, of course, being the most widely read comic strip. In the cartoon strip, Charlie Brown and Lucy are engaged in a game of croquet. Lucy smacks Charlie Brown's ball with her mallet so hard that it takes him five cartoon panels to walk to it. At this point, Charlie Brown enters a nearby phone booth and places a call, instructing the unknown person at the other end of the phone line, "Yes…Call me when it's my turn, will you? The number here is 343-2794…" When the comic strip ran, Mendelson's phone began to ring at six a.m. and rang steadily throughout the day until nine p.m. that night. Each time the producer answered, the voice on the other end, whether it was a child or an adult, would always utter the same line: "It's your turn, Charlie Brown."[21]

Finally, after an anxiety-ridden three weeks of waiting, Mendelson received his much anticipated call back from John Allen. The producer held his breath while listening to Allen's words. "Well, once again I have good news and bad news," he said. "The good news is that Coca-Cola wants to buy *A Charlie Brown Christmas*, but the bad news is they want it for early December. That gives you just six months. Can you do it in six months?"

Mendelson had no experience in producing an animated television special. He had employed a few minutes of animation in the Schulz documentary, but he could not have fully appreciated the amount of work involved in the painstaking process of producing an animated program—preparing the script, as well as an original music soundtrack, and casting voice talent and then editing and postproduction. But the producer was not about to let this incredible opportunity slip away. "Of course!" he blurted out, recognizing full well that what he was committing to might be an impossibility and could be, after the Schulz documentary, *another* embarrassing failure, the cumulative impact of which could irreparably damage his career. "Good," Allen said. "You'll hear from our business affairs people tomorrow. Get to work. And congratulations!"

Reflecting upon it, however, would bring another perspective to Mendelson's mind. His previous failure, the unsold Schulz documentary, had brought him to McCann-Erickson's attention when they were seeking a Christmas special. It was a vindication of the producer having struck out on his own. It was a validation of the notion that failure is not the opposite of success but is a part of success. Mendelson allowed himself a few moments of utter exhilaration, which were suddenly swept away by sheer and utter panic. He needed an animator. There was never any question of who that would be. Bill Melendez was the only man Charles Schulz would allow to animate his *Peanuts* characters. The producer picked up the handset and placed his index finger in the rotary dial and placed a call to Los Angeles.[22]

THE DIRECTOR
BILL MELENDEZ

✦

Billy, if we don't do it, who will?
—Charles Schulz to Bill Melendez

Bill Melendez answered the phone at his studio on Larchmont Boulevard in Los Angeles. "Can we do an animated half hour in six months?" asked Lee Mendelson. Without hesitation, the always upbeat animator replied, "Of course!" Mendelson had some concerns that Melendez was putting on a false front of confidence, just like he had done minutes earlier with McCann-Erickson. (Truthfully Melendez knew that the time frame would be extremely tight. "I wasn't sure it was possible," he later told an interviewer.) The two men agreed to meet with Schulz that weekend, which was Memorial Day weekend, at the cartoonist's home in Sebastopol to plan for the production and sketch out some additional themes that could be explored in the script. Melendez had first met Schulz when he had animated the *Peanuts* characters for some Ford Motor Company television commercials promoting the Ford Falcon. He had later also prepared a couple of minutes of animation for the unsold Charlie Brown documentary.

The three men met inside Schulz's studio, which looked out on his property's wooded acreage. They reviewed the original one-page outline that had been sent to Coca-Cola three weeks earlier, which contained the following elements: winter scenes like ice skating, a school Christmas play, a scene that included a biblical element, and a soundtrack with a mixture of jazz and traditional holiday music.

Mendelson suggested the script could have something to do with a Christmas tree. He related to his two colleagues that during the prior Christmas he and his wife had both read "The Fir Tree," a short story by Danish writer Hans Christian Andersen. The fairy tale, first published in 1844, tells the story of the life of a small fir tree. In its infancy, the tree is embarrassed by its diminutive height and is envious of trees that have grown large enough to be chopped down and used for the masts of ships. As a youth, the tree is cut down and brought inside a family's home, where it is wondrously decorated and topped with a gold star and listens, enchanted, to a tale told of a princess. The next day, the tree is discarded in the home's attic, where it relates the story of the prior day's festivities to rats, who belittle the fanciful tale. In the spring, the tree, now withered and brown, is taken outside, cut into pieces, and burned. The depressing story with a sorrowful ending immediately resonated with Schulz, who responded, "We need a Charlie Brown–like tree!"

The producer then noted, matter-of-factly, that a lot of animated programs included a "laugh track," the recorded sound of an audience laughing. "I assume we will have a laugh track," Mendelson said. Schulz said, "I quit," then stood up and left the room. The cartoonist found the idea of cuing the audience when to laugh to be

insulting to the viewers and thought it didn't allow them the opportunity to absorb the humor and decide for themselves when to laugh.
The producer and Melendez exchanged stunned looks. "Well, I guess
we won't have a laugh track," joked Melendez. Schulz reentered the
room, and the meeting resumed.[1]

The musical soundtrack was also a topic of discussion. The three
men decided that the opening song would be something that was
neither jazz nor traditional holiday music. It was also important to
create a memorable scene that would fully utilize Vince Guaraldi's
stellar piece "Linus and Lucy." Although the song had been written
for the unsold 1963 *Peanuts* documentary, it was felt that the music
was so compelling that it should be given new life in the special.
Schulz also wanted to insert a scene where Schroeder would be playing Beethoven.

Snoopy, the most surrealistic of all the *Peanuts* characters, would
be given his usual scene-stealing roles. Schulz refused to allow the
beagle to ever speak, but he would allow the animal to squawk or
utter sounds. Voices of the human characters were also discussed.
It was important that Charlie Brown's voice be "blah" to match his
bland personality. Lucy's tone had to match her assertive crabby
temperament. Linus, perhaps Schulz's most well-adjusted *Peanuts*
character, had to combine both intelligence and childlike innocence.
Schulz also insisted that the voices of the characters should be actual
children, not professional adult voice talent.

The most contentious issue arose when Schulz proposed having
Linus recite from the Book of Luke. "We can't do this; it's too religious," said Melendez. "Sparky, this is religion. It just doesn't belong
in a cartoon." Lee Mendelson voiced the same concerns. The Bible
had never been animated before, not by Warner Bros., not by Disney, and not by Hanna-Barbera. The men were exposing themselves

to potential attacks from both religious and non-religious viewers. Churchgoers might object that animating the Bible and having its sacred verses spoken by cartoon characters was sacrilegious. Those who were less religious might be turned off by what they might perceive to be preachy moralizing. Animated cartoons had served many purposes—they had been educational (like in military training films), they could be funny, even wackily funny, they could be racy even, but no one had attempted to preach, and certainly no one had ever animated the Bible. As Mel Blanc noted in his biography, "[T]he Warner cartoons never proselytized morality—the surest way to alienate kids."[2] Schulz looked at Melendez and said determinedly, "Billy, if we don't do it, who will? We can do it."[3]

At one point, the three men took time to relax in the Schulzes' swimming pool. Schulz, a war veteran, lamented to Mendelson that the Memorial Day holiday's true meaning had been lost in what was now merely a kickoff to the summer season and an occasion to barbecue. It had once been called Remembrance Day, Schulz recalled. Now the cartoonist feared that the same thing was happening to Christmas. The real meaning of the holiday was being lost in a secular celebration of Santa Claus. The true meaning could be found in the Book of Luke, and the special would need to work in the Nativity story somehow.[4]

There were also business affairs to wrap up, including the budget for the program. The business partners in the special's production—United Feature (the cartoon syndicate behind *Peanuts*), Charles Schulz (the creator of *Peanuts*), Lee Mendelson (the producer), and Bill Melendez (the director and animation studio)— would split the ownership and any economics from the special four ways. Melendez, who had only recently set up his own shop, had no idea what to charge for the production, an indication of how his prior experience had been separated from grappling with business affairs. His previous work was strictly on the creative side as an animator. He had never before directed his own television entertainment special. His limited directorial experience was in corporate training films and commercials.

"I didn't know what to charge, because nobody had done any specials," Melendez later explained. Seeking help, he called up Bill Hanna, whom he considered to be a good friend. "What should I budget for this thing?" Hanna refused to answer, citing competitive reasons. Melendez would receive $76,000 to produce the program. (It would eventually cost more than $20,000 more. As soon as the program first aired, the first call Melendez received was from a seemingly gleeful Hanna. "Heeeeey! You lost your shirt didn't you?" he crowed.)[5]

When Coca-Cola accepted the business terms for the special's production they sent Schulz and Mendelson the following telegram:

CONFIRM SALE OF CHARLIE BROWN FOR
CHRISTMAS TO COCA-COLA FOR DECEMBER
BROADCAST AT YOUR TERMS WITH OPTION ON
SECOND SHOW FOR NEXT SPRING. GOOD GRIEF![6]

Coca-Cola's acceptance of the business terms, without any attempt to negotiate, would seem to confirm that Melendez had indeed misestimated the cost of the production and underbid the job.

Bill Melendez was born on November 15, 1916, in Hermosillo, Sonora, Mexico. His father, Ramon, was a Mexican cavalry officer. His mother, Sarah, came from a wealthy ranching family. As a baby he had been presented to a Catholic priest for baptism, but when Ramon told the priest he wanted to have the boy christened as Cuauhtémoc, an Aztec name meaning Descending Eagle, the priest refused, saying he would only baptize the boy with a Christian name. (Cuauhtémoc had been the name of the last Aztec emperor.) When the stubborn father proceeded to take his baby away, the priest relented, and a compromise was reached—the boy would be christened as José Cuauhtémoc.

When the boy was nine years old, his mother took him and his two siblings, Carlota and Ralph, to the United States. She separated from her husband and drove her children north in her 1915 Cadillac and they settled in Douglas, Arizona, located in the southeast corner of the state. Young José Cuauhtémoc, known in the family as "Temoc," was enrolled in kindergarten to learn English, a humiliating experience. After two or three years the family relocated again, this time moving west to Los Angeles, where they had many relatives.

Melendez graduated from John H. Francis Polytechnic High School in 1935, then located in a neoclassical building in downtown Los Angeles, on the corner of Washington Boulevard and Flower Street. When the boy turned seventeen his mother showed him a letter from his father. The correspondence revealed that the boy's parents had an understanding that when he turned seventeen and graduated from high school, he would return to Mexico and undertake military studies, joining his father, who was now a general. The young boy desperately wanted to return to Mexico, but his mother hoped the boy would remain with her. She looked into his eyes. "Hijo mío," she said, "you don't want to go back, do you?" The dutiful son acceded to his mother's wishes and stayed in the United States.

Upon graduation, Melendez went to work in a lumberyard in Los Angeles. Although he had graduated with honors, he mistakenly believed that because he was not a US citizen he was not eligible to attend college at a California university like UCLA, where his good grades almost certainly would have gained him admission. Instead, Melendez toiled for two years doing physical labor before a friend offhandedly mentioned that there was a company named Disney that was hiring people who could draw. The friend had obviously been aware of Melendez's gift for art, a talent that he had exhibited since childhood. "What's Disney?" Melendez asked. "It's a cartoon studio," his friend replied. A determined Melendez appeared at the Disney studio on Hyperion Avenue the following day, where he ran across a man named George Drake outside the building. Drake was an animator whose job was to hire and train all the new talent. A Hollywood historian described him as "a hatchet-faced martinet" and "the most hated man at Disney."[7] Drake lacked solid animation skills, which is perhaps why Walt Disney had recycled him in an administrative role. "Are you looking for artists?" asked the twenty-year-old Melendez. "Yes. Are you an artist?" Drake asked. "Yes," the young man replied. Drake then asked Melendez for his samples, a request that seemed to confuse the young man. Drake explained, "Samples of your work. Examples of your drawings." Melendez said, "No, but I can bring some tomorrow." The aspiring artist then raced home and made a bunch of sketches that he brought back again the next day. Drake inspected the work carefully. "Well, you can obviously draw, but you haven't had much training, have you?"

Despite his lack of formal art instruction, Melendez received a job offer and began working at Disney in 1938. An offer letter that Drake issued to another young prospect around the same time provides the details of the offer that was likely made to Melendez as well. Applicants were brought into a try-out training program. The first four weeks were a probation period, where a trainee was supervised and their talents assessed. No salary was paid during this time, but they would receive $2 per day, except on Sundays. If a trainee was deemed suitable, they would be hired under a three-year contract beginning at between $18 and $25 a week, depending on skill level, and rising to $40 per week in the third year.* "Stipulated periodical increases in salary are provided for based on the very minimum we believe any artist would be worth to the Studio, if he were worth keeping at all."[8]

Melendez was thrilled to begin his new career at Disney. "This is it! The doors are beginning to open. I'm in the motion picture industry!" When he came across Walt Disney in the halls, the new trainee greeted him respectfully as "Mr. Disney." Melendez was elated when the studio chief warmly responded, "Call me Walt." The new trainee would eventually learn that Walt's moods could be more volatile than the sunny disposition he had exhibited in their first encounter. The young trainee also learned that Walt was not a gifted artist, and that he actually couldn't even draw a good Mickey Mouse. (In fact, the famous mouse was originally drawn by Ub Iwerks.) Walt would become frustrated when excited fans would beseech him for a sketch of his iconic creature, knowing he was capable of producing only a sad replica. Melendez was present when Fred Moore, the studio's best Mickey Mouse animator, sat down with Walt Disney himself as his student to instruct the studio chief how to sketch a three-quarter

---

* Sometime earlier in the 1930s one of the trainees who was living on turnips and bruised fruit had toppled over at work, dropping right out of his chair. Ben Sharpsteen, who was running the training program, discovered the malnourished artist on the floor. He then went to Walt Disney and suggested that those going through the "tryout period" should have their wages adjusted to $18 a week. Then they could at least dine at the popular greasy spoon across the street. Walt agreed and their pay was increased (Jack Kinney, *Walt Disney and Assorted Other Characters* [Harmony Books, 1989], 34).

angle of Mickey Mouse. This would be the typical mouse that Disney would draw and sign "Walt."

The new trainee also learned that Walt would not tolerate certain gags in the office, especially not from the rambunctious animators. When a pay raise bumped the wages of some of the lowly paid "inbetweeners" (those who create the intermediate frames of animation between two frames), the pay after taxes rounded out to a paycheck of $17.76. The night before the next payday, an artist named Curtis Barnes stayed late and put up red, white, and blue bunting with signs saying SPIRIT OF '76. When the paychecks were distributed at the end of the day, Barnes had his check and a pink slip terminating his employment. To Melendez, when Disney abandoned its Hyperion Avenue studio and moved to Burbank (its current location), the workplace became even more "corporate" and less freewheeling. The new offices were beautiful, with new chairs and desks, but the boisterous animators missed the old offices, where they could push pins into the wall and act with more reckless abandon.

However, Walt Disney's studio was unmatchable in one regard: training. Animators at Disney had the opportunity to avail themselves of courses five nights a week on topics including life drawing, animal drawing, action analysis, and character design. Each class lasted two to three hours and was taught by some of the best animators working at the studio, as well as by outside experts who were brought in as teachers. Some of the notables hired to guest lecture included architect Frank Lloyd Wright, color theorist Faber Birren, Italian American artist Rico Lebrun,* and French American muralist Jean Charlot. Melendez took in every class. "I just loved it." He

---

* Lebrun worked during the preproduction phase of *Bambi*, bringing a live deer into the studio as a model for the animators, and he prepared the deer skeleton guide for the film's animators.

also availed himself of the Disney library. He learned all about art history, art appreciation, the Impressionists. Working at Disney was an art and animation master class, and it was all free.

When Melendez entered the field of animation there were dozens of cartoon characters appearing in short films produced by eight full-sound production studios: Fleischer Studios (Poppy the Sailor, Betty Boop, Koko the Clown); Terrytoons (Farmer Al Falfa); Walter Lantz Productions (Oswald the Lucky Rabbit); Ub Iwerk's Celebrity Productions (Flip the Frog, Willie Whopper); Charles Mintz's productions for Columbia Pictures/Screen Gems (Krazy Kat, Scrappy); MGM (the Happy Harmonies series); Leon Schlesinger Productions, distributed by Warner Bros.; and Walt Disney Productions. The process of animation had been established around 1914. Characters and backgrounds were inked on the front, painted onto clear celluloid ("cels"), and then filmed frame by frame.[9] It was essentially the same process at every studio, but Disney was distinctively different. As Ben Sharpsteen, who ran the Disney training program in the 1930s, said:

> *You could have picked out the best animators in other studios and plunked them in Disney's, which happened time and time again, and they had to go through a very humble indoctrination: learning how to animate the way we did, learning how to pick your work apart, learning how to diagnose, learning to cooperate with others, learning to accept criticism without getting your feelings hurt, and all those things. We had a saying, "Look this is Disney Democracy: your business is everybody's business and everybody's business is your business." If you did not have that attitude, you were not going to stay very long.[10]*

Melendez began working at Walt Disney Productions the same year the studio made history by releasing the first animated feature

film in American movie history, *Snow White and the Seven Dwarfs*.*
Walt had been working on the film since 1934, and it was his most
ambitious undertaking since he and his brother Roy had opened
Disney Brothers Cartoon Studios fifteen years earlier in 1923. The
studio had been releasing animated shorts, like *Steamboat Willie*,
which featured Mickey Mouse, as well as *The Skeleton Dance* and
The Moose Hunt, featuring Mickey's dog, Pluto. *Snow White* was a
monumental production involving 2 million drawings and had cost
Disney $1.6 million in production costs alone, an incredible sum for
the time and way over budget. Hollywood thought Walt had gone
mad, and many began referring to the cartoon as "Disney's Folly."
Within months of the film's release, however, the film had grossed
$8 million in revenue, making it Hollywood's highest-grossing film,
a record it would hold until *Gone with the Wind* was released the following year. Walt would be awarded an honorary Academy Award
for the film, accompanied by seven miniature Oscar statuettes, one
for each dwarf.[11]

Melendez originally went to work at Disney's tiny garage studio at 2719 Hyperion Avenue** in the Silver Lake neighborhood of
Los Angeles, which Walt had been able to set up thanks to a $500
loan from his uncle.[12] It was at Disney that Melendez would first
come to be called Bill. When he had asked that his animation work

---

* The film's world premiere was on December 21, 1937, at the Carthay Circle
Theater. The Art Deco theater was built in 1926, and it was one of the movie
palaces of Hollywood's golden age. It would also serve as the location for the
West Coast premiere of *Fantasia*. A meticulous reproduction of the building
is located on Buena Vista Street at the Disney California Adventure Park in
Anaheim. On the second floor of the building is an upscale restaurant.
** The street name of the studio, Hyperion, would be used by the company to
name various operations, including Café Hyperion in Disneyland Paris and
the Hyperion Theater in both Disney California Adventure and Disney's
Hollywood Studios. The original studio building on Hyperion Avenue was
torn down and is now a Gelson's Market grocery store.

in a film be credited as Cuauhtémoc Melendez, his bosses resisted, arguing that such a long name would hog the credits on the screen. It would probably be safe to speculate that, like the priest who had baptized the young Melendez, the Disney executives also considered the Aztec name to be unacceptable. So a second compromise was reached on the young animator's name, and he would be credited as Bill Melendez.

In 1941 Walt Disney's relationship with many of his employees would be so strained that the studio workers undertook a strike. Melendez joined the strikers' ranks and marched on the picket line outside the studio's Burbank offices. The strike was led by Art Babbitt, a talented animator. Babbitt was one of the most highly compensated individuals at the company, but he sympathized with the working conditions, compensation, and lack of credits given to the lower-level employees of the studio. Disney and Babbitt almost came to blows once when the studio chief drove his car past picketers. Babbitt heckled the studio chief through a bullhorn, Disney exited his vehicle, and the two men had to be separated. The strike lasted five weeks, and Walt never forgave the striking employees, whom he felt had betrayed him, including Bill Melendez. The young animator would never forget the pained look he had seen on Disney's face when he had returned to work. Shortly after the strike ended, so would Melendez's employment at Disney.

Now much more confident in his craft, Melendez joined Warner Bros., the maker of the Looney Tunes and Merrie Melodies series of cartoons, as an assistant animator. The culture of Melendez's new employer was very different from that of Disney, as divergent as the wise-cracking, Brooklyn-accented Bugs Bunny and the amiable Mickey Mouse. Warner Bros. didn't have the prestige that Disney had at the time. It didn't have someone with Walt Disney's singular devotion to excellence. It didn't have the Academy

Awards that Disney had. But it did have some incredible talent—directors like Friz Freleng, Frank Tashlin, and Tex Avery, and animators like Chuck Jones, Rod Scribner, Emery Hawkins, Sid Sutherland, and Bob McKimson.

There was a playfulness and an irreverence with which the Warner Bros. employees approached their work that was missing from the halls of Disney's Burbank offices. This was despite the fact that WB's animation studio was relegated to a ramshackle cottage on the Warner Bros. lot known as the "Termite Terrace." As Melendez recalled, the wooden building was never professionally cleaned, it was infested with bugs, and it had holes in the floor. Gags and practical jokes were a constant work hazard. When one animator proudly bought himself a stylish, wide-brimmed Panama hat bearing his initials, some of his colleagues had two more of the same exact hat style made, but one a size larger, and one a tad smaller. The man's coworkers would constantly switch out the hats, watching at the end of the day when their friend would be suddenly puzzled that a hat that had fit perfectly in the morning now seemed too small or too large.

The Warner Bros. studio also had production quotas—something that Disney did not have. "I was shocked when I left Disney to find out that everybody else was drawing twenty-five feet per week and at Disney we could do two feet, one foot, ten feet, no one was counting. What was important to Walt was the quality of the work, and he would cancel a whole goddamn picture we'd spent tons of money on…If it's not right, do it again. We gotta start from scratch. Start with the storyboard…He puts his money where his mouth was. That was very admirable."

Warner Bros. also had the services of perhaps the greatest voice talent of all time, Mel Blanc. "The Man of a Thousand Voices" had been smoking a pack of cigarettes a day since the age of eight, but his inventive mind and elastic vocal cords could produce an incredibly wide range of voice styles and characterizations. The Jewish, San Francisco–born voice actor was able to vividly bring to life the off-the-wall characters like Porky the Pig, Elmer Fudd, Bugs Bunny, Yosemite Sam, the Road Runner, Wile E. Coyote, Speedy Gonzalez,* Foghorn Leghorn, and Pepé Le Pew.[13]

Blanc had lived near the old Disney Studios on Hyperion Avenue, which he could see when he looked down the hill from his home's front door. The voice talent had repeatedly tried to get an audition with Walt Disney himself, but he was unable to get past the studio head's secretary until one day when he performed his impression of a drunk for the young woman. Unbeknownst to Blanc, Disney needed voice talent for Gideon the Cat, a character in his *Pinocchio* film. The secretary was impressed enough that she retrieved her boss, who gave his visitor an audition on the spot, and Blanc was hired.

"My *Pinocchio* dialogue was recorded in sixteen days, at fifty bucks per day. After I collected my eight hundred dollars, I waited like everyone else for the film to open. When it finally did…to my great surprise Gideon was mute. Between the time I'd been taped and the picture released, Disney, concerned that children might think the cat was a lush, edited out every utterance; except for one hiccup. At eight hundred dollars, it undoubtedly remains the most expensive glottal spasm in the annals of motion pictures."[14]

Melendez found Blanc to be a joy to work with. He was unselfish, funny, and "a wonderful human being." He also remembered that the voice actor would always discuss his stock market portfolio and share investment tips with the animators. "Buy this and you're

---

* In "The Pied Piper of Guadalupe," a 1961 Looney Tunes cartoon featuring Speedy Gonzalez and Sylvester, Sylvester takes flute lessons from a music teacher named J. C. Melendez, which is a nod to José Cuauhtémoc Melendez.

going to make money!" was Blanc's frequent suggestion to his colleagues at Termite Terrace.

Melendez and Blanc, like many of the employees of WB, would also have comical run-ins with the rotund Leon Schlesinger regarding their requests for pay raises. Schlesinger's counterarguments, sometimes melodramatic and at times nonsensical, were legendary. "What do you want more money for? You'll only have to pay more taxes." Another oft-repeated response was the two-word phrase "Insufficient profits."[15] When Melendez and some other animators entered Schlesinger's office to demand a raise to $27.50 a week, the overweight producer suddenly seized his chest, shouting, "Oh my God, oh my God!" The cartoonists thought he was having a heart attack, so they rushed to the front desk, where an ambulance was called. Melendez and the others were guilt-ridden, thinking they had killed the man. The next day they were surprised to see a vigorous Schlesinger back at the office. "Leon, how do you feel?" the puzzled animators asked him. "I'm fine," he responded, as if nothing had happened. The animators' anger simmered through the rest of the year, when they again entered Schlesinger's office, now demanding $35 a week. Schlesinger dropped to the floor again, feigning another heart attack, but this time his dramatic performance failed to elicit any sympathy. Schlesinger stood up. "Okay, you bastards, you got me this time. But next year I am gonna get you."

The Warner Bros. animation style was a drastic departure from that of Disney. Where Walt insisted on a realistic devotion to life-like detail, the animation at Warner Bros. was often surrealistic and often defied the laws of real-world physics. Its cartoons were energetic and outrageous, spilling forth with irreverent, wordplay-laden humor. One of the driving forces of the zany style of Warner Bros. was a young animator named Bob Clampett. His rubbery and wacky cartoons and his influence helped the other Warner directors shed the final vestiges of the influence of Disney. An animation historian would admirably praise Clampett for "putting the word *looney* in *Looney Tunes*." Melendez admired Clampett's crazy stories and wild animation styles. It was Clampett who had made Melendez an animator, promoting him from his position as an assistant animator, saying, "I'm wasting money on you. You start animating!"

Melendez departed Warner Bros. when he was drafted into the US Army during World War II. He went to basic training at Camp Wolters in Mineral Wells, Texas, which was the largest American infantry center of the war, located an hour west of Fort Worth. Melendez would go into the city when he got a weekend pass, or perhaps to nearby Dallas, farther east. Melendez also became a US citizen while in the Army. One day a sergeant gruffly instructed anyone who was not an American citizen to line up. The gathered group was then marched off to appear in front of a judge, who had the men raise their right hand and swear an oath to defend the Constitution of the United States against all enemies, foreign and domestic, and to bear arms on behalf of the country.*

The animator turned soldier actually enjoyed military life, and after basic infantry training, he was selected to go to Officer Candidate School because he had achieved a high score on his Army intelligence exam. He was shipped off to Fort Benning, Georgia, where he volunteered for Jump School, the Basic Airborne Course at the Army Airborne School. At this point in the war it seemed likely that Melendez and the other troops he trained with were being prepared for an assault on Japan. Melendez's brother, Ralph, had been fighting in the Pacific since the war had begun, and he warned his sibling not to get himself shipped out to that theater because

---

* Over 300,000 immigrants served in the US armed forces during World War II, 109,000 of whom were noncitizens. Over 100,000 noncitizens that served during the conflict would receive naturalization for their service.

he wouldn't last, apparently concerned that his gung-ho brother was too incautious to survive combat. (Ralph Melendez was a member of the famed US Army's 6th Ranger Battalion, which liberated over five hundred American POWs in a daring raid on the Philippine Islands.) Ultimately, the atomic bombs dropped on Hiroshima and Nagasaki spurred the surrender of Japan, likely sparing Melendez and his cohort of fellow soldiers from the invasion of the country.

With the war concluded, Melendez returned home and resumed his job with Warner Bros. The studio's culture had changed, however, with the firing of animator and director Bob Clampett. The Ireland-born artist, who had lived next to Charlie Chaplin as a boy, had embodied the groundbreaking animation style of Warner Bros., but he had crossed producer Edward Selzer, who ran the studio. Selzer was viewed with contempt by most, if not all, of the animators for his interference with their work. For example, the producer had objected to the pairing of Sylvester and Tweety in the carton *Tweetie Pie*. The cartoon went on to win Warner Bros. its first Academy Award for Animated Short Film, and the duo proved to be an enduring cartoon combination. Melendez himself would also cross Selzer when, after having worked for over a decade in the industry without a vacation, he took a day off to attend the funeral of his father-in-law. When the animator received his next paycheck, he noticed that he had been docked his pay for that day. "I thought you knew I was at a funeral that day," Melendez told the producer. "Well, you weren't here, were you?" replied Selzer. Melendez resigned immediately.

The animator's next stop was at a newly formed studio called United Productions of America (UPA). Melendez called it the best place he ever worked. UPA had been formed in 1941 by former Disney employees in the wake of the strike there. The studio had been able to secure work in the booming field of army-training films and other war-related work. In 1944 they made a reelection film for

President Franklin D. Roosevelt, and they also produced the 1945 animated short film *Brotherhood of Man* for the UAW. After the war ended, UPA gained many employees who had completed their wartime service at "Fort Roach," the First Motion Picture Unit (a US Army Air Force unit), which operated out of Hal Roach Studios in Culver City.* It was while working at UPA that the animator first grew the broom-like mustache that he would proudly display for the rest of his life.

UPA pioneered a brand-new style of cartooning known as "limited animation." Very flat (two-dimensional), stylized, and economical, it eliminated all detailed backgrounds. Character movements were limited to the basics, and stock close-ups were employed as much as possible. A five-minute short that had previously required 25,000 drawings could now be produced with only 1,500. Hanna-Barbera enthusiastically embraced the new production style and employed it when animating characters like Quick Draw McGraw, Yogi Bear, and Huckleberry Hound. Anyone who has seen the same rock and tree go by repeatedly when watching an episode of the cartoon *The Flintstones* has a sound grasp of the concept of limited animation.[16] Melendez was schooled in the concept at UPA and also utilized the same simple, clean animation style when producing *A Charlie Brown Christmas*. The two obvious advantages of limited animation were its much lower cost and the greatly shortened production time.

While working at UPA Melendez faced troubling accusations. In October 1947 the House Un-American Activities Committee held hearings to investigate Communist influence in Hollywood. A group of filmmakers and screenwriters refused to cooperate and were blacklisted in the industry. Melendez received a threatening

---

* Captain Ronald Reagan was one of the Hollywood workers who did his wartime service at Fort Roach while a member of the First Motion Picture Unit.

phone call from the labor management lawyer at Columbia Pictures, the company that distributed UPA's films. "There's reason for people to believe in this town that you have communist leanings and sympathy." The lawyer continued on that some people were saying that Melendez was "psychologically unfit to work in this business." The animator suspected that maybe Walt Disney himself had submitted his name to the government, perhaps still resenting his former employee's participation in the strike against the Disney studio. Melendez pushed back on the caller's accusation. "If you openly charge me with being a communist, I'll sue the hell out of you. You have to prove it." The Columbia attorney responded by saying, "I'm not saying I believe you're a communist...the word is going around that you're psychologically unfit to work, and they're gonna get you out. They're going to kick you out." Melendez promised to fight any attempt to terminate him, but he also said that if he was successfully removed from his position, the job wasn't worth having.

Melendez departed UPA shortly thereafter, possibly because of the harassment of the Columbia lawyer, and went to work at Playhouse Pictures. Ade Woolery had formed Playhouse in 1952 after selling his interest in UPA, where he had been a cofounder. Woolery and Melendez had known each other since working at Disney, where Woolery had been a cameraman on much of the final footage for *Snow White and the Seven Dwarfs*. At UPA and at Playhouse, Woolery pioneered the use of animation for television commercials. In 1960 Playhouse Pictures took home top honors at the International Advertising Film Festival in Venice, winning three of the four top prizes. Two of the award-winning spots were directed by Bill Melendez, who had now made the jump from animating to directing as well.

One of Playhouse's biggest clients was Ford Motor Company. In 1958 Playhouse Pictures was approached by J. Walter Thompson,

Ford's ad agency, to produce some advertising spots for the new Ford Falcon. Ford had employed characters from the *Peanuts* comic strip in their print advertising. (They had earlier also used characters created by Ted Geisel, better known as Dr. Seuss.*) Now Ford wanted to create a television commercial that animated Charlie Brown and his quirky gang. Charles Schulz had expressed reservations about animating his characters, however, so it was necessary for Schulz to personally approve the animator selected to oversee any commercial that would bring his characters to life.

Melendez was chosen to work on the project and was set up to "audition" with the *Peanuts* creator for the assignment to animate his characters for Ford. The animator was familiar with the comic strip, but while he had enjoyed the storyline, he thought the artwork of the cartoon was terrible. Melendez was anxious about his first meeting with the now famous cartoonist. He had been cautioned by agency executives to expect a frosty reception given Schulz's Midwestern disdain for people from Hollywood (as well as for New Yorkers). Melendez jokingly said that he would simply introduce himself as being from Mexico. When Melendez and an adman from JWT drove up the driveway to Schulz's Sebastopol home in northern California, they were greeted by two signs. Schulz, aware that perhaps he had telegraphed his regional antipathies a bit too strongly, had, with perhaps a slight sense of irony, inked two carboard signs which he had posted in his front yard: *Welcome Los Angeles. Welcome New York.*

The visitors to Schulz's home were informed that no smoking was allowed. There would also not be any alcohol served, since Schulz didn't drink. Melendez's first impression was that this was completely different from the freewheeling business environment

---

* Before becoming known as Dr. Seuss, the world famous children's book author and illustrator Theodor Seuss Geisel was an ad agency illustrator.

that animators typically worked in. He presented a sample reel of his work to Schulz, including an animated commercial Playhouse had made for Falstaff beer, featuring a comedic actor named Eddie Mayehoff as the "Old Pro." Schulz liked Mayehoff and seemed impressed with some of the work Melendez had done. Perhaps the most persuasive comment the visitor had made, however, was telling the cartoonist, "There is no need to change your drawings, the idea is to make them come to life and to animate them just the way they are." To Schulz, who jealously protected the comic strip children he had created, it was the perfect thing to say. Schulz cautiously gave permission for Melendez to animate one commercial.

Although both men were highly intelligent and had a shared talent for drawing, Schulz and Melendez could not have been more different in their personalities. Schulz could be depressed and anxious; Melendez was ebullient and optimistic. The cartoonist was shy and contemplative; the animator was outgoing and expressive. One was a clean-shaven Republican from the Midwest; the other was a mustachioed Democrat from Mexico. One was a cartoonist who never cursed, living an hour away from the city; the other was a Hollywood animator who loved martinis and who punctuated his stories with expletives. But Schulz would grow to love the infectious smile of his new friend, whose rambunctiousness not only made him smile but could also make him erupt in laughter.

About two weeks after the 1965 Memorial Day weekend meeting in Sebastopol, where Charles Schulz, Lee Mendelson, and Bill Melendez finalized the story elements of the Charlie Brown Christmas special from the one-page outline that had been approved by Coca-Cola, Schulz completed a working draft of the script. The draft was about sixty pages in length, and with its completion Bill Melendez was now able to begin to storyboard the production. Storyboards, a visualization of the script, are the director's interpretations of the writer's words and are a critical part of the preproduction process known as previsualization or "previz." The director decides how each scene will be presented on the screen, what will be the focus of the viewer's eyes, including what elements will appear onscreen and from what angle. Character designs were readied outlining the look and feel of each character as guides for the animators.

A pencil test, or animatics, was also prepared, which is a video using only rough black-and-white sketches from the storyboards, sometimes set to a basic soundtrack, to give a director an early sense of how the production will look. At about this stage, Melendez received a worried call from Lee Mendelson. The producer had just been informed that McCann-Erickson wanted to get an in-person update on the production. The ad agency naturally wanted to ensure a quality program for one of their biggest clients. John Allen would not be coming out from New York. Instead he would be sending the head of McCann's West Coast operations, an experienced television producer based in Los Angeles named Neil Reagan.

That meeting would jeopardize the production itself.

THE ADMAN
NEIL REAGAN

✦

If I give the McCann office my honest opinion of
this production, they'll shut it down right now.
—McCann executive Neil Reagan to producer Lee Mendelson after
reviewing the storyboards for *A Charlie Brown Christmas*

In the summer of 1965 Neil Reagan was a very busy man. He was
supervising the Los Angeles office of McCann-Erickson as well
as managing his own accounts and clients. When he wasn't working he was also plotting a possible race for the California governor's
office for his younger brother, former actor Ronald Reagan. And
when he wasn't working or dabbling in politics, he was golfing at
Bel-Air Country Club or piloting his large sailboat from its harbor
in Newport Beach to the San Diego Yacht Club. But now the New
York office of McCann had asked Reagan to fly to San Francisco and
report back on the status of one of their most important projects,
an animated Christmas special being produced for the firm's premier client, Coca-Cola. Reagan would have to fly to San Francisco,
meet with the principals, and report back on the show's content and
production status.

Neil Reagan's proximity to San Francisco as well as his extensive background in entertainment made him a natural choice for the assignment. His first job after moving to Los Angeles had been at KFWB, a commercial radio station owned by the Warner Bros. movie studio. Warner had started the station to promote and publicize the studio's actors and its movies, and not coincidentally one of those contract actors was Neil's brother, Ronald. Neil had started out as a radio announcer at the station, and by 1944 he had become the station's program director.[1]

Reagan left KFWB for a job as a director with CBS, which allowed him to have greater interaction with talent. At CBS he managed a show sponsored by the Edwards Coffee Division of Safeway Stores, which starred Jack Bailey, a prominent radio and television star of the time who was known for a program called *Meet the Missus*. Bailey went on to host the show *Queen for a Day*, which ushered in big-prize giveaway shows featuring contestants from the audience, a staple of television programming that continues today. Bailey and Reagan were good friends, and Bailey loved to engage in a recurring, nerve-racking gag to tweak his pal at the end of a show: when Reagan, as the show's director, gave Bailey the signal to wind up and take the show off the air, Bailey would turn away and continue talking as if oblivious to the show's time limit. Reagan would then have to face questioning from higher-ups on why he had allowed the show to run over.

Reagan's work at CBS drew the attention of Clarence Olmstead, the manager of the McCann-Erickson office in Los Angeles. Olmstead called Reagan and invited him to meet for lunch the following day at the Brown Derby restaurant at 1628 Vine in Hollywood. Olmstead was preparing to launch *The John Charles Thomas Show*, a big weekly musical production on the Radio Westinghouse Program featuring band and vocal performances and narrated stories. Each show was expressly addressed to the troops fighting in World War II and opened with an angelic chorus of voices. The program featured John Charles Thomas, a singer for the Metropolitan Opera and one of the great baritones of the twentieth century.

Olmstead made Reagan a lucrative offer to join him in the advertising agency's Los Angeles office managing *The John Charles Thomas Show* as well as other client assignments. Reagan quickly accepted the offer and eventually took over for Olmstead when he retired. Beginning an advertising career in the early years of television promised to be exciting, and Neil Reagan had a front-row seat to the new industry. He recounted his involvement in a notorious incident in one live broadcast involving actress Betty Furness, a spokesperson for Westinghouse, showcasing all the company's modern electronic home appliances to 1950s housewives:

> *We had her doing Westinghouse commercials, and I fought my way through the time she couldn't get the refrigerator door open. They were doing live shows and live commercials then. They weren't filmed. She gives two or three yanks and then turned around and right into the camera and said, "I can't get the goddamned door open." Coast to coast, you know. Well, of course, the phone started jangling right then from over in Ohio at the Westinghouse offices. And she was getting $100,000 a year.*[2]

Another show Reagan produced was *Death Valley Days*, a syndicated half-hour television series that ran from 1952 until 1970. The program had been conceived by McCann-Erickson for its client Pacific Coast Borax Company. The show featured a host who would introduce and conclude the program with forty-five seconds of narration bracketing a dramatization of a story from the old American West.

The show's original host was Stanley Andrews, who presented in character as the Old Ranger. Andrews was a veteran of radio and film whose first big role was on radio as Daddy Warbucks in the *Little Orphan Annie* series. He eventually appeared in over 250 movies, including *Mr. Smith Goes to Washington, Beau Geste, The Ox-Bow Incident, The Lemon Drop Kid*, and *State of the Union*. But by 1963 the aging acting veteran would have difficulty remembering his lines. As Neil Reagan recalled to an interviewer years later, "The Old Ranger... was so old that it took more time for us to shoot the forty-five second opening and forty-five second close...than it did to do the rest of the show. Put three words together, and he couldn't remember the middle word or maybe the last word...you couldn't go on with it; so the client, U.S. Borax, agreed that we're going to have to replace him. Well, the question becomes, now, who?"[3]

To Reagan, the answer to his question was easy: the new host for *Death Valley Days* should be no one other than his brother, actor Ronald Reagan. The younger Reagan had just been released from his GE contract, which required him to travel to the company's plants and facilities and speak to employees. Neil felt that his brother's pride might be hurt from no longer being in demand in Hollywood. When the ad executive suggested casting his brother to the executives at Borax, they immediately responded very favorably. But Neil had a more difficult time convincing the actor to take on the role. As he recalled later:

> So, I went to him and asked him, and he said, "No way I don't want to do anything, I don't want to do anything." But I kept after him and got turned down for over a period of a few weeks. Finally, it got to the place where I was going to have to do something. Then I got the brilliant idea, "Why don't I go to his agent? Because his agent doesn't make anything off of him if he isn't working."

Neil Reagan approached William "Bill" Meiklejohn, his brother's agent. Meiklejohn had originally taken the younger brother to Warner Bros. and secured the contract that had brought him out to California from Iowa. Meiklejohn had sold his agency to MCA, but he left after several years to once again launch his own firm, but he was not finding much success. Neil Reagan explained to the agent how his brother had rejected his prior entreaties regarding the *Death Valley Days* hosting job. "Well, leave it to me," Meiklejohn responded.[4]

A few days later Neil Reagan entered the Brown Derby restaurant in Hollywood, where he ate lunch every day. The ad agency executive had a booth that was permanently reserved for him in a prime location as guests entered the restaurant. Behind his booth were caricatures of famous actors and Hollywood power brokers, including one of Neil Reagan himself.* The ad exec entered,

---

* For years, even after Ronald Reagan was president, Neil would tease the former actor that he was never as important in Hollywood as his older brother because Neil had a caricature in the Brown Derby and Ronald didn't. (In 1981 Neil Reagan would recount in an oral history project at UCLA: "Every once in a while I call that to his attention: 'Don't forget, I've still got my picture on the Derby wall, and you never did.'") However, in the research for this book, I discovered that Ronald Reagan did indeed have a caricature on the Derby wall that was sketched in 1941. I think it's noteworthy to point out that the actor endured his older brother's teasing, never correcting Neil's mistaken belief that of the two brothers only Neil had been deemed important enough to have earned having his face sketched at the restaurant. Ronald Reagan's caricature was an 11×14-inch sketch of Reagan in left profile by world-famed caricaturist Frank "Pancho" Willmarth, signed "Pancho" and dated "41." Reagan had inscribed the artwork "Good luck Bob + plenty of runs, hits & no errors. Sincerely, Ronald Reagan." Bob was almost certainly Robert "Bob" Cobb, co-owner of the Brown Derby and creator of the Cobb salad. The artwork sold at auction in 2009 for almost $4,500. See this link at the Heritage Auctions website: https://entertainment.ha.com/itm/movie-tv-memorabilia/autographs-and-signed-items/ronald-reagan-signed-sketch-from-the-brown-derby/a/7004-49209.s.

recognized friends, and was conversing with them when he heard his brother's familiar voice over his shoulder. "If it wasn't for you, I wouldn't have to be here this noon, dressed up with a tie on." Feigning ignorance, Neil responded, "What do you mean, because of me?" The actor replied that he was having lunch with Bill Meiklejohn. "Well, good," said Neil. "I hope he has something for you."

After lunch with his agent, the actor exited the restaurant without stopping by his brother's booth. Meiklejohn, however, did stop by. "Go ahead and write the contract up and send it out to him. He'll sign it," he said. The ad agent's plan to corral his reluctant brother had worked perfectly. Two or three days later Neil was sitting in his booth at the Brown Derby when Ronald appeared and immediately began needling him about what kind of trouble he had gotten him into with the *Death Valley Days* contract. The two brothers were extremely close but never physically demonstrative or capable of expressing deep emotions with one another, and Neil recognized that the actor's faux whining was his way of expressing his appreciation for his assistance in landing him a new job.

Neil Reagan had another motivation for securing his brother a high-visibility position. He knew it would keep Ronald in the public eye, which would be helpful if the actor decided to run for governor in 1966.

✦ ✦ ✦

John Neil Reagan entered the world on September 16, 1906, in Tampico, Illinois, a town with a population of around 1,200. He was the first of two sons born to Jack and Nelle Reagan.

He was born at home—a rented five-room flat over a bakery on Main Street with no indoor toilet facilities. An outside pump supplied water to the kitchen, and a stairway in the back of the flat led from the dining room to an outhouse. Water was heated on a coal-burning stove that also served to provide heat to the flat's occupants.[5]

The newborn's baptism became a point of contention when a priest from the Catholic church paid the child's parents a visit shortly after Neil's birth. Nelle, who was a Protestant, resisted having the child baptized as a Catholic. The priest insisted that Nelle must have agreed to raise her children Catholic when she had married her husband. Nelle denied ever having made such a promise, a claim that was confirmed by Jack, who maintained that both he and the priest had forgotten to inform his wife of the agreement.[6]

The couple eventually reached a compromise—John Neil and any subsequent child would be baptized and raised Catholic, but when they reached an age when they could think for themselves, they would be given the liberty to freely choose their faith. Nelle Reagan would herself be baptized less than two years after giving birth. She professed her faith in Christ at the Christian Church of Tampico (Disciples of Christ) on March 27, 1910, and shortly thereafter she become pregnant with her second child, who would be born on February 6, 1911, following a terrible blizzard. That child was named Ronald Wilson Reagan, but his father quickly bestowed him with the nickname Dutch.*

Neil Reagan was less than thrilled by the entrance of his younger brother into his world. Neil had stayed with a neighbor while Nelle was in labor. Upon returning home, the older brother refused to enter the room where his mother was recuperating with his new sibling. He had been promised a sister by his mother and father and was disappointed that the newborn was a boy.

---

* "For such a little bit of a Dutchman, he makes a hell of a lot of noise, doesn't he?" Jack Reagan said upon viewing his crying newborn. The nickname Dutch stuck with the child.

The two Reagan boys would soon embark on childhood adventures together with the older brother always leading the way. Three months after Ronald's birth, the family moved to a small white wood-framed bungalow built in the 1870s. This home had indoor plumbing and was located across from a park and near the railroad tracks. One day when Neil was five years old he took his younger brother by the hand and led him toward a wagon he had spied on the other side of the railroad tracks. Neil had plans to take some of the ice from the wagon. The two boys crawled beneath a train that was parked in the station, and, as their horrified mother looked on from the front porch of her home, the train began to lurch forward. Her terror turned into relief as she saw the boys emerge safely from the other side. When the boys returned home their father unbuckled his belt and drew the leather from his belt loops. Punishment was meted out solely to Neil for having led his younger brother astray and putting them both in serious danger.[7]

Ronald recalled another childhood experience that he considered "a thousand times worse" than any physical punishment the brothers ever received from his father: the day their father bought a carload of secondhand potatoes on which he hoped to turn a profit by reselling them. "My brother and I were ordered to the siding to sort the good potatoes from the bad. It was a unique experience. No one who has not sat in a stinking boxcar during hot summer days, gingerly gripping tubers that dissolve in fingers with a dripping squish, emitting an odor worse than that of a decaying corpse, can possibly imagine the agony we suffered. We did this hideous chore for days. At last we got so queasy at the very look of spuds that we simply lied about the rest and dumped them all, good or bad." Jack Reagan made a little money, but the two boys developed a near permanent dislike for potatoes in any form.[8]

Young Charles M. Schulz. From the earliest age Schulz had the ambition to become a cartoonist. *(Courtesy of the Charles M. Schulz Museum and Research Center, Santa Rosa, California)*

Schulz earned a combat infantryman's badge serving in Europe with the US Army's 20th Armored Division in World War II. He was promoted to staff sergeant and was the squad leader on a mechanized halftrack. *(Courtesy of the Charles M. Schulz Museum and Research Center, Santa Rosa, California)*

Schulz working at his home studio at Coffee Grounds in Sebastopol, California. The creator of the *Peanuts* comic strip worked on the same drawing board he had purchased at the beginning of his career for $23. He had learned to draw from an art correspondence school. *(Getty Images)*

Charles M. Schulz with a drawing of Charlie Brown, January 1, 1962 *(Photo by CBS via Getty Images)*

US Army soldiers during the Battle of Ia Drang in November 1965. Televised images of the war may have triggered Charles Schulz's PTSD from his World War II combat service. *(US Army photo/Alamy)*

J. Paul Austin, president of the Coca-Cola Company. Austin joined the board of directors of General Electric in 1964, the same year that company sponsored *Rudolph the Red-Nosed Reindeer*, likely spurring the competitive Austin to seek a Christmas special for Coca-Cola the following year. *(Alamy)*

Marion Harper Jr., the brilliant head of McCann-Erickson, secured the prestigious Coca-Cola account for the ad agency. Harper forged the model of the modern advertising agency. In 1965, McCann-Erickson was tasked with finding a Christmas special for Coca-Cola to sponsor. *(Getty Images)*

A program analyzer designed by CBS president Frank Stanton and social researcher Paul Lazarsfeld. McCann-Erickson contracted for the exclusive rights to the device. *(CBS via Getty Images)*

James T. Aubrey, CBS Television Network president. Aubrey had a strict policy against specials, which he believed drove viewers to competing networks. Aubrey's firing by Frank Stanton in February 1965 opened a path for the network to broadcast the Charlie Brown Christmas special. *(CBS via Getty Images)*

CBS president Frank Stanton at the setup for the first presidential debate between John F. Kennedy and Richard Nixon on September 26, 1960. Stanton had worked for years to institute televised debates between leading presidential candidates. *(CBS via Getty Images)*

While driving over the Golden Gate Bridge in 1963, producer Lee Mendelson first heard Vince Guaraldi's Grammy-winning song, "Cast Your Fate to the Wind." He contracted with the musician to compose music for his documentary on Charles Schulz. Several weeks later, Guaraldi composed the signature *Peanuts* song, "Linus and Lucy," while driving across the bridge. *(Getty Images)*

Jazz pianist Vince Guaraldi, circa 1960. Guaraldi composed the music for the Charlie Brown Christmas special. *(Getty Images)*

Vince Guaraldi recording with a quartet in a studio, circa 1965 *(Photo by Michael Ochs Archives/Getty Images)*

Neil Reagan and his younger brother, Ronald, then a Hollywood actor, reviewing a script. In 1965, Neil was head of West Coast operations for McCann-Erickson and provided an upbeat assessment of the Charlie Brown Christmas special despite his misgivings about the program's quality. The same year, Ronald Reagan was plotting his first run for political office. *(Getty Images)*

Director and animator Bill Melendez recording dialogue for the animated TV special *It's the Great Pumpkin, Charlie Brown*, a year after producing the Charlie Brown Christmas special *(Photo by Ted Streshinsky/ CORBIS via Getty Images)*

CBS president Frank Stanton. Network executives were so concerned about the Charlie Brown Christmas special that they discussed it directly with Stanton, who personally watched the program before its broadcast. *(Photo by CBS via Getty Images)*

Lee Mendelson, Charles M. Schulz, and Bill Melendez accepting the Emmy Award for Outstanding Children's Program for *A Charlie Brown Christmas* on May 22, 1966 *(Courtesy of the Charles M. Schulz Museum and Research Center, Santa Rosa, California)*

Schulz's grave marker notes his service in World War II but makes no mention of his role as the creator of the world's most popular comic strip. Schulz considered the combat infantryman's badge he had earned during the war to be the greatest honor he had achieved. *(Tifani Beecher Photography)*

A bench was later added next to Schulz's grave with the inscription "Charlie Brown, Lucy, Linus, Snoopy…How can I ever forget them…" The words are taken from the farewell message Schulz wrote in his final cartoon, which ran in newspapers on February 13, 2000. The cartoonist died the previous day. *(Tifani Beecher Photography)*

Ronald was eleven years old when he confronted a bracing reality that his older brother had dealt with earlier: their father's alcoholism. The young boy came home one evening and discovered his father flat on his back on their home's front porch. Jack was passed out drunk, and no one else was home to help. "I stood over him for a minute or two. I wanted to let myself in the house and go to bed and pretend he wasn't there. Oh, I wasn't ignorant of his weakness. I don't know at what age I knew what the occasional absences or the loud voices in the night meant, but up till now my mother, Nelle, or my brother handled the situation, and I was a child in bed with the privilege of pretending sleep."[9]

Jack Reagan was a tall, muscular, handsome man of Irish ancestry. He was a sharp dresser and a great storyteller, and he had a thirst for Irish whiskey.[10] Politically he was a sentimental Democrat who sympathized with the workingman and supported labor unions and workers' rights, but he also had a strong belief that, while all men were created equal, after that a man's own ambition determined what happened to him.[11] Jack also taught his boys to stand up against racism. When the film *The Birth of a Nation* came to town, Ronald and Neil were the only two kids not to watch it. "It deals with the Ku Klux Klan against the colored folks, and I'm damned if anyone in this family will go see it," Jack Reagan told his sons.[12] Years later, during the Depression, Jack refused to check in to a small-town hotel that did not permit Jewish guests. "I'm a Catholic," he told the clerk, "and if it's come to the point where you won't take Jews, you won't take me either." The elder Reagan instead spent the night in his car in the snow.[13]

Evenings in the Reagan household centered around the kitchen table. Jack would sit at one end of the table, focused on reading the newspaper. At the other end, Nelle sat with the two boys. The family shared handfuls of buttered popcorn from a huge bowl in the middle of the table or snacked on apples and salted crackers. Nelle would read aloud to her sons from books, including stories of the Three Musketeers and King Arthur and the knights of the Round Table.[14]

Nelle Reagan was strikingly different from her husband. She was a small woman with auburn hair and blue eyes "who had the conviction that everyone loved her just because she loved them." She was as unfailingly optimistic as her husband was cynical. Where her husband loved to tell off-color jokes, Nelle's humor was more restrained. Her husband was Irish Catholic, and Nelle was Scots-English Protestant.

Nelle frequently tended to those in need, whether it was preaching the gospel to prisoners or feeding the poor or caring for the sick. These goodwill missions could take her away from her family for hours at a time. During one of her absences, her two boys became scared as nightfall approached. With neither Jack nor Nelle at home, the children decided it was best to begin to scour the city for their parents. They carefully blew out the gas lamp and then wandered two or three blocks from home, where they encountered a friendly drunk who chastised the boys for being out late. Nelle returned home to an empty, gas-filled house and immediately became frantic. She ran into the street looking for her missing boys just in time to find them being urged to return home by the intoxicated stranger. It was a rare occasion when Nelle lost her temper and righteously accepted her husband disciplining the boys.[15]

On December 26, 1920, the Reagans moved to Dixon, Illinois, where the family rented a boxy white two-story framed home with three bedrooms and an indoor toilet. The boys shared one room, the parents took another, and the third was Nelle's sewing room. Jack Reagan worked at the Fashion Boot Shop, where he had been made a partner, although his ownership interest was yet to be earned and would be paid for by deducting commissions above his meager salary.[16]

Neil Reagan made friends in their new town more quickly than his younger brother. His new classmates at South Central quickly nicknamed him Moon because of his resemblance to the comic strip character Moon Mullins. The name stuck and the Reagan boys were each known to their friends and family by their respective nicknames, Moon and Dutch. Neil was a good athlete, better than his scrawnier and nearsighted younger brother. One of Neil's new best friends was Winston "Wink" McReynolds, a sixth grade classmate and a good football player. Wink became a frequent visitor to the Reagan household. The McReynolds family was one of only twelve Black households in Dixon, and while the town was certainly not free from racial prejudice, there was less racial intolerance than in many American cities. The Reagans preached and practiced racial equality.[17]

The two brothers would occasionally tussle with one another, but they would always defend one another if an outsider picked on one of them. "When someone started taking picks at me, [Dutch]'d stick in, and if somebody starting taking picks on him, I'd stick in," Neil recalled. To outsiders, however, the boys did not appear particularly close. "I knew when he had down moments, but I never said anything to him. There was no such thought of, you know, putting my arm around his shoulder and saying, 'Let's talk this over,' or anything like that...I always operate on the theory that [Dutch] doesn't even know I'm breathing—but that's the way it's always been with my dad, [Dutch,] and myself."[18]

The two Reagan boys were baptized on the same date, June 21, 1922, in the newly built Christian Church at 123 Hennepin. Nelle was the spiritual leader in the family, and Neil claims that he was eighteen years old when he learned that his father was Catholic.

Nelle took her boys' religious instruction and matters of faith seriously. The boys attended Sunday school, followed by church services, then Christian Endeavor* Sunday evening, followed by another church service. There was also a prayer meeting on Wednesdays.[19]

Nelle Reagan was loved by everyone in her congregation and respected as a leader. There was also a strongly held belief by her fellow churchgoers that Nelle's prayers were answered. Her personal ministry extended beyond her local church and included visits to the state mental hospital and to prisoners in the local jail as well. In addition to preaching from her Bible, she brought cookies or apples to the inmates and when she was finished reading she allowed the prisoners to hold the holy book in their hands.

Nelle was not only in demand for her Bible readings and prayer, but many in the congregation also believed that she had been divinely gifted the power to heal. "She never laid hands on or anything like that. It was the way she prayed, down on her knees, eyes raised up and speaking like she knew God personally, like she had had lots of dealings with him before. If someone had real troubles or was sick, Nelle would come to their house and kneel and pray. Maybe she didn't always pray herself a miracle, but folks could bear things a lot better after she left."[20]

Neil attended South Dixon High School, which he continued to attend after his family moved to a small, less expensive home in Dixon. The new location meant that Ron entered a different high school, North Dixon. It was the beginning of a schism between the two boys that would see them develop more individual personalities as well as split in ways including eventually politics and religion. The South Dixon boys were a rougher crowd, visited poolrooms, and

---

* Christian Endeavor is an international youth fellowship organization that was founded in 1881 in order to "bring youth to accept Christ and work for Him."

considered the boys at North Dixon to be "sissies." North Dixon was newer and more affluent and cultured.

Neil graduated from high school in the summer of 1926, but when the class voted that the boys would wear tuxedoes to the senior prom and graduation, he knew that his family's budget would not accommodate purchasing such fancy attire. "We were poor, and I mean poor...There was no way," he recalled to an interviewer years later. Neil matter-of-factly announced to his surprised parents at dinner that he would not be attending graduation. Jack and Nelle were immediately concerned that in actuality their son had not passed his required coursework. The boy reassured them that he met the requirements to graduate but then reluctantly explained the class vote on the required attire. He thought that was the end of the conversation until a week before graduation when his father invited him for a walk, which ended at O'Malley's clothing store. There the proprietor was already awaiting them, prepared with a selection of tux coats and trousers.[21]

Neil Reagan had no desire to go off to college and instead was able to secure a job working at the Medusa Portland Cement Company for a salary of $125 a month. The money helped to support the Reagans, but Nelle was disappointed that her oldest boy was not continuing his education. "She always said Dutch would have succeeded if he had gone to college or not, but Moon was another matter," an old friend of Nelle's recalled.[22]

An even bigger blow to Nelle was that at the age of eighteen Neil suddenly decided to leave his mother's Christian Church and convert to Catholicism. "I was eighteen years old and decided I was dissatisfied with the church and went out shopping for a church, and went home and told my mother I was going to join the Catholic church. She then, with a tear in her eye, told me [for the first time] I had been baptized Catholic when I was six weeks old."[23] Neil's conversion to

Catholicism, his father's religion, was further confirmation that the older boy's personality and character were more akin to Jack's than to Nelle's. As Moon explained years later, "I always say that Ronald is my mother's boy, and I'm my father's boy."[24]

Ron graduated from high school two years after his brother and with the help of a football scholarship was able to enroll in Eureka College, a small liberal arts school affiliated with the Christian Church in Eureka, Illinois. He became a member of the Tau Kappa Epsilon fraternity and, even as a freshman, established himself as a leader on campus. Nelle, however, had never given up on her dream for her older son to also head off to college. "I've got news for you," Nelle announced to Ronald one day when he had returned home from school. "Your brother Neil doesn't think college is a joke anymore. He doesn't want to work, he wants to be educated. He wants to come to Eureka."[25] Ron, ever the dutiful son when his mother made a request, make extensive arrangements for his older brother to be able to attend college with him.

Nelle, however, may have oversold her older son's commitment to his education. As Neil recounted later: "[Ron] came home at the end of the second year down at Eureka…and he made the announcement that he had it all arranged for me to go to college—a scholarship for football, a job at the girls' dormitory hashing, and then he would see that I was pledged to the fraternity that he was a member of, so that all I'd have to raise was the ten dollars a month to pay for my room at the fraternity house. And I just laughed." The next day Ron returned to school but left his precious steamer trunk at home. When Neil returned home from work, he spied his brother's luggage and was confused. "Nelle, I thought Dutch was going back to school today."* Nelle replied, "He did, and you ought to be ashamed of

---

* The Reagan boys always referred to their parents as Jack and Nelle.

yourself. He left the trunk, thinking you'd change your mind." This prompted another laugh from Neil.[26]

The next day at work, as he related the prior day's events to his supervisor, Mr. Kennedy, Neil slowly realized that his boss did not find the story amusing. At ten o'clock Mr. Kennedy's secretary approached Neil and handed him his paycheck. "Paycheck?" Neil asked. "It's not payday." "It is for you," she replied. "Well, do you mean I'm fired?" he asked. "Call it what you want to. Mr. Kennedy says if you're not smart enough to take the good thing your brother has fixed up for you, you're not smart enough to work for him." Neil left work, headed to the bank to cash the check, then went home and began to pack the steamer trunk his younger brother had left for him.[27] He was enrolled in college before the end of the week.

At Eureka, Neil was now in his younger sibling's shadow, and he was referred to on campus as "Dutch Reagan's brother." Their change in rank was demonstrated most painfully at the fraternity house, where pledges were struck on their behind with a wooden paddle drilled with one-inch holes. Neil later recalled, "When I was a pledge, any time I heard the shout, 'Assume the position, Reagan,' and I grabbed my ankles, when they each took their whack, I knew that the whack I got from him was going to be worse than the others, because he felt he had to, otherwise they'd accuse him of showing partisanship."[28]

Ron's role in shaping his older brother's life extended beyond college. When he finished school, Neil intended to attend law school at Northwestern University. Ron was working for a radio station in Des Moines, Iowa, and he had just purchased a brand-new Nash convertible. He asked his younger brother to pick up the car from the dealer and drive it out to Des Moines, casually adding, "Plan to spend two or three days out here and see the station and meet the guys at the station."

The day after Neil delivered his brother's new vehicle, Ron brought him into the station, where introductions were made to the program director and announcers. At the station Ron also arranged for a surreptitious audition for his brother. Neil was asked to announce a few imaginary plays of a college football game in the announcer's booth. "Being a football player and very interested in sports, I knew all of the football players in the Big Ten teams and Notre Dame especially. So I went in and did Iowa-Northwestern, two or three plays." The program director was listening in to the audition, liked what he had just heard, and asked for the candidate to be brought upstairs for a meeting. He was oblivious to the fact that the effortless and knowledgeable sports announcing he had just listened to had been done by Ron Reagan's brother. Initially irritated, thinking he was being pranked, the program director eventually offered Neil the position as announcer of a program called *Scoreboard of the Air* sponsored by the Deep Rock Oil Company. It was a fifteen-minute program that involved reading the sports scores for Saturday's college football games as well as a series of dramatized commercials. The pay was meager, but Neil was able to save money by living with his brother, and so he put aside his plans for law school.

Soon the Reagan brothers put together a new show that would be broadcast on Friday nights. The pair would sit across from one another and discuss their predictions for winners and losers for the next day's football games. A faux argument would erupt whenever the two siblings picked different teams to win the next day's contest, fueling the drama of the show. The following week the two men would roast each other over how poorly their picks may have fared the previous Saturday.[29]

While working in Des Moines, Neil met a young woman named Bess Hoffman, and the two very quickly fell in love. Bess was from

Des Moines and was a graduate of Drake University. Just two weeks after meeting they decided to get married. Bess was cute and slender, as well as intelligent and a stylish dresser. Dutch liked Bess but he understandably thought his brother was simply moving too quickly. "Two weeks—that's way too fast," Dutch counseled his brother. The younger brother would protest the marriage right up until the wedding. A mutual friend of the two brothers drove Ronald to his brother's wedding and recalled that Reagan complained bitterly the whole way. "He said, 'Now here's your very best friend in the world, he's only known this girl for about two weeks, and they're gonna get married, and what kind of friend are you?' And I kept saying, 'Well, she's a lovely woman, she's a lovely girl.' He says, 'That doesn't make any difference,' and gave me a hard time."[*, 30]

Neil was the first of the two brothers to defect to the Republican party, which he did in 1932, causing great distress to his parents and brother, who all still looked to President Roosevelt and Democratic policies to rescue the country from the woes of the Depression. In the 1940s on Sunday evenings there would be a gathering of a dozen or so Hollywood celebrities at the home of Ronald Reagan and Jane Wyman. The guests included names like Jack Benny and George Burns, and a political argument frequently erupted between the Reagan brothers. "[Ron's] statement to me always was: 'That's the trouble with you guys. Anybody who voted for Roosevelt is a Communist,' and I used to agree with him heartily, at which point he'd get the screaming meemies," recalled Neil.[31]

---

* Despite his brother's concerns, Neil and Bess would be married for sixty-one years, until Neil died on December 11, 1996. Ron's first marriage, to actress Jane Wyman, would end in divorce in 1949 after nine years.

Ron would eventually migrate in his political leanings, but he would not officially switch parties until 1962.* A group of businessmen approached Reagan to convince him to challenge the more liberal Republican Thomas Kuchel in the Republican primary for the US Senate. Kuchel was the incumbent in the race, and Reagan wisely refused their entreaties. (Kuchel would be reelected to his second full term in office, carrying every county in California.) "The whole idea of entering politics was alien to my thinking," said Reagan, who would instead go on to host *Death Valley Days*.[32] By 1965, however, Ronald Reagan was seriously considering challenging Pat Brown, the Democratic incumbent governor of California, in the November election the following year.

Beyond his television production and advertising experience Neil Reagan brought two other talents to bear in being able to evaluate the Charlie Brown Christmas special. He had a special emotional connection with children, and he had an extraordinary attachment to the Christmas holiday.

Neil discussed his bond with children in an interview with a historian: "I've always been a real pigeon for children...if a three-year-old girl were to come through that door right now and we both stood up, the three-year-old girl would come right over to me. And I'd pick her up, and there'd be no fright or anything." Neil then related a story of when he first moved to Los Angeles and he learned of a tragedy involving the family of an elderly woman who was his next-door neighbor. The woman's son lived in Virginia with his wife and young child. The wife was killed in a car accident, and the

---

* Reagan campaigned as a "Democrat for Nixon" in the presidential election of 1960.

daughter, only three or four years of age, was inconsolable and had been crying nonstop for days, so much so that her eyes had practically swollen shut. The grandmother invited her son and granddaughter to her home hoping that she would be able to comfort the distraught child. Two days after the family reunited in Los Angeles, the Reagans' doorbell rang. When Neil's wife, Bess, answered the door she was greeted by their neighbor and her son and granddaughter, whom the Reagans had never met. The trio entered, and even before introductions were completed, the little girl, upon seeing Neil, instantly jumped into his arms, where she eventually fell asleep. The small child's father was astounded at the calming influence Reagan had. For days afterward, the little girl and her grandmother would visit Reagan after work, or the Reagans would stop by their neighbors' home and visit with her. Some days the busy adman would even travel home for lunch, and the little girl would join him for a glass of milk.

Neil's bond with children extended to his own brother's offspring as well. Ron was a great swimmer and had served as a lifeguard, but it was Neil who taught Maureen Reagan, Ron's daughter with his first wife, Jane Wyman, to swim before she could even walk. Neil never criticized his brother's parenting, nor did he provide any advice. But he knew his brother was "really not a demonstrative guy" and believed that Ron was "more the type that thinks [children] should be on their own."[33]

The Reagan brothers were poor growing up, as were most families during the Depression. As one Christmas holiday approached, their mother asked the boys what they wanted Santa Claus to bring them on Christmas Day. Neil responded to his mother's question with only one request: "I want an electric train." As a child he could not appreciate that the item was not within the family's meager budget. As Christmas approached, his mother began repeatedly saying that "maybe Santa doesn't have electric trains," a maternal attempt to soften the blow when her boy awakened on Christmas morning to the crushing disappointment of not having received his most desired gift. On Christmas Eve, however, Neil and his brother were awakened by the sound of laughter and the clacking of metal. The two boys exited their beds and carefully snuck partway down the stairway unseen, where they spied their father playing with a childlike joy with an electric train engine pulling one car and a caboose in front of the Christmas tree. The two boys kept the secret of what they had witnessed that Christmas morning from their parents until they were adults.

The mere presence of a Christmas tree in Neil's recollection of that particular Christmas indicates that if the Reagan family was more typically poor than prosperous, there was perhaps a greater prosperity that year in their household. Ronald Reagan wrote in a letter in August 1981 that "There were very few decorated trees in the years of my growing up. We couldn't afford them." Instead Nelle Reagan would decorate a table with ribbon and crepe paper or create a cardboard fireplace out of a packing box. Ron also recalled that his mother always reminded her boys whose birthday it was and made sure they knew the true meaning of Christmas.[34]

While the Reagans were not particularly well-off, neither were they destitute, and some Christmas memories took on the sheen of a Currier and Ives lithograph of the holiday season in rural America. At Christmastime the Reagans would often travel by train to visit Nelle's relatives who lived on a farm near Morrison, Illinois. The family would then depart the train station in a sleigh with jingling bells, with hot bricks at their feet to stave off the cold, and wrapped up in thick lap blankets.[35]

Ronald also recalled that one of the most cherished Christmas gifts he had ever received was a simple letter from Neil. "I must have presented something of a problem to my brother after we were grown up and in our middle years. A problem with regard to what might be a suitable gift. He solved the problem with a letter." In his letter Neil recounted that he had found an especially needy family with small children who were all too painfully aware they would not be receiving any gifts from Santa Claus. Neil decided to change that, and he took on the role of Santa Claus himself, providing the family with a tree, turkey, toys, and gifts. His letter described in detail the joyful faces of the children and the grateful happiness of their mother. To Ron, Neil's letter to him was a gift "truly in keeping with the spirit of the day."[36]

Sometime in the summer of 1965, most likely in late June or early July, Neil Reagan arrived at the Sebastopol home of Charles Schulz.[37]

Reagan was the logical candidate to be sent by McCann-Erickson to review the project. The production was being broadcast on a major television network, CBS, and was being sponsored by Coca-Cola, one of the premier advertising clients in the world. This demanded a senior executive's attention, and not only was Reagan, based in Los Angeles, nearby, but he was the head adman overseeing McCann's West Coast operations, and he had over two decades of experience in film and television production.

In attendance for the presentation were all three of the principals behind the production: Charles Schulz, the cartoonist and scriptwriter; Lee Mendelson, the producer; and Bill Melendez, the head of animation and director. The team walked Reagan through the special's story and presented storyboards (black-and-white illustrations of key scenes) and a "pencil test" animation using rough pencil sketches of the characters and scenes without color or backgrounds added.

Reagan's reaction was swift and negative. "I've got to be honest with you. This is not very good. If I go back and tell everybody what I see here, they may not want to do the show."

Mendelson pleaded with the McCann executive. "Please, you're looking at it with one-third of the show there. Just put your trust in Charles Schulz and the *Peanuts* characters and trust us." Schulz, Mendelson, and Melendez tried to reassure their visitor that the special would have more bounce once the color and music was added. Reagan gave Mendelson a long look. "Okay, it might cost me my job, but I'm not going to say anything."[38]

THE JAZZ MUSICIAN
VINCE GUARALDI

I gotta play something for you; it just came into my head!
—Vince Guaraldi to Lee Mendelson,
having just composed "Linus and Lucy"

In 1963 Lee Mendelson was driving back to his home in Burlingame, south of San Francisco, after a meeting with Charles Schulz at the cartoonist's home in Sebastopol. The producer was excited about the documentary the two men were making about the life of the famous *Peanuts* creator. Along the ninety-minute drive home, Mendelson pondered all the pieces he was pulling together to make *A Boy Named Charlie Brown*, including video footage shot of the cartoonist in his home studio drafting the comic strip interspersed with family moments such as Schulz playing with his children and driving them to school, as well as a couple of minutes of animation of the *Peanuts* cartoon characters.

One important missing piece was finding the right composer to prepare a suitable soundtrack to accompany the animation. Mendelson knew that a musical soundtrack would be critical to how the two-dimensional characters came to life on the television screen and how viewers related to them. He thought jazz would work well with the comic strip's quirky characters, but he had been unable to find a suitable musician who was available. Ideally, he had hoped to find a composer who had children and who enjoyed the *Peanuts* comic strips. Overtures had been made to local musicians Dave Brubeck and Cal Tjader, but both men had turned Mendelson down, claiming that they were too busy to take on the project. Now the producer was running out of time.

Mendelson pondered his predicament as he drove south across the Golden Gate Bridge, his eyes darting momentarily down to the sailboats in the San Francisco Bay. The bridge held special meaning to Mendelson. It had been the subject of his first documentary, and he had had tremendous luck in sourcing film footage of the bridge's construction. The images had been invaluable to the filmmaker in telling the story of the bridge and the people who had built it. The same good luck was about to shine on Mendelson again as he crossed the suspension bridge's almost two-mile span. It was as if the bridge were bestowing a kiss of good fortune on the producer, in appreciation for his previous attentions.

As he drove, Mendelson was listening to KSFO, San Francisco's most listened to radio station. Mendelson had tuned in to a jazz program on the AM station that was hosted by a popular disc jockey named Al "Jazzbo" Collins when he heard a song that completely captivated him. As Mendelson later described the tune, "It was melodic and open, and came in like a breeze off the bay." At that moment, Mendelson recognized that he had found the sound that he had been searching for to accompany his Schulz documentary.

The song the producer had heard was "Cast Your Fate to the Wind" by a local jazz artist named Vince Guaraldi. When he arrived home, Mendelson reached out by phone to Ralph Gleason, a music critic and columnist for the *San Francisco Chronicle*, and asked the writer if, by chance, he happened to know Guaraldi. "I just had lunch with him," Gleason replied. Mendelson asked for an introduction, and Gleason happily obliged.

Mendelson and the musician arranged to meet at Original Joe's restaurant, a well-known upscale eatery located at 144 Taylor Street in San Francisco's Tenderloin district. Mendelson felt an immediate rapport with the jazz musician, whose round face was framed by long sideburns, thick black eyeglass frames, and an outsize mustache. Guaraldi's warmth, smile, and laugh made an instant positive impression, but Mendelson was also struck by the diminutive pianist's short, stubby fingers. *How can he play the piano with hands like that?*

Mendelson quickly got down to business, explaining that he was producing a documentary about the life and work of *Peanuts* comic strip creator Charles Schulz and was interested in having a jazz soundtrack to accompany some of the production. Guaraldi immediately expressed his interest. He was a fan of the comic strip and enjoyed reading it with his two young children, David and Dia. Mendelson explained that he didn't have a lot of money to pay the musician. His production company was new, and the documentary was not a big-budget Hollywood show. The two men were able to quickly agree to business terms, and Guaraldi enthusiastically took on the assignment.[1]

Not two weeks later, Guaraldi also found himself driving across the Golden Gate Bridge when inspiration struck him. The musician began to compose a catchy tune that built on some of the same elements as "Cast Your Fate to the Wind," the song that had mesmerized Mendelson on the same bridge days earlier. As soon as Guaraldi arrived home he sat at his piano and began to play the notes that he had already pieced together in his mind. Guaraldi next called

Lee Mendelson on the phone. "I've gotta play something for you," said the pianist. Mendelson responded that he didn't want to hear it over the phone, explaining that it wouldn't be possible to catch the highs and lows of the piece. "I've got to play it now or I'm going to explode. I don't want to forget it," said Guaraldi excitedly. Mendelson relented, and Guaraldi put down the phone handset and began to play. The producer was immediately enchanted by what he heard. "I just knew instantly that it was so right and so perfect. I even remember thinking, 'This is going to make this show happen.' It was just perfect. It was like a godsend." The moment was electrifying for the producer. "I have no idea why, but I knew that song would affect my entire life."[2]

The tune the producer heard over the phone would eventually be titled "Linus and Lucy." It was released in October 1964 by Fantasy Records on an album titled *Jazz Impressions of a Boy Named Charlie Brown*. Charles Schulz himself prepared the artwork for the album cover—a black-and-white photo of Guaraldi's head pasted on a cartoonish body seated behind the keys of Schroeder's piano and admired by a besotted Lucy; to the side is Schroeder, looking miffed, while Linus plays bass, Charlie Brown plays guitar, and Snoopy dances.

Mendelson was wrong when he thought that it would get the Charlie Brown documentary made. He would be frustrated when, even a year after trying to find a network or a sponsor, no one was interested in buying *A Boy Named Charlie Brown*. However, the producer was correct when he felt that the song would change his life. The tune would eventually become the signature melody for the *Peanuts* franchise, when two years later it would find its way into *A Charlie Brown Christmas*.

✦ ✦ ✦

Vincent Anthony Dellaglio was born on July 17, 1928, in San Francisco, the son of nineteen-year-old Carmella Marcellino and a bricklayer named Vince Dellaglio. When Vince was four years old, his father moved out of the family home and his parents divorced, a stigma that embarrassed the family in the strong Italian Catholic neighborhood that the boy grew up in. Vince would eventually take the last name of his mother's second husband, Tony Guaraldi. That marriage would also end in divorce, and the boy would largely be raised by his mother and grandmother Jenny.

Music played a big part in the boy's childhood, and he was always surrounded by some type of musical entertainment. His mother played the piano by ear, and her father loved to entertain friends with his singing. Two of Vince's uncles, Joe and Muzzy, played big band music and would become bandleaders during World War II. Vince was intrigued watching his uncles practice, and when he was seven years old, his mother began giving her son piano lessons. The boy exhibited a natural feel for the piano, and he had the ability to hear a piece of music and be able to immediately play it.

In 1946 Guaraldi graduated from Lincoln High School, and after a summer of playing gigs at a resort in Yellowstone with a combo group he had formed, he headed off for a two-year hitch in the US Army during which he was stationed in Korea. He returned to San Francisco in the summer of 1948, enrolled in music courses at San Francisco State University, and began looking for new gigs to play.

In the 1950s Guaraldi honed his craft playing with Cal Tjader, a prominent American Latin jazz musician. Guaraldi quickly became known for playing with a certain reckless abandon. Jazz critic Doug Ramsey recalled watching Guaraldi "playing an upward series of arpeggios" and seeing the piano player play himself "right off the end of the piano bench on to the floor." Guaraldi then "got up as if nothing had happened, and went back to work" finishing the piece. Later, Ramsey talked to Tjader about what he had seen, and the musician said, "Yea, he's done that before."[3]

In 1959 Guaraldi began to pursue his own projects full-time and in 1962 Fantasy Records released his album *Jazz Impressions of Black Orpheus*. The record contained both original works by Guaraldi as well as covers of songs from the 1959 French Brazilian film *Black Orpheus*. Fantasy Records released one of the songs from the album as a 45 rpm single, a bossa nova piece named "Samba de Orpheus." On the record's B-side was Guaraldi's original composition, "Cast Your Fate to the Wind." Radio DJs gave the song considerable airplay, and the tune slowly became a hit, earning Guaraldi the Grammy for Best Original Jazz Composition. (When the jazz musician appeared for the awards ceremony at the Beverly Hilton Hotel in Beverly Hills, he was turned away because he was not suitably dressed in a tuxedo.)[4]

"Linus and Lucy," the piece that Guaraldi had excitedly played for Mendelson over the phone, would build on many of the same elements found in "Cast Your Fate to the Wind." As pianist and writer Ethan Iverson wrote in the *New Yorker*, "Many details are exactly the same. The main argument of 'Fate' is a strong, syncopated, even eighth-note melody harmonized in diatonic triads floating over a left-hand bagpipe and bowed bass, followed by an answering call of gospel chords embellished by rumbles in the left hand borrowed from Horace Silver. This general scheme is followed for 'Linus and Lucy,' even down to the same key, A-flat."[5] The good fortune associated with "Cast Your Fate to the Wind" was yet to reveal itself, however.

✦ ✦ ✦

In October 1963 Episcopal minister Charles Gompertz was reading his Saturday newspaper, looking for any news on the ongoing reconstruction of Grace Cathedral. The original church had been destroyed in the 1906 San Francisco earthquake, and the cathedral's reconstruction had been a decades-long project that was finally nearing completion. As Gompertz flipped the pages of the newspaper he spied a photo of Bishop James A. Pike speaking with teenagers who were part of the Episcopal diocese. The caption for the photo noted that the bishop was suggesting to the teens that they organize a "holy hootenanny" for the celebration of the cathedral's christening. Gompertz indulged a rash impulse to call the bishop's office and express his opinion that a "holy hootenanny" didn't seem to quite bestow the dignity that the completion of one of the world's greatest cathedrals warranted. The priest was surprised when he reached Bishop Pike directly, and the young cleric seized the opportunity to voice his opinion directly to the church official in charge. To Gompertz's shock, Pike immediately agreed with Gompertz, "Yes. And it's your job. Fill the cathedral. In May 1965." The bishop then hung up.

Gompertz stared at his phone in stunned silence, wondering what he had just done, and thinking his career in the ministry might be over. He drew a hot bath to allow himself time to collect his thoughts. While he contemplated the impulsive phone call he had just made as well as the bishop's response, Gompertz heard a haunting tune on the radio outside his bathroom. When the song finished playing the DJ announced the song's title: "Cast Your Fate to the Wind." The irony of the song's title immediately struck Gompertz. "That's what I just did!" the minister thought to himself. After a moment's reflection, it occurred to Gompertz that perhaps this was more than just irony; this might be his solution. He noted the name of the performer, Vince Guaraldi, whom Gompertz had never heard of before, and he sprang into action, abandoning his bath. He called a friend, seeking any information that he might have on Guaraldi, and the friend mentioned that he knew that the jazz musician recorded on the Fantasy Records label. The friend also said he thought his cousin might have the phone number for a direct line at the record company. Gompertz hung up, and minutes later the friend called back with the number.

Max Weiss and his brother, Sol, had founded Fantasy Records fourteen years earlier. In addition to jazz musicians, the record company also recorded beat poets like Lawrence Ferlinghetti and Allen Ginsberg as well as groundbreaking comic Lenny Bruce. Max and Sol Weiss worked out of the same office, sometimes both talking loudly on a phone at the same time. Max was known for sitting behind his desk, stacked high with paperwork and albums, and twirling the cylinders of a revolver.[6]

The minister immediately dialed the digits he had just scribbled down and was surprised to reach Max Weiss at work on a Saturday morning. Gompertz outlined his concept for having Guaraldi be a part of church history by composing and performing music for Grace Cathedral's christening. Weiss listened patiently to the minister before pointing out that, since he was Jewish, he was perhaps not the right person to weigh in on the merits of Gompertz's proposal. However, he helpfully offered the minister the phone number for Guaraldi's wife, Shirley, who acted as the pianist's screener for anyone inquiring regarding booking her husband.

Gompertz then made his fourth phone call that Saturday morning, and once again he reached his intended target. The minister introduced himself to Shirley Guaraldi and explained his concept of arranging for an appropriate musical entertainment for the occasion of the opening of the new Grace Cathedral, and why he thought her husband would be appropriate for the assignment. After listening attentively, Shirley asked Gompertz to wait for a minute. After five minutes, she returned to the phone and conveyed good news. Yes, her husband was interested, and she repeated her husband's self-assured, somewhat cheeky response: "Bach, Brahms and Beethoven all wrote masses, so why not me?"[7] After arranging to meet Guaraldi for lunch the following week, Gompertz hung up and paused for a moment to reflect on his good fortunes. In a matter of hours he had been able to reach everyone necessary to pull off his proposal, one that he had not even conceived of when the day had begun. It seemed like everyone had been in place waiting for his phone calls. This was more than just a wonderful coincidence. It seemed like divine intervention.

The jazz pianist and the Episcopal minister met for lunch the following week at a popular restaurant and jazz club called the Yacht Club (now the Trident), which is nestled in a spot overlooking the water in Sausalito. Guaraldi frequently performed at the club, and as the two men sat on the deck outside, the jazz musician was constantly greeted by people who knew him, even occasionally by those passing by in boats. As they ate, Gompertz put forth his detailed vision for the inaugural mass at the new cathedral: "I gave him my idea of taking the Marbach Setting of the Eucharist—the plain chant setting—and having that as the core, and having him improvise around it. During the service, there would be a long block of time when people come up to take Communion, when he could improvise and do anything he wanted. And we'd put in some absolutely familiar hymns, so that there'd be nothing new or radical, in terms of the music we chose. What would be 'new and radical' was what Vince would do with it."[8]

Neither man ever discussed the topic of money. The challenge itself seemed to be tantalizing enough for Guaraldi. The moment also had to seem redemptive to the former Catholic altar boy, whose mother felt excommunicated from her church after her divorce from her first husband. Now Guaraldi was being asked to compose music for the city's grandest cathedral.

Gompertz also wisely prepared for any incoming criticism for the unprecedented introduction of jazz into a church service. To many churchgoers jazz was the music of beatniks and rebels and the soundtrack for the counterculture. It was played in cocktail lounges, not in churches. The minister sought to insulate the service from such critics by protectively cloaking the rest of the service in the most conservative rituals possible such as the use of the plainsong setting of the Missa Marialis. "You couldn't get more conservative than that," pointed out Gompertz. Whenever critics assailed his use of jazz music, the minister would always respond, "Well, then, how do you explain the plain chant? You don't hear a lot of plain chant in cocktail lounges!"[9]

Gompertz and Guaraldi became good friends, spending hours talking on the phone and sitting around the baby grand piano in Guaraldi's home. They discussed more than just the important liturgical project both men were working on, broaching the topical events of the times, as well as the difficult personal challenges each man had faced. Gompertz remembers Guaraldi typically dressed casually in a T-shirt and a pair of Levi's jeans, constantly smoking cigarettes while playing on his piano and occasionally stopping to scribble notes.

Gompertz also organized a choir by working with Barry Mineah, the organist and choirmaster of St. Paul's Church in San Rafael. Mineah's choir had sixty-eight members from half a dozen churches, including a range of voices from children to senior citizens. Rehearsals for the "Grace Cathedral project" took place from seven to nine p.m. every Wednesday, nine a.m. to noon on Saturday, and before service on Sunday mornings. Guaraldi was typically present for the Saturday morning practice sessions.

The choir members, especially the children, were often mesmerized by Guaraldi's performances during their rehearsals. The choir was trained to perform consistently, just as they had done in prior practice sessions, but the jazz musician could not resist the impulse to improvise, riff, alter harmonies, or suddenly insert a bossa nova beat. Some of the singers found themselves so fascinated with Vince's performance that they would halt mid-song, engrossed in watching the piano player's inspired take on their music. When a hunched-over Guaraldi would take a moment to look up from his piano keys and glance over at the choir, it made the singers feel like they were part of his jazz ensemble.

Guaraldi had an instant rapport with the children in the choir. During breaks the youngsters would typically run outside the church to play on their skateboards while the adults gathered to drink coffee or smoke. Guaraldi frequently accompanied the kids outside, often hopping on a skateboard for a thrilling ride down the street. Guaraldi's playfulness terrified the church rector, Father John Riley, as well as Gompertz, who feared that if the musician fell and broke an arm, it would literally bring the plans for a jazz mass to a crashing halt.

As the preparations for the cathedral's consecration proceeded, Bishop Pike requested a meeting with the Grammy-winning musician responsible for arranging and performing the music for the momentous reopening of his most important church. Gompertz scheduled the unusual meeting between the piano player and the bishop for after midnight, following one of Guaraldi's regular club gigs. Like Guaraldi, the bishop was also accustomed to working late, so the odd hour was an accommodation to both men's busy schedules. Gompertz drove to the club where Guaraldi was performing, and then the two men drove together to the bishop's office.

Bishop James Pike was a high-profile religious leader in the United States in 1965. He had been raised a Catholic but became an Episcopalian after attending Easter Sunday services at the National Cathedral in Washington, DC: "[I]t looked like a church ought to look." Although highly intelligent, he was not a scholarly theologian, but he enjoyed intellectual debates and thrusting himself into contemporary political and social issues. In a manner that had parallels in much of the 1960s counterculture, Pike would publicly discuss his own intellectual paroxysms, including agonizing soul searching over fundamental church doctrines such as Original Sin, the Virgin Birth, the Trinity, and the Resurrection. Such a public questioning of established orthodoxies infuriated many Episcopal clergymen, who came to see him as a grandstanding self-promoter. His hyperactivity and nonstop devotion to work also seemed to mask inner turmoil. He had separated from his wife, and the prior year the bishop had confronted his own alcoholism, joining Alcoholics Anonymous.[10]

Guaraldi and Pike enjoyed a pleasant conversation about a wide range of topics. After the meeting, Guaraldi expressed his shock at the size of the massive ring that the bishop wore on his finger. "That's an Episcopal ring," explained Gompertz. "That's what bishops wear." Guaraldi jokingly responded, "No, no. That's not a ring, man. That's a TV set!"[11]

As May 21, 1965, the date of the scheduled consecration of the church, approached, the plans for a jazz mass gained more publicity. The upcoming service had been promoted in newspaper and magazine advertisements as well as on radio. Announcements were printed in parish bulletins from Northern California to the middle of the state. Public anticipation grew, but so did hostility from some quarters. Gompertz received threatening letters and phone calls, including threats of death. "They were scary. These people felt that I was bringing Satan into the church: bringing the music of the cock-tail lounge—the den of sin and iniquity—into the holy and sacred precinct," recalled the cleric.[12]

Sitting on top of Nob Hill, the newly reconstructed Grace Cathedral was a stunningly beautiful house of worship, and it remains as one of the largest Episcopal cathedrals in the country. Designed by architect Lewis Hobart in the French Gothic style, the building's cruciform plan, twin towers, central flèche (spire), and polygonal apse are all French in origin. Influences on the cathedral's design include the cathedrals of Amiens, Paris (Notre Dame), Beauvais, and Chartres. Grace Cathedral is 329 feet long and 162 feet wide at the transepts, and the building's nave vaulting rises to 91 feet. Because of the seismic susceptibility of San Francisco, the cathedral was framed with a skeleton of riveted steel lattices, beams, and rebar, which was encased with wooden and plastic forms, into which was poured semi-liquid concrete.[13] The cathedral's massive bronze doors are reproductions of the doors of the Florence Baptistery by Lorenzo Ghiberti, also known as the "Gates of Paradise." Considered to be a masterpiece of the Italian Renaissance, the door's ten panels recreate scenes from the Old Testament.[14] The cathedral's stunning design is accentuated by murals by Jan Henryk de Rosen, two labyrinths, and colorful stained-glass windows, as well as a forty-four-bell carillon and three organs.

When May 21 arrived, Guaraldi entered the cathedral a couple of hours before the eight p.m. mass and took up position with his trio in the chancel beside the altar. The huge cathedral was a drastically different venue than the small, smoky clubs he typically performed in. Now he was "playing the big room," as he referred to it. "I had one of America's largest cathedrals as a setting, a top choir, and a critical audience that would be more than justified in finding fault. I was in a musical world that had lived with the Eucharist for 500–600 years, and I had to improve and/or update it to 20th-century musical standards. This was the most awesome and challenging thing I had ever attempted."[15] That Friday evening was the culmination of eighteen months of composing, rewriting, and rehearsal, including with a sixty-eight-voice choir. This was the moment of truth. It would soon be seen whether Gompertz's and Guaraldi's attempt to coherently blend together spoken and chanted prayers, choral music, and pure instrumental performances had been a far too ambitious undertaking. The evening would also reveal whether jazz music would be compatible with a Eucharist celebration in the cruciform of a medieval-style gothic cathedral.

Guaraldi's piano playing was accompanied by Tommy Beeson on double bass and Lee Charlton on drums. Gompertz didn't take an active part in the liturgy so that he could be available to troubleshoot any problems that might arise during the church service. Choir director Barry Mineah warned his choir that the acoustics would be drastically different in the massive space of the cathedral than in the small rehearsal space at St. Paul's church in San Rafael. The lag time for an echo in the cathedral was around four seconds, which Mineah knew could be disruptive and distracting to singers, especially when they were already unsettled by the intimidating venue and the attention of thousands of churchgoers, including the bishop. "When I start you, just keep going!" he instructed his choir members.[16] The mass and performances went off without a hitch, however. The biggest issue was that so many attendees went up to receive the Eucharist that Communion took perhaps half an hour or more, which required Guaraldi's trio to improvise for an extended period of time, a challenge that the experienced jazz performers were more than capable of handling.[17]

A continuation of the new cathedral's celebration was held a week later on March 28, 1965. The highly anticipated sermon for that day's ten a.m. service was delivered by Martin Luther King Jr. By sunrise there were five thousand people spilling forth from the cathedral, out onto the steps, into the parking lots, and into the streets. King had been invited to speak by Bishop Pike. The two men were friends, and Pike was also a civil rights advocate. Just three days earlier King had led thousands of nonviolent demonstrators to the steps of the state capitol in Montgomery, Alabama, after a five-day, fifty-four-mile march from Selma. At the conclusion of the march the civil rights leader spoke to the assembled crowd and told them that there never was a moment in American history "more honorable and more inspiring than the pilgrimage of clergymen and laymen of every race and faith pouring into Selma" to face danger at the side of the embattled Black Americans who lived there.[18]

King appeared weary from the recent protest march, and as he began his sermon he accidentally began to greet the assembled crowd as "Los" (Angeles), before quickly catching himself to say "San Francisco." In his inimitable powerful style of speech, with its rising and falling cadences, he then repeated one of his most powerful phrases: "Injustice anywhere is a threat to justice everywhere." Speaking for almost forty-five minutes without notes, King addressed the ongoing struggle for civil rights, especially in the Deep South. "A man must be judged not on the color of his skin but on the content of his character…We must learn to live together as brothers or we will all perish together as fools."

King addressed the importance of each individual reaching their full potential "no matter how small it may be according to the world's standards" for it has "cosmic significance if it is for the building of humanity." King said, "So if you can't be a pine at the top of the hill, be a scrub in the valley. But be the best little scrub on the side of the rill. Be a bush, if you can't be a tree. If you can't be a highway just be a trail. If you can't be the sun, be a star. For it isn't by size that you win or you fail. Be the best of whatever you are."

The Nobel Prize–winning preacher's optimistic conclusion was tinged with the dark foreshadowing of death. "I do believe we shall overcome. Deep in my heart, I do believe we shall overcome…Before the victory is won, some of us will get scarred up a bit…Before the victory is won, maybe somebody else will have to face physical death…[but] we shall overcome."[19]

✦ ✦ ✦

Within weeks of the successful jazz mass at the consecration of the Grace Cathedral, Charles Gompertz received a call from Max Weiss of Fantasy Records asking if the minister was available for lunch that day. The Jewish record label owner was inviting the Episcopal minister to a lunch at Original Joe's on Taylor Street, where the Fantasy Record label owners had a regular table. Gompertz had dined there several times during his work on the Grace Cathedral consecration, which had also been produced as a live performance album by Fantasy Records and titled *Vince Guaraldi at Grace Cathedral*.

This lunch meeting invitation felt different, however, and Gompertz probed further, asking why his presence was being requested. Weiss explained that he was hoping to release the musical soundtrack to a Christmas special for which Vince Guaraldi was providing the music. "Well, we're all Jews, and Vince is a Catholic, and we're gonna meet this Christian guy…so you gotta be there, and you gotta wear the black shirt and the white collar." Gompertz agreed to attend the lunch, and when he appeared at the restaurant he discovered that "the Christian guy" in attendance was none other than Charles Schulz, the creator of the *Peanuts* comic strip. The special for which Vince Guaraldi was preparing the soundtrack was, of course, *A Charlie Brown Christmas*. Weiss had obviously been made aware that Schulz was a committed Christian, and the record label owner was apparently seeking Schulz's blessing to produce the album recording of the Christmas show's soundtrack. Weiss seemed to hope that demonstrating his amicable relationship with an Episcopal minister might favorably dispose Schulz to allow Fantasy Records to work on the project. Gompertz sat beside Guaraldi, Schulz, and Lee Mendelson, the show's producer. He recalled a wide-ranging discussion, including about the personalities of all the *Peanuts* cartoon characters.[20] Whether his presence was needed to persuade Schulz is uncertain, but Max Weiss and Fantasy Records did move forward to produce the special's soundtrack.

Bill Melendez, the Christmas special's director, found Vince Guaraldi a joy to work with. The two men had previously teamed up on the earlier, and still unsold, production, *A Boy Named Charlie Brown*. "Vince was perfect for all of us," Melendez recalled later. "He was easy to work with, like Schulz. When I finished the storyboards for *A Charlie Brown Christmas* and showed him my bar sheets, the pages that show the music and dialogue cues for each scene, he'd say, 'Just tell me how many yards you want.' By yards, he meant seconds of music."[21]

The two men developed a solid friendship. Both Melendez and Guaraldi shared an artistic sensibility, a passion for life, and each man proudly sported an impressive mustache. "When Vince was in town, he'd always spend an evening with me, at my home. We were very good friends, and he was easy to get along with. We'd sit and chat: sometimes about nothing, once in a while about the story of our next show. Then, eventually, I'd say, 'Okay, Vince; we've talked about this long enough. Let's get in the hot tub and have some wine!' and he'd say okay."[22]

After reviewing the storyboards with Bill Melendez, Guaraldi spotted two scenes that he felt required original compositions: the production's opening scene of the *Peanuts* characters skating on a frozen pond and a scene that takes place on stage when the same characters disregard the instructions from their director, Charlie Brown. Guaraldi filled the opening scene with a slow-paced, somber instrumental called "Christmas Time Is Here." For the scene on the theater's stage, Guaraldi composed "Christmas Is Coming," a peppy bossa nova piece. "Linus and Lucy," the song Guaraldi had excitedly played over the phone for Lee Mendelson, would be reprised from the *Peanuts* documentary and inserted during another scene on the stage, accompanied by the characters dancing. Guaraldi would also stand in for Schroeder playing "Für Elise," a composition by Beethoven, of course. Since a part of the storyline focused on Charlie Brown's search for a Christmas tree for the school play, the soundtrack includes Guaraldi's own cover of "O Tannenbaum," the traditional German folk song that became associated with Christmas. For the special's conclusion the jazz composer prepared a traditional rendition of the Christmas carol "Hark! The Herald Angels Sing."

Guaraldi's compositions would be accompanied by a bassist and a drummer, but the question remains, who were they? The identities of the other two members of the pianist's trio remains mired in a mess of confusion, controversy, and conflicting claims, all likely resulting from Guaraldi's own inattention to detail and record keeping. Guaraldi biographer Derrick Bang, author of *Vince Guaraldi at the Piano*, believes that there were two recording sessions, one that took place in Los Angeles at the Glendale Whitney Studio and the second one in San Francisco. Elements from each may have been used for both the television special as well as the soundtrack album. Bang believes that first recording session used bass player Monty

Budwig and drummer Colin Bailey. The Bay Area recording used Fred Marshall and Jerry Granelli. The LP that was issued for the special's soundtrack gave no credits for a bassist or the drummer. Fantasy Records would eventually attempt to research and resolve the question, and their determination was that Budwig and Bailey's session had been used for the score that appears in the television special, while the Guaraldi soundtrack album should have been credited to Marshall and Granelli. Bang also notes that four others also claim to have contributed tracks for the special: bassist Eugene "Puzzy" Firth and drummer Paul Distel, as well as bassist Al Obidinski and drummer Benny Barth.[23]

Concerns similar to the objections raised over the use of jazz in a liturgical setting would be raised about the making of *A Charlie Brown Christmas*—was an animated cartoon character an appropriate figure to recite Scripture? The even bigger question faced in the making of the television special wasn't whether jazz entertainment was appropriate for a religious setting, but whether religious content was appropriate for animated entertainment (or appropriate in entertainment at all).

THE ANIMATORS
AND ACTORS

◆

I think we've ruined Charlie Brown.
—Bill Melendez to Lee Mendelson, after screening a rough cut
of the Charlie Brown Christmas special

When Lee Mendelson began working on his documentary about Charles Schulz in 1963, he suggested to the cartoonist that they include a few minutes of animation to break up the video footage and to give people a sense of the *Peanuts* characters brought to life. Schulz responded cautiously: "You know the great thing about being a cartoonist is that you have 100 percent control of the comic strip—you are the writer, producer, director and stage manager all at once. So it's scary to turn your characters over to other people in a completely different medium." After some further discussion the cartoonist said, "Well, if we are going to do this, there is only one person I would trust. His name is Bill Melendez."[1]

Bill Melendez Productions operated out of three adjacent homes that had been turned into film studio offices. The properties were located at 429 N. Larchmont Boulevard, just south of Hollywood, in the upscale Hancock Park neighborhood of Los Angeles near the Wilshire Country Club. The wide boulevard had been the setting for the Keystone Cops series and other silent film slapstick comedies. Paramount Studios was less than a mile away, and Warner Bros. was a six-mile drive north through a pass in the Hollywood Hills into Burbank. Melendez had moved his operations into these homes in 1964, a year after opening his own animation studio.

The animators enjoyed the relaxed and comfortable atmosphere of their workspaces, a sharp departure from the shabby offices of Warner Bros.'s Termite Terrace, as well as the stuffy studio of Walt Disney, places where Melendez and many of his employees had toiled years before. Nearby was Larchmont Village, a stretch of shops and restaurants, and the studio employees frequently strolled to a nearby delicatessen for lunch. "It was nice pulling up to the studio, this quaint little house in a neighborhood," recalled Dale Baer. "You'd walk in and you felt at home. Everybody was busy. Bill was there and he was reachable. He wasn't one of those guys behind closed doors someplace."[2]

Before the work of animating the Charlie Brown Christmas special began, Lee Mendelson made one more attempt to head off what he felt was a potential disaster in the making. The producer had not realized how lengthy Schulz had intended to make the program's Bible recitation. With the script now in his and the director's hands, and animation on a highly compressed schedule, the producer knew he could not waste time or money producing a scene that might be edited later by a network. Mendelson made one last attempt to confront Schulz on the lengthy scene over its overt religiosity. Religion and entertainment simply do not mix, he argued to the comic strip artist. "He just smiled," Mendelson later wrote, "patted me on the head and left the room."[3]

Once Schulz had completed the script, Melendez began to prepare storyboards. Each page of his storyboards contained six squares, and each square would represent a scene from the special. The dialogue from each scene would be written underneath each storyboard square. In total the production had about 480 scenes. Each one of those scenes would have to be animated, requiring approximately ten thousand drawings. It was a massive undertaking. At some point the network had discussed making the special one hour in length, but it would be impossible to complete the work for an hour-long animated program in the remaining four months. Melendez wasn't even sure he could complete a half hour of animation in the time he had left.[4] Accounting for about four minutes of commercials, there would have to be about twenty-six minutes of animated content.*

One scene would be cut from Schulz's script before voice talent was recorded. It would be excised in order to fit the time constraint of the program. Scene 8B was to fall between Charlie Brown's argument with Violet over her not sending him a Christmas card and Patty's suggestion to "try to catch snowflakes with your tongue":

"Pig-Pen. You're the only person I know who can raise a cloud of dust in a snow storm," says Charlie Brown to his perpetually dirty friend. "What's the paper?"

"That's my Git-List," replies Pig-Pen.

"What's your Git-List?" asks Charlie Brown.

"This is what I figure to git for Christmas from my mom and dad, and my two grandmas and two grandpa[s], and my cousins, and my..." explains Pig-Pen.

---

* Today the amount of commercials in a half hour of television programming has doubled to nine minutes versus four and a half minutes in 1965.

"Where's your Give List?" asks Charlie Brown.

"My what?" replies a confused Pig-Pen.

"I knew it!" exclaims Charlie Brown, finding one more example of a selfish take on the Christmas holiday.[5]

✦ ✦ ✦

With the script written, voice talent had to be auditioned, and then dialogue had to be recorded. Schulz had already noted his requirement to use real children and not adults who were professional voice talent. Mendelson, Schulz, and Melendez auditioned all of the voice talent together. Three children who had performed well for the Ford television commercials were cast again in the Christmas special: Peter Robbins, the blah voice of Charlie Brown; Chris Shea, the innocent voice of Linus; and Tracy Stratford as the crabby voice of Lucy. All three had had some professional experience.

Peter Robbins had appeared in the movie *A Ticklish Affair* and on several television series including *Rawhide*, *The Munsters*, *F Troop*, and *Get Smart*, as well as dozens of television commercials. His godmother was Hazel McMillen, a well-known Hollywood agent. McMillen had also suggested Chris Shea, calling Mendelson and telling him, "I have this wonderful actor but he has a very slight lisp. He can read with great emotions, however." As soon as Mendelson, Schulz, and Melendez heard Shea read his first few lines of dialogue, they all agreed that they had found their Linus. His lisp gave him a childhood innocence, but his delivery also had an intelligence and authority to it that would be critical for the Bible verses he was going to recite.

Tracy Stratford was an experienced young Hollywood actor who could enthusiastically deliver a wide range of personalities demanded by the character Lucy—Charlie Brown's nagging nemesis, Schroeder's saccharine suitress, and the stunned victim, recoiling in horror at the sloppy smooch of a mischievous Snoopy.

The rest of the voice talent were all amateurs that were largely sourced from Melendez's own network in his Burlingame neighborhood. Sally Dryer was cast as Violet. Cathy Steinberg, at only six years old, was the youngest performer, and was cast in the role of Sally, Charlie Brown's sister. Chris Doran provided the voice for the piano-playing Schroeder. Anne Altieri played Frieda. Jeff Ornstein was Pig-Pen. Mendelson's second cousin, Karen Mendelson, played the role of Patty.

The recording session was done at United Western Recorders, which operated out of two adjacent buildings at 6050 and 6000 Sunset Boulevard. The studio had won many awards for technical excellence. Rock groups like the Doors and the Beach Boys recorded there, and many of the biggest hits of the 1960s had been taped there. With Melendez by the microphone and Mendelson and Schulz in the sound room, the young voice talent recited their lines.

The youth of the voice talent impacted the ability to quickly record the dialogue for the special. Peter Robbins later described the chaotic recording session. "I thought it was going to be very easy; a voice-over, compared to acting on camera. But once I got in the studio I found it was chaotic, with a bunch of kids, six to nine years old, running all over the place and too excited to calm down." Children were playing with drum sets and tambourines that were left in the recording studio. Eventually all the young talent had to be separated and would record their lines individually.[6]

The high energy of the performers was not the only issue presented, however. Schulz's dialogue dealt with some very adult topics that were foreign to the young voice talent. Words like *depression* would have to be explained to a mystified Robbins, who would then respond, "But why would anyone be depressed at Christmastime?" Sometimes a line would have to be repeated ten times by a young performer before they delivered their rendition with the appropriate tone, correct emphasis, or proper delivery.

Some of the children, including Chris Shea, when handed their scripts with their lines of dialogue, stared back at Melendez in stunned silence. They had not yet learned how to read. This necessitated having the director recite the lines to some actors, sometimes just pieces of dialogue, and then having the child recite the words back. At times a single word had to be broken down into bite-size syllables, even for the actors who could read. Melendez then had to edit the separate recordings back together.[7] The end result was that much of the dialogue in the special has an uneven, choppy cadence to it. Some children, instructed by Melendez to repeat back exactly what he had said, would innocently repeat back their dialogue with the director's distinctive Sonoran Mexican accent. The comical interaction greatly amused Schulz as he looked on from the wings.[8] This prompted Lee Mendelson to step forward from the recording booth to handle some of the actor coaching duties.[9]

Melendez assembled a team of about twenty animators at his Larchmont studio to work on the special. They were a combination of employees and freelance contractors, and Melendez had worked with many of them before, going all the way back to his days at Disney. The talented group had a mix of skills—character designers, inbetweeners, background colorists, assistant animators, and animators. Melendez treated his employees like they were members of his family. Whether it was a conscious decision to adopt this management style, prompted by the ugly fracture that had erupted at Walt Disney's studio, or more likely just the warm personal style of the man himself, the employees seemed to respond well to their chief's enthusiasm and kindness.

Many studios flex their headcount up and down depending on the vagaries of their production cycle, but Melendez was always reluctant to lay off any staff when things were slow. Cheryl Barnes, who worked at Bill Melendez Productions during the making of *A Charlie Brown Christmas*, would on at least one occasion approach her boss, guilty about accepting a paycheck when she wasn't working on a production. "Bill, there's no work. I can find work somewhere else." But her boss would keep her on the payroll, saying, "No. When I need you, I'll need you. I don't want you somewhere else where I have to pry you away."[10]

Melendez also instituted a more equitable pay system for his animators. In most studios animators were paid a rate per footage of the scenes that they animated. This completely ignored the varying complexity of the work of the scene. If animators became friends with the production manager, the manager could steer the simpler scenes to their friends, allowing them to be paid the same amount as their colleagues but for doing much less work. Melendez would institute a rating system for each scene, depending on its difficulty. A moderate difficulty or average scene, that perhaps did not show a character's whole body, would be paid at the standard rate. A more complex scene would be paid at that rate times 1.5. Scenes with multiple characters would be paid at the standard rate times 2.0 or 3.0 or possibly more.[11]

One of the most experienced animators working on the Charlie Brown special was a veteran of animated studios named Ed Levitt. The forty-nine-year-old animator was just seven months younger than Melendez, and the two men had worked together since the earliest days at Disney. Levitt had immediately started working on *Snow White* on his first day at Walt's studio. He also worked on other

Disney classics such as *Pinocchio, Fantasia*, and *Bambi*. Like Melendez, Levitt was also on the picket line during the Disney strike of 1941. After the settlement he worked on a film that Walt financed personally in hopes that it would help shape military strategy in World War II. Titled *Victory through Air Power*, the film was based on a book by Alexander de Seversky, a Russian American aviation pioneer. Seversky argued that the strategic employment of air power could be decisive in war. Levitt departed Disney during World War II, enlisting in the Marine Corps, where he made training films in Quantico, Virginia. After the war he produced the film *Where Will You Hide?*, warning of the apocalyptic effects of another world war using nuclear weapons and advocating for world peace. He had also worked closely with Melendez at Playhouse Pictures, where the two men produced the Ford commercials using the *Peanuts* characters. Levitt teamed up with Melendez again when Bill Melendez Productions was set up in 1964.

Another experienced animator working at Melendez's studio was Rudy Zamora Jr. Like Melendez, Zamora had also been born in Mexico. The artist had an irrepressible rebellious streak and a wicked sense of humor, but he was also one of the fastest animators in Hollywood, something that Melendez desperately needed for his new assignment. Zamora had begun working in animation in 1927. He was first employed by film producer Pat Sullivan, for whom Zamora animated Felix the Cat. The always-joking Zamora would be quoted in 1931 in *Motion Picture Daily* as saying, "My dreams were to become a respectable dope fiend, but I could not accomplish this so I lost all self-respect and became a cartoonist." After a stint at Fleischer Studios, the artist joined Disney in the early 1930s, where he animated the Silly Symphony cartoons.

Despite his obvious talent, Zamora's irreverent humor would cause him problems throughout his career. It was a practice at

Disney that once the studio had completed a short film, it would be previewed at the Los Feliz Theater at 1822 N. Vermont Avenue. Employees who had worked on the film would watch it with an audience, and afterward Walt would gather his employees in the theater's lobby to provide his thoughts on their work. Zamora was unable to disguise his disregard for his boss's long-winded critiques. After one film, the artist retreated to a corner of the lobby, where the lifetime smoker lit up a cigarette. Walt became miffed when he noticed his employee's insouciance. "Rudy, aren't you interested in what we're saying? What are you doing standing over there?" A diffident Zamora coolly blew out a puff of smoke from his cigarette. "There is one thing I want to know, Walt. What really makes a good move?" The animator was asking the studio head the best way to seduce a woman, with the word *move* carrying a more vulgar connotation in that era than it might today. Zamora's inquiry, both inappropriate and insubordinate, resulted in him being fired the next day.[12]

Zamora would have similar issues at his next stop, Metro-Goldwyn-Mayer's cartoon studio, where he would also cross his new boss, Fred Quimby. MGM produced the award-winning *Tom and Jerry* cartoons. Quimby enforced a production requirement per animator of twenty-five feet per week. Zamora would quickly finish his daily quota and then enjoy provoking his boss by conspicuously loafing. "Why aren't you at your desk working, Rudy?" questioned Quimby. With his boss then baited, Zamora pointed out he had completed his required workload. On one occasion he brought a bowling ball to work and began bowling in the hallway. At Melendez's studio Zamora's chain-smoking produced burn marks all over his office. Melendez would become just as exasperated with Zamora's antics as all his prior employers. He frequently fired the fellow immigrant, but then Melendez would just as quickly forgive the talented animator and hire him back.

One of Zamora's fellow animators at MGM, where he worked on *Tom and Jerry*, was Bill Littlejohn. Littlejohn also joined Melendez's studio, where he worked on the Charlie Brown Christmas special. During the time of the Disney strike, Littlejohn, a licensed pilot, would race to the airport on his lunch hour and fly his airplane over the picket line, showing his support by waggling the plane's wings. The Disney strikers would cheer and wave their signs at the plane's appearance. (Union organizer Herb Sorrell, a rotund man, tried to accompany Littlejohn on one flight, but the small plane tipped to one side with Sorrell inside, and Littlejohn couldn't get the plane airborne.) After encouraging the strikers, he would then land his plane and race back to his desk so as not to incur the wrath of his boss, Fred Quimby, the same producer that Zamora had enjoyed irritating. During World War II, Littlejohn trained pilots for the military, and later he became a test pilot, flying supersonic jets. He did not return to animating until the 1950s. He and Melendez had worked side by side at Playhouse Pictures to produce Ford's animated commercials using *Peanuts* characters. Littlejohn proved particularly gifted at animating Snoopy. Melendez would single out Littlejohn for praise, saying he was "the best animator that I've worked with, the most creative and productive."[13]

Other key animators included Herman Cohen, Frank Smith, Manny Perez, and Ruth Kissane. Herman Cohen was originally from New York, where he started animating for Fleischer Studios in the 1930s, before moving to Los Angeles, where he worked at Leon Schlesinger Productions on Warner Bros. cartoons. While toiling away at Termite Terrace, he worked for legends like Friz Freleng and Bob McKimson. Frank Smith had been born in Michigan, but he left home as a teenager and became a hobo, illegally riding freight trains. His drifter life eventually brought him out to Los Angeles in 1930. He began work at Fleischer Studios, which was Walt Disney's main competitor, producing animated films in the 1930s. He worked for a time at UPA, and he also directed and produced films in Paris, France, in the 1950s. Manuel "Manny" Perez was born in Arizona but attended high school in Los Angeles, where he was a star athlete. He also worked at Leon Schlesinger Productions making Warner Bros. cartoon characters like Bugs Bunny, Porky Pig, Tweety, and Sylvester. Ruth Kissane was born in Cleveland, Ohio, in 1929. She had begun her career in animation only five years before undertaking work on the Charlie Brown Christmas special. Kissane had worked alongside Melendez animating the title sequence for the successful comedy film *It's a Mad, Mad, Mad, Mad World*.

Other animators who worked on *A Charlie Brown Christmas* were Eleanor Warren, John Walker, Beverly Robbins, Bernard Gruver, Bob Carlson, Dean Spille, and Reuben Timmins.

One animator would not be available to work on the *Peanuts* Christmas special—Sterling Sturtevant. Born in 1922, Sturtevant was one of the few women working in animation studios since the 1940s. Born in Redlands, California, she had attended the University of Redlands and then studied at Chouinard Art Institute, before starting her career at Walt Disney Studios where she co-wrote the Pluto cartoon "Bone Bandit." After Disney she joined UPA, where she worked on Mr. Magoo. She employed her talent for character design, giving the gruff old character a more appealing baby-doll appearance. After UPA she joined Bill Melendez at Playhouse Pictures, where she worked on television commercials, including the Ford commercial using the *Peanuts* characters. Schulz himself would praise Sturtevant's talent in bringing his work to life, praising "Sterling's touch." Sturtevant died of pancreatic cancer in 1962.[14]

✦ ✦ ✦

After Schulz first gave Melendez permission to animate his characters for a Ford commercial, the cartoonist came down to Los Angeles to visit the studio where the animator was then working in order to gain a better understanding of the animation process. Melendez showed his visitor a stack of drawings of the *Peanuts* characters that was eight inches high. "I don't make that many drawings in a year!" exclaimed Schulz. The cartoonist began flipping through the drawings. He admired the first couple of sketches before pausing at the third one. "That's a terrible drawing. No, that's not acceptable." Melendez then handed the cartoonist a pencil and said, "Here you are, Mr. Schulz, you draw Snoopy in that position." The visitor responded, "I never draw him in that position." Melendez then carefully explained that when animating a character it was necessary to draw it in unfamiliar poses for fleeting moments to be able to depict it in motion. It was a departure from the flat, two-dimensional cartoon panels that the *Peanuts* kids inhabited. Characters that had always been portrayed in a comic strip from the side or in three-quarter view now had to be rotated. It was Schulz's first lesson in animation.[15]

Since working on the Ford commercials, the two men had developed a mutual respect and admiration for one another's professions. Both were artists but with different skills. As Melendez recalled later: "What made it easy to work with Sparky was that he established our roles from the very start, saying, 'I'm a cartoon strip artist and you're an animator. You can't do my cartoon strips and I can't do your animation. Therefore, if you do your job well and I do my job well, everything will work.'"[16]

Schulz himself would readily admit that he was not quite as humble as Bill Melendez had portrayed him. "Bill has so many great qualities. What helps us work together is that we each appreciate what the other does. I've heard Bill say many times, 'I could never draw a comic strip,' and I like to have somebody admit that he could not draw a comic strip because a lot of animators probably think they could—there's nothing to it. I'm not sure I could be an animator, but I'm not as humble as Bill, and I won't say that I don't think I could be an animator. I think I could be an animator, but I don't want to be one."[17]

One element that made *Peanuts* adaptable to animation was that the characters actually conversed with one another. It was not merely a gag cartoon. They interacted and spoke in meaningful sentences. They were not merely feeding each other gag lines punctuated with punchy one-liners. Artistically, however, Schulz's characters were incredibly difficult to render in animation. They had large round heads, making it difficult to gather them together in a scene without their oversized skulls banging into one another. Their arms couldn't reach the top of their heads, restricting certain movements, and their short stubby legs made walking look awkward. Melendez also had to take care that when he animated the characters he was still true to their look from the comic strip. Ironically, the minimalism of Schulz's drawings made them more difficult to animate. Because there were so few points of reference on their faces, if an eye were a little too far to the left or right, the character would look disfigured. As Bill Littlejohn explained: "The *Peanuts* characters were not designed for animation. Just try to make one of them turn slowly, or try to turn Charlie Brown's head on an angle or a tilt. It's not round! And it's a different shape at every angle, with that little glob of hair on his forehead changing completely from front view to a profile. It was big trouble trying to make them turn slowly until we figured out how to start a turn and then zap to the last position."[18]

The one exception was Snoopy. He could be animated and made into rubbery poses that would be familiar to anyone who was a fan of Looney Tunes cartoons. His face could be contorted, and he could be put into weird positions that were not possible with the human characters. "Snoopy saved me because Snoopy is more like a real animated character. He can do anything—move and dance—and he's very easy to animate, whereas the kids are nearly impossible!" said Melendez.[19] Snoopy's scenes gave the animators license to do the more expressive movements that they were used to with other cartoon characters.

The beagle did have one restriction, though. Snoopy couldn't think out loud anymore, like in the comic strip where his thoughts appeared in bubbles over his head. Schulz refused to allow the dog to talk. When the *Peanuts* characters were used in the Ford commercials, the J. Walter Thompson ad agency had sent Hollywood character actors who auditioned funny voices for Snoopy's thinking, but Schulz wouldn't budge.[20] Melendez also attempted to persuade Schulz to allow the beagle to talk in the animated special. He recorded a talented friend who could speak in a high-pitched, cartoonish voice reciting dialogue from the cartoon strip, and he sent the tape recording to Schulz. The cartoonist listened to the recording and found it humorous, but he told Melendez he couldn't use it. "Snoopy's a dog and he can't talk."

Schulz, Mendelson, and Melendez all agreed that the animation for the special would be the limited animation pioneered by UPA, not the realistic animation of Walt Disney. This special was to be more like *The Flintstones* and less like *Fantasia*. It was a concession to budget, time, and the realities of the program's economics. Television ad rates did not support full-blown animation. Melendez still felt comfortable that the program would be able to present a certain style that was consistent with the *Peanuts* characters. He did not want the special to be lacking in a certain recognizable look and feel. Merely because the animation would be simple didn't mean that it would not have a definitive style. It should not leave the viewer feeling like they were being denied something.

When it came time to produce the credits for the special, someone promoted the idea that instead of breaking out the usual hierarchy of animators by distinguishing painters from checkers, animators from assistant animators, and character designers from inbetweeners, they should have a more egalitarian approach and put everyone under the same heading. Perhaps this reflected the rushed nature of the production, where everyone at the studio, working very closely together, had finished the special in a four-month sprint to completion. Perhaps Melendez wanted to erase the stratifications that had erupted at Disney between the poorly paid junior artists and those more senior. Melendez ultimately decided that in the credits for the Christmas special all the animators would be lumped into the same category, using a new designation that was created by Ed Levitt, the former Marine—"Graphic Blandishment."*

Despite the undeniably rough nature of most of the Christmas special's animation, the production displayed some truly beautiful artwork as well as some inspired directing. It remained to be seen, however, if those moments shone brightly enough to soften the harshness of the special's more uneven cartoon work. The stylized, geometric shapes of the Christmas trees in the tree lot with stunning

---

* The odd appellation "Graphic Blandishment" would become a hallmark of the credits for the Charlie Brown specials for the next ten years. It would finally be discontinued with the production of *It's the Easter Beagle, Charlie Brown!* in 1974. Phil Roman, that special's director, persuaded Melendez to end the practice and credit everyone for the work they had actually performed (Charles Solomon, *The Art and Making of Peanuts Animation: Celebrating Fifty Years of Television Specials* [Chronicle Books, 2012], 26).

tropical colors stand in sharp contrast to the round-headed figures of Linus and Charlie Brown. The sharp uneven stars of the night sky look like they are from a Matisse painting. Sometimes Melendez frames a scene that looks like it could be hung in a museum's exhibition of Impressionist art. The end product was both undeniably crude as well as unmistakably moving.

The production included some truly inspired pieces of directing. The surreal Snoopy established himself as a scene stealer. In one scene Schroeder plays a jazz riff, and Snoopy begins dancing on top of his piano. Linus and Lucy notice, the music stops, and the embarrassed beagle stops dancing and slinks away. At first Charles Schulz didn't like the scene. He felt it deviated too much from his style. "He wanted the whole film to be talking heads, doing his dialogue," said Bill Littlejohn.[21] But the cartoonist eventually relented and would come to embrace a more animated Snoopy in his cartoon strip as well.

During the special's climactic scene, when Linus recites from the Gospel of Luke, there is a tiny detail that only the most astute viewers noticed. As soon as Linus utters the words "fear not" he releases his security blanket, letting it slip through his fingers. The moment is handled without any attention being brought to it, but it is rich with significance, both in the context of the character and the words being spoken. Linus had been clinging to the security of his blanket since its introduction to the comic strip on June 1, 1954. Lucy had constantly conspired to dispose of the blanket, even burying it once. Snoopy continually tried to snatch it away. Linus's grandmother detested it, and her grandson would mail the blanket to himself when she came to visit. The words "fear not" or "be not afraid" are rich with biblical import too, and are reportedly the most common phrases in the Bible, found 365 times in Scripture.

As risky as it was to have the lengthy recitation from the Bible, how it was executed is truly bold as well. As Andrew Stanton, the Oscar-winning director of *Finding Nemo* and *Wall-E* noted, "They stopped everything: just a single spotlight on a kid standing onstage, saying this long passage. It was very moving because of the stillness, because of everything stopping for the simplicity of it."[22]

✦ ✦ ✦

About three weeks before the special's scheduled broadcast, Mendelson gathered with Melendez and about half of the animators at the Universal studio lot to watch the first cut of the entire production. While watching the end credits, Mendelson winced as he noticed that Schulz's name had been misspelled as "Schultz." It seemed a bad omen and perhaps indicative of the whole production's rushed quality. A dejected Melendez turned to the producer. "I think we've ruined Charlie Brown," he said, perhaps unconsciously mimicking the forlorn tone of Charlie Brown in the special when the round-headed character utters, "I've killed it," after the small Christmas tree buckles under the weight of the one ornament he attempted to adorn it with. The entire room seemed to share the same negative reaction, except for Ed Levitt. The senior animator stood up and pronounced, "This show is going to run for a hundred years."[23]

Melendez was understandably pained by what he saw projected onto the screen. In their rush to complete the production, his animators had committed a number of errors that were easily observable.

- When Lucy approaches her psychiatric booth, it has no snow on it, but when she arrives she has to wipe away snow before sitting down to consult with her patient, Charlie Brown. In the same scene, her sign sometimes says "The Doctor is Real In" while at other times it says "The Doctor is In."

- When Lucy is dispensing psychiatric advice to Charlie Brown, she refers to fear of cats as "ailurophasia." The correct term is actually *ailurophobia*.

- Charlie Brown's nose disappears when he is addressing Lucy while discussing the need for a Christmas tree for the play.

- When Linus and Charlie Brown select the fragile, small Christmas tree, it first has only three branches. In subsequent scenes it has six or more branches.

- When Linus makes his speech on stage reciting from the Gospel of Luke, Schroeder's piano, which had been on stage in the earlier scene, is now missing. In the same scene, Charlie Brown is first seen wearing his trademark zigzag shirt, but then when the camera angle is from the side of the stage, he is wearing his coat.

- Also during the Linus speech scene, an American flag can be seen stage left. But when the camera angle shifts to a side view, the flag is not there.

- In the final scene, where all the children shout, "Merry Christmas, Charlie Brown!" and sing "Hark! The Herald Angels Sing," Snoopy also speaks and sings—perhaps the only time Snoopy ever speaks—and it is a violation of Schulz's directive that Snoopy never be allowed to actually talk.*

---

* Some of these errors would be corrected before the special was broadcast again the following year. Even years later Bill Melendez would grimace when discussing the quality of the program's animation.

After previewing the production, Mendelson made a frantic, last-minute attempt to lift the mood of the special's opening scene, where all the *Peanuts* characters are seen skating on the ice. Guaraldi's song "Christmas Time Is Here" plays in the background, and Mendelson thought that adding lyrics would elevate the tone and give the scene a less plodding feel. He reached out to several lyricists but was unable to find anyone who had the availability to quickly take on the assignment. Undeterred, the producer sat down at his own kitchen table and began to pencil out some lyrics on the back of an envelope. To his surprise the words came to him freely. The effort took him only ten minutes. Not one word of the lyrics would change from the producer's initial draft.[24]

Mendelson was a gifted writer. He would bristle whenever his friend, Bill Melendez, described him as a salesman—"He can sell the Eskimos refrigerators!" the animator liked to say. The producer had wanted to inject some of his own creative impulses into the special's script, but Schulz jealously guarded his writing from any outside influence. Melendez was embarrassed at times watching Mendelson make a script suggestion, only to see Schulz respond with indifference. As soon as the cartoonist left the room, the producer and the animator would look at one another, knowing that Schulz would never use the idea that had been proffered by the producer.[25] Now, however, Mendelson's words would find themselves sung in the special's opening scene. (In an ironic twist, the lyrics for the special's opening were composed by a Mendelson, and the music for the special's concluding song—"Hark! The Herald Angels Sing"—was composed by a "Mendelson" of sorts, classical German composer Felix Mendelssohn.)

Now Mendelson had to rush to arrange for a children's choir to sing the lyrics for the special's opening song in the recording studio. In September 1965 Lee Mendelson enlisted the help of his friend Vince Guaraldi, who was able to recruit choir members from St. Paul's Episcopal Church in San Rafael, north of San Francisco.* Guaraldi had used the choir in the jazz mass he had produced for the consecration of the newly rebuilt Grace Cathedral earlier that year. The children did three separate recording sessions, on school nights, at Fantasy Records in San Francisco. They recorded both "Christmas Time Is Here" and "Hark! the Herald Angels Sing," a traditional Christmas carol, which, like Linus's pivotal speech, was also derived from the Gospel of Luke's nativity story. Afterward the young performers were treated to ice cream.[26]

One last decision remained to finish the production of the Christmas special. What to do about Snoopy's vocalizations? Melendez had previously recorded gibberish that was then sped up on a tape recorder and held as a place filler for the dog until a proper voice actor could be found. No one had met with Schulz's approval. There was no more production time left. The editor told Melendez that they had to fill in Snoopy's lines or they would not finish the picture. Melendez directed him to just use the gibberish he had recorded for the manic canine.

---

* The children who were choir members who participated in one or more of the Charlie Brown Christmas special recording sessions include: Dave Willat, Kristin Mineah, Candace Hackett Shively, Dan Bernhard, Mark Jordan, Marcia Goodrich, Cary Cedarblade, Nancy Goodrich, Debbie Presco Nelson, David Hertzel, Dianne Johnston Garcia, Claudia Kendell Sullivan, Steve Kendell.

THE TELEVISION CRITIC
RICHARD BURGHEIM,
TIME MAGAZINE

✦

The Bible thing scares us.
—CBS executive to Lee Mendelson after screening
A Charlie Brown Christmas

Just a week before *A Charlie Brown Christmas*'s scheduled broadcast on December 9, 1965, Lee Mendelson headed from his home in Burlingame, California, to San Francisco International Airport, just five miles away. From there he flew to New York by himself to screen the special for CBS. Incredibly, although it was just a week from the special's scheduled broadcast, it would be the first time the network's executives would actually see the production. There were no plans for either of Mendelson's creative partners, Charles Schulz or Bill Melendez, to join him. Schulz's worsening anxiety about leaving home was likely enough to keep him in Sebastopol. Melendez's absence may have been a tacit admission that the poor quality of the program's animation would likely be discussed at the meeting, and it was perhaps thought best to save Melendez the embarrassment of having his work criticized in person. So it had been decided that Mendelson would fly to New York by himself and handle the task of screening the production to CBS alone.

As he boarded the aircraft for the transcontinental flight Lee Mendelson was full of trepidation. This was a pivotal moment in his career as a producer. If the anticipated broadcast of *A Charlie Brown Christmas* performed well, or even just respectably, Mendelson would likely be able to break out from his work as a producer of regional, Bay Area market documentaries broadcast on local San Francisco television. However, his career could be over if the upcoming Christmas special was badly received (or perhaps even mocked) for its poor production quality or if its content missed the mark. His reputation would likely be irreparably damaged for having tainted the *Peanuts* franchise, one of the most valued pieces of intellectual property in the world. Indeed, a disastrous reception for the animation production could even possibly be a *Peanuts* extinction event. Given Mendelson's most recent stumble with *A Boy Named Charlie Brown*, this was a make-it-or-break-it moment for Mendelson to either redeem himself or fall even further into a narrowing career crevasse.

With the introduction of transcontinental jet service six years earlier, flight times across the country were essentially the same as today, five hours from California to New York. But in many other ways, flying was drastically different. Passengers smoked freely on the aircraft, flicking their cigarette ashes into ashtrays built in to the armrests of the seats. Storied carriers such as Pan Am and TWA, which had launched the airline industry, were still among its most dominant operators. Most men boarded their flights wearing suits and ties; women typically wore dresses and heels. Overhead bins were preceded by overhead racks. Service was remarkably better, and on some transcontinental flights American Airlines had a branded 21 Club service, using items such as china and linens from the upscale New York city club of the same name.*

Flight attendants, then referred to as stewardesses or air hostesses, were exclusively female, attractive, thin, young, and single and were required to not have had children. Like many airlines, American had an age ceiling of thirty-two years for continued employment as an air hostess. Getting married was grounds for termination.[1] Films such as *Boeing Boeing* (released in December 1965) and *Come Fly with Me* (1963) portrayed stewardesses as young women seeking adventure and romance, and men as seeking, well, stewardesses.[2] American Airlines would humble brag in its advertisements in 1965 that "It's got to the point now where we can't keep our girls more than 2 years." Why not? "Well if you must know, one of you married her. In fact, one or another of you has practically married every stewardess we've ever had."[3]

It is most likely that Mendelson flew to New York City on American Airlines, which, in 1965, offered five daily nonstop flights (four on the weekends) between San Francisco and New York's John F. Kennedy International Airport, the most of any carrier from SFO. Mendelson's flight would have included Astrovision, the airline's newly introduced in-flight video and audio entertainment system, consisting of a closed-circuit television with input from a transistorized Sony video tape player weighing 145 pounds, which was mounted in the rear of the cockpit. In-flight entertainment also included two channels of tape-recorded stereophonic music played through pneumatic hollow tube headsets available to each passenger.[4] Each month, a new musical program was circulated throughout the appropriate aircraft fleet. In November 1965 the three-hour

---

* The 21 Club is located at 21 West 57th Street, directly east of Mendelson's meeting at CBS headquarters.

music program included eighteen recording artists in sixty-five performances, including Frank Sinatra, Vic Damone, Sammy Davis, Buddy Ebsen, Duke Ellington, the Everly Brothers, Dean Martin, Trini Lopez, Dinah Shore, and the Paul Smith Trio.[5]

But no amount of upscale service, in-flight entertainment, or winsome stewardesses could distract Mendelson from his mounting anxiety over the quality of the special and the impact that a ratings bomb would have on his career. If the Christmas special performed badly in the ratings, Mendelson also had to be concerned over its impact on his friendship with Charles Schulz. When Mendelson hadn't found a buyer for the Schulz/*Peanuts* documentary, he had maintained the relationship by sourcing the animated Christmas special opportunity from Coca-Cola. Schulz had been a loyal partner and had been forgiving of the documentary's failure, but this project's collapse and its negative impact on the *Peanuts* franchise might exhaust even Schulz's goodwill. And a ratings bomb would ensure there would be no other opportunities to market another televised Charlie Brown program even if Mendelson was able to salvage the friendship from the ruins.

All of this must have weighed heavily on Mendelson's mind as he pushed through the revolving doors of the looming flannel gray skyscraper known as Black Rock at 51 West 52nd Street in New York City, where above each bay of swinging doors, set in polished bronze-finished aluminum against a solid black background, were the gleaming letters CBS.

✦ ✦ ✦

In late 1965, CBS had just opened its stunning new headquarters building on Sixth Avenue (Avenue of the Americas) between West 52nd Street and West 53rd Street in Midtown Manhattan. The thirty-eight-story building rose 490 feet tall and had 872,000 square feet of office space. The building's design was admired by many, respected by most, and despised by a few. Its somber dark gray tone was seen as dignified by some and funereal by others, and its modified brutalism style was either revered or reviled. But the building made a powerful visual statement and its imposing presence, like William Paley's burgeoning network, could not be ignored.

The new headquarters signified CBS's arrival as a giant corporation to be reckoned with by Wall Street and media competitors. NBC's offices at 30 Rockefeller Plaza, six blocks away, were considered to be architecturally undistinguished. ABC was housed in rented offices in a nondescript modern building sometimes mockingly referred to as "the package the CBS Building came in."[6]

The building's look had been conceived by Eero Saarinen, a Finnish American architect and industrial designer known for a wide range of designs, including buildings, monuments, and office furniture. He had designed the main terminal at Washington Dulles International Airport; the TWA Flight Center at JFK Airport, a *Jetsons*-like, futuristic thin-shell structure; the Kresge auditorium at MIT, also a thin-shell structure; the 630-foot stainless steel Gateway Arch in St. Louis; and a number of pieces of office furniture for Knoll furniture company, including the Tulip chair and Womb chair.

Saarinen's self-described goal was to build "the simplest skyscraper in New York." The CBS Building was the city's first postwar reinforced-concrete high-rise, a looming rectangular tower. Its concrete piers were sheathed in smoky granite sourced from Canada, which earned the structure the enduring sobriquet "Black Rock." The building's exterior consists of V-shaped piers alternating with relatively narrow five-foot-wide window bays of plate glass tinted black. When the building is viewed from an angle, the V-shape of the pier eclipses the view of the receded glass presenting the viewer with a stark but stunning view of somber stone. The austerity of the building is enhanced by the almost complete absence of any interruptions in the façade.

The CBS headquarters building was constructed in a stretch of Sixth Avenue that was experiencing an architectural makeover that had begun in 1958. Before Saarinen's skyscraper asserted its presence, the preexisting pattern of undistinguished buildings and irregular public plazas made the neighboring skyline look like a smile with broken and missing teeth.

When William S. Paley first viewed a model of Saarinen's proposed building in the architect's Detroit office, the CBS chairman did not find it appealing. On a second visit, however, Paley's opinion changed. "I saw what I had at first thought of as austerity really come through as strong, exquisite, ageless beauty. In 1961 I decided to go ahead with Saarinen." Thus the decision was made to move CBS's offices from its headquarters at 485 Madison, which it had occupied since 1929, as well as to consolidate offices in dozens of other buildings around Manhattan.[7] The building's construction ultimately took four years to complete.

The details of every inch of the interior of the building were reviewed in excruciating detail by CBS's president, Frank Stanton. Furniture and fixtures all had a modern, sleek look dominated by glass and chrome, punctuated by modern art, reflecting Stanton's own personal tastes. The network's head even carefully directed the location of each plant in the thirty-eight-story building.[8] But if Stanton was the unofficial, corporate "architect" for the building's interior details, there was one feature of the building that was the exclusive domain of William Paley. Besides his own office, Paley dominated the design, décor, menu, and naming of the restaurant that was featured on the building's ground floor—which he christened with the uninspired appellation the Ground Floor.

Paley's extraordinarily expensive tastes and gourmet palate clashed with those of Jerry Brody, the more business-minded and experienced restaurateur who was hired to be the restaurant's first manager. Brody had suggested that the Ground Floor be a northern European steakhouse, but Paley, a Francophile who visited France every year, vetoed Brody's proposal and instead dictated that the restaurant serve a menu of French cuisine. Almost every day, Paley would be in the restaurant's kitchen, sampling soups and other items, to the inevitable frustration of the manager, and without measurably improving the restaurant's dismal financial performance.

CBS executives notoriously avoided confronting Paley with the unassailable truth about the Ground Floor's business affairs, fearful for the blowback that it could have on their own careers. One afternoon Stanton and Paley met in Paley's office with two other CBS executives, Fred Friendly, head of CBS News, and Bill Leonard, one of Friendly's subordinates at the news division. As soon as the meeting commenced, Paley inquired if the men had eaten at the restaurant. In fact, all three men had just eaten there, and they all thought it was terrible. Fearful of Paley's wrath, Stanton and Friendly mumbled that yes they had eaten there and yes, it was fine, just fine. But Bill Leonard, a journalist and a man who loved food as much as Paley, was incapable of dissembling as convincingly as his corporate colleagues. "It was awful. The food was terrible. Fred had a fish dish and got sick. The service was bad and the prices were way out of line," blurted out Leonard, to the shock of the CBS executives and to Paley's dismay. The meeting ended shortly thereafter, much sooner than expected, and as soon as Friendly returned to his CBS News office at West 57th Street, his phone was ringing. It was Stanton calling with a message for Friendly's deputy news chief. "Tell Leonard that he has just set the News Division back ten years. He's wrecked everything. All Paley can talk about now is the restaurant."[9]

✦ ✦ ✦

After six frenetic months, the moment had arrived. Mendelson sat down with two CBS network vice presidents and screened *A Charlie Brown Christmas*.[*, 10] With just a week left prior to its scheduled broadcast, expectations—and anxiety—were high all around the table. Only a couple of weeks earlier Mendelson had screened a slightly earlier cut of the production with Bill Melendez and his team of animators, after which Melendez had turned to the producer and said, "I think we've ruined Charlie Brown." The director's distressing words had to still be ringing in his ears.

Mendelson carefully scrutinized the men's faces as they watched, noting that neither executive laughed once during the special. When the lights came on, the two CBS men looked at each other and then at Mendelson. The producer instantly knew that both men were disappointed by what they had just seen. There was a moment of silence before one executive turned to Mendelson and said flatly, "Well, you gave it a good shot." Then, like a boxer unleashing a flurry of punches before the bell, came the onslaught of criticisms and objections:[11]

- *It seems a little flat…a little slow.*
- *The music is all wrong.*
- *The script is too innocent.*

---

* One of the mysteries surrounding *A Charlie Brown Christmas* is, who were the two CBS executives for whom Lee Mendelson screened the special? The producer refused to ever identify the men by name, stating that he did not want to embarrass them. Mendelson did mention that the men he met with were both vice presidents and at the very top positions at the network. The top two programming executives at CBS in December 1965 were Michael Dann and Irwin Segelstein. I believe it is highly likely that it was these two men who were in the meeting with Mendelson.

- *The Bible thing scares us.*
- *The animation was crude—couldn't it be jazzed up a bit?*
- *The voice talent was unprofessional—you should have used adults.*
- *The music didn't fit—who ever heard of a jazz score on an animated special?*
- *And where were the laughs?*[12]

Mendelson absorbed each blow like an aging palooka no longer able to slip punches. Then came the kill shot.

- *Well, we will, of course, air it next week, but I'm afraid we won't be ordering any more. We're sorry; and believe me, we're big* Peanuts *fans. But maybe it's better suited to the comic page.*

The CBS executives had almost certainly expected another *Rudolph the Red-Nosed Reindeer*, but instead of Santa Claus, reindeer, elves, and traditional holiday music, they had been served up a buffet of Bible study, holiday angst, and a searing attack on commercialism. In any rendition of the meeting that he ever gave, Mendelson never claimed to have countered the executives' critique of the Charlie Brown special at all. Given that he and Bill Melendez had both protested to Schulz regarding the lengthy recitation from the Bible scene, it had to have been especially painful for him to hear the network men raise the same concern.

Mendelson could have pointed out that one of the most popular songs in the country for the past month—indeed it became the number one ranked Billboard Top 100 song for the week of December 4—took its lyrics from the Bible. The American folk rock-group The Byrds had a chart topper with the song "Turn! Turn! Turn!

(To Everything There Is a Season)." In fact, The Byrds' recording label was Columbia Records, which was owned by CBS. Except for its title, repeated throughout the song, and the final two verses, the song's lyrics consist of the first eight verses of the third chapter of the King James Version of the Bible's Book of Ecclesiastes, although they are rearranged for the song. The song culminates in a plea for peace, a powerful message that resonated with listeners at a time of escalation during the Vietnam War. Notably, in the Charlie Brown Christmas special, Linus's recitation from the Bible's Gospel of Luke (also from the King James Version) concludes similarly as The Byrds' song, with a message for peace—"Glory to God in the highest, and on earth peace, good will toward men."

But if Mendelson provided any defenses or counterarguments to the litany of concerns voiced by the disappointed CBS executives, the producer never mentioned them whenever he recounted his painful reception at Black Rock. What Mendelson did do next, however, as the meeting concluded, was critical. Having critiqued the special, one of the network executives turned to the other and said, "What should we do about Burgheim?" Without hesitating, the other executive responded, "We shouldn't show it to him." Mendelson, not knowing if the men were perhaps referring to another CBS executive, asked, "Who's Burgheim?"

"Burgheim" was Richard Burgheim, a writer for *Time* magazine. The CBS men had invited him to the meeting in anticipation of showing the critic the TV special after watching it themselves. Burgheim was planning to write a review of the show that would run prior to its broadcast. None of this was known to Mendelson beforehand. If he had any doubt how the network execs felt about the program before, he certainly knew now—they had so little confidence in the special that they thought better of showing it to a reviewer whom they had already invited to screen it and who was right now waiting patiently outside.

But Mendelson feared that not showing the program risked becoming its own, even worse, story—that CBS executives were so shocked by the poor quality of the Charlie Brown production that they were not showing it to a television critic for a prebroadcast review. Mendelson, grasping at straws, said, "Won't it be worse if we don't show it to him?" The two executives looked at each other for a few seconds and then relented. Richard Burgheim was ushered into the screening room as the CBS executives exited. The writer watched the special in silence while Mendelson closely inspected the man's face for any flicker of emotion. There was none. When the screening concluded, the critic stood up, politely thanked the producer, and left the room. Mendelson was devastated.[13]

After the brutal honesty of the CBS executives, Mendelson hoped that Burgheim would provide some positive reaction to what he had just seen, but the *Time* critic's impassivity was crushing to the producer, seemingly further confirmation that what he, Schulz, and Melendez had toiled away at for the past six months had been an abject failure, destined to be a ratings bomb. The San Francisco producer exited the CBS building in a daze, like a gull that had crashed into one of the polished windows of Black Rock.[14] For hours he walked around the streets of New York, feeling the same sense of defeat and depression that was the very essence of the *Peanuts* special's protagonist, Charlie Brown.

In December 1965 Richard Burgheim (known as "Dick" by his friends and colleagues) was a thirty-two-year-old contributing editor at *Time* magazine, where he focused on show business and television.

He had been born on July 5, 1933, in St. Louis, to Nathan H. Burgheim, from Missouri, and Mary (Rudman) Burgheim, originally from New York.

Mary had earned a bachelor degree and graduate degrees from Washington University.[15] She had also attended Columbia University in New York. Before Richard was born, she taught English at Clayton High School. She resumed teaching again in the 1960s and 1970s, after raising her two children, leading courses in communications and public speaking at Washington University and at St. Louis Community College at Forest Park. She remained active even after retiring, volunteering to teach an English course for foreign-language students.[16]

Her husband, a native of St. Louis, had attended St. Louis University at night but left college after one year. He became a prosperous life insurance salesman and a prominent member of the local community, participating in business, social, and religious affairs. He did well enough financially that the family could afford a live-in servant in their stately home, which was situated on over two acres of land in the wealthy Frontenac neighborhood of St. Louis.[17] He had started working for Northwestern Mutual in 1926 and would spend his entire career with the company, commuting every workday morning to his downtown office.

The senior Burgheim was an active leader in the local Boy Scouts, leading a group of scouts to a jamboree in London in 1929. He also served as president of the Liberal Forum of the Young Men's Hebrew Association, which brought prominent speakers to St. Louis. His other civic roles included serving as a board member of the United Way, the Jewish Federation, and Jewish Family Services.[18]

Nathan Burgheim and his wife were among the first members of Temple Shaare Emeth, where he was president of the congregation. He also played a notable role in rescuing dozens of Jews who were living in Germany when Adolf Hitler rose to power. From 1938 to 1940 the St. Louis native supplied affidavits and sent money that enabled people to bribe their way out of Germany. He then provided financial assistance to Jewish refugees as they established themselves in their newly adopted countries, including far-flung locations like Australia, Bolivia, and Chile.

The Burgheims could afford to send their son to St. Louis Country Day School,* an elite private boys' college prep school educating the sons of affluent upper-class families of the St. Louis area. Graduates of the school typically went on to attend Ivy League schools. Some notable alumni of the school at the time the young Burgheim attended included Morton May, chairman of May Department Stores; actor Vincent Price; William McChesney Martin Jr., the Federal Reserve chairman; and poet T. S. Eliot.[19]

Richard Burgheim thrived at St. Louis Country Day, where he was affectionately known by the nicknames Burgie, Captain Bugs, and Heim. His high school yearbook noted that he often disrupted class with his "sharp, irrepressible wit." ("Fumigate your mind, Burgheim!" was the frequent retort of the biology teacher to the teenage boy's suggestive classroom eruptions.) His intellect was recognized when he received the Harvard Prize Book, an achievement award from the Harvard Alumni Association given to the outstanding high school junior from more than two thousand high schools. The future *Time* writer served on the school newspaper throughout high school, assuming the role of editor-in-chief his senior year.

Also held in high regard by his fellow students for his integrity, Burgheim was elected by his classmates to the school's five-member Student Court his junior and senior years; in his senior year, he was selected by his fellow court members to serve as chief justice. In weekly

---

* Now Mary Institute and St. Louis Country Day School, after the school's combination with Mary Institute in 1992.

meetings, the student court adjudicated any disciplinary reports submitted by the school's administration, faculty, or students.[20]

Upon graduating from prep school Burgheim headed to Harvard College, where he majored in government and played soccer. He also wrote for the *Crimson*, the school newspaper, becoming its sports editor, and served on the editorial board of the *Harvard Alumni Bulletin*.[21] While in college the industrious writer also worked as a stringer for the Associated Press.

One of Burgheim's strongest college memories came as a junior, on a cold autumn day in 1953. The wind whipping across the nearby Charles River had not deterred students from filling a lecture hall to capacity to listen to the new dean of Harvard's Faculty of Arts and Sciences. Only thirty-four years old, this was the youngest dean in the school's history, and perhaps its most impressive young thinker. As Burgheim absorbed the dean's lecture, he was incredibly impressed by the speaker's clarity, perception, and grasp of international issues. He knew it was only a matter of time before the speaker would be employing his talents in government service, using his brilliance to further America's goals in world affairs. The speaker was McGeorge Bundy, who, as Burgheim correctly foresaw, would indeed impact foreign policy when he was selected to be President Kennedy's national security adviser.[22]

After graduating from Harvard, Burgheim served in the Coast Guard for almost four years, becoming aide to the admiral in the Fifth District at Norfolk, Virginia, who oversaw operations responsible for securing the safety and security of the oceans and coastal areas of America's mid-Atlantic. The Harvard graduate's writing talents were employed to rewrite *The Coast Guardsman's Manual*.[23] While in the service, Burgheim was also able to do some reporting for the *Virginian-Pilot*, the Norfolk daily newspaper.

Burgheim joined *Time* in 1960, where he first served an apprenticeship on the magazine's employee publication before being assigned to the magazine's "People" section. From 1962 to 1964 he was assigned to Montreal, where he reported on Canada before returning to New York City. In Montreal Burgheim met his future wife, Nona Mary Macdonald, a graduate of the University of Toronto and the daughter of a doctor from Calgary in Alberta, Canada. It was there that Macdonald had begun her own career in media at CBC Radio-TV.

The couple were married on January 15, 1965, in a Protestant service held in the chapel of the United Nations. The location was a popular site for interfaith marriages, but the more likely reason that the couple chose the site for their nuptials is that Burgheim's bride worked at the United Nations in the radio and visual department. The chapel is located on the first floor of the twelve-story Church Center for the United Nations, a private building that is located across the street from the United Nations headquarters complex but with no official connection to the UN itself. The building, which was constructed in 1963, was founded, owned, and operated by the Methodist Church. The officiating minister at the couple's wedding was Elfan Rees of Geneva, Switzerland, who was also an adviser for the World Council of Churches on refugee affairs. Rees was an outspoken authority on the issues of humanitarian crises, especially refugees and displaced persons in war-torn countries.

At *Time* Burgheim was known as a talented writer, albeit disorganized. In appearance he was mild mannered, disheveled, and unprepossessing. His colleagues noted his workaholic intensity and drive. His tendency to mumble may have been employed at times to mask his biting wit.[24] Fond of puns, Burgheim wrote in a review of the movie *Peyton Place*, based on the eponymous, best-selling novel, that "the movie cut some of the sex and violence from [the author's] hugely profitable peeping tome."[25] But lacking a mentor, and perhaps because of his unassuming manner, Burgheim found himself typecast as a "back of the book" writer for *Time*, relegated to the less glamorous "Television" and "Modern Living" sections of the magazine.[26]

Lee Mendelson flew home to San Francisco two days after his disastrous meeting at CBS, nervously awaiting the publication of the December 10 issue of *Time* magazine and Burgheim's all-important review. In the interim, the December 4 issue of *TV Guide* carried a two-page color teaser for the upcoming Charlie Brown special. Consisting of fourteen frames of a special cartoon strip drawn by Charles Schulz, the teaser covered the same themes as the upcoming special: the commercialization of Christmas, Charlie Brown's depression, Linus's upbeat message ("Don't let them get you down, Charlie Brown. Just think of Christmas as a time of joy... friendship...love.").

Mendelson had obvious reasons to be concerned over the impending *Time* magazine review. He had no illusions about the quality of *A Charlie Brown Christmas*'s animation. He had twice voiced his own concerns about the program's biblical content. The CBS meeting had been disastrous. Burgheim's impassive body language when watching the show had not been promising. Most distressing of all was the fact that even a cursory inspection of Burgheim's recent reviews for *Time* revealed withering criticism of television's current offerings.

About two months prior to Burgheim's meeting with Mendelson, *Time* had published a review of the three networks' fall television lineups: eighty-eight premieres, thirty-four of them brand-new. In a lengthy piece titled "Television: The Overstuffed Tube," Burgheim unloaded a double-barreled, blistering broadside against the new programming.[27] Some samples:

- "For never have the TV gristmills ground so ponderously and turned out such thin gruel."
- "But even by TV's own mass-entertainment standards, the content of the new shows was deplorable, hackneyed, timid and banal."
- "The new season fielded one barely passable show for every seven that were artistically bankrupt and boring."
- "If the season seemed to have a theme, it was, what's new copycat?"

CBS did not escape Burgheim's barrage. Going after the network's newly launched show *The Wild, Wild West*, a program set in the 1870s about Secret Service agent James West working to foil threats posed by megalomaniac villains to President Ulysses S. Grant and the country, the *Time* writer punctured both the program's major plot theme and its preening protagonist by posing the question: "Except for President Grant, who needs him?"

Time magazine went to press on Saturday; finished articles (known as "final takes") were due on Friday. This meant that for Burgheim's review to get "into the book" (correspondents' jargon for making publication) for the magazine published on Monday before the program's broadcast date, he had only two or three precious days after his screening with Mendelson to sit alone at his desk, pull a piece of blank paper from a drawer, spin it under the roll band of his typewriter, and peck out his critique of *A Charlie Brown Christmas*.[28]

Although the special's CBS broadcast date was Thursday, December 9, and the date printed on the magazine carrying Burgheim's review was Friday, December 10, *Time* released the magazine on the Monday prior to its printed publication date. For Mendelson, this meant the crucial issue would arrive on newsstands on Monday, December 6. Mendelson also recalled that for some reason, the weekly issue of *Time* was on the newsstand at San Francisco airport a day earlier. So on Sunday, December 5, Mendelson jumped in his car and raced north up the 101 freeway, making his third appearance at the airport that week.

Pulling into the airport parking lot, Mendelson parked his car and ran to a magazine stand, where he purchased the new edition of *Time*. His hands shook as he turned the pages, frantically searching for the magazine's TV section.[29] On the periodical's cover was a painted portrait of Harold Keith "Johnny" Johnson, the US Army chief of staff. Angled across the upper left of the portrait was an italicized quote from the four-star general: "The Battlefield Is a Lonely Place." With the escalating conflict in Vietnam, it was *Time*'s eighth magazine cover that year focused on the conflict there. The Battle of Ia Drang, the first major battle between the United States Army and the People's Army of Vietnam (aka the North Vietnamese Army or NVA), had taken place just two weeks before the magazine went to press.[*]

Mendelson flipped rapidly through the periodical's pages, past ads for the new 1966 Cadillac, Ballantine's Scotch, Boeing, Hertz, and Republic Steel. He may or may not have noticed a brief entry on

---

[*] General Johnson headed to Vietnam in December 1965, where he would spend Christmas with the troops and correctly assess that, contrary to Army reports, the Battle of Ia Drang had not been a victory at all, and that the US commander in Vietnam, General William Westmoreland, was executing a flawed strategy. Johnson was a World War II veteran who, like Charles Schulz, also emerged from his wartime experience a man of strong faith. Johnson spent forty-one months as a prisoner of the Japanese, during which time his religious convictions were reawakened and strengthened.

page ten, where noteworthy television programs, theater plays, movies, books, and album releases were highlighted. In the television section, below a Danny Thomas special on Wednesday, December 8, was this brief but positive note:

THURSDAY, DECEMBER 9

A CHARLIE BROWN CHRISTMAS (CBS, 7:30–8 p.m.).
Happiness is the Peanuts strip, animated.

(This entry's wording played off of the title of Charles Schulz's best-selling book, *Happiness Is a Warm Puppy*, published in 1962.)

He flipped through seemingly countless ads on alcohol, perfume, automobiles, and appliances (including a full-page color advertisement from General Electric featuring the red-nosed reindeer, Santa, and elves from the *Rudolph* Christmas special the prior year, who were now hawking the company's clocks, blenders, can openers, and portable hair dryers). Mendelson turned past a story on the Supreme Court rejecting the State of Maryland's requirement that jurors swear that God holds them "morally accountable," a piece on the origins of Christmas holiday customs, and an article on the challenges facing Western media reporters in Moscow. Then, turning to page 89, he spotted the show business section with the subheading "Television"…and there it was.[30]

The page was divided into three columns of text. The first entire column and the top of the second contained three chunky paragraphs, just over three hundred words, devoted to *A Charlie Brown Christmas*. In the lower left corner of the page, taking up two columns of width and about two inches high, was a photo of an animation cel from the production. The cel contained two *Peanuts* characters staring at the miniature, needle-bare Christmas tree: Charlie Brown on the left, with a warm smile, and Linus on the right, clutching his ever-present blanket, with a look of pure sadness. Each character is flanked by a very tall, very full Christmas tree, strewn with decorations.

The photo was credited to David Gahr, an American photographer who would become well known in the 1960s for photographing folk, blues, jazz, and rock musicians. Gahr completed thousands of assignments for *Time* or its related publications. (Four months before snapping the Charlie Brown photo, Gahr was at the Newport Folk Festival photographing Bob Dylan, where the musician famously made his first appearance with an electric guitar.[31] The singer had just released "Like a Rolling Stone" five days before the festival, and the concertgoers were shocked by Dylan's shift from acoustic folk into electrified rock and roll.[32])

The article carried no byline for Richard Burgheim, as it was not customary for many magazines and newspapers to credit reporters or writers with bylines until around 1970.

Heart racing, Mendelson's eyes plunged in, reading the review.

TELEVISION: SECURITY IS A GOOD SHOW

December is the gruelingest month, the time when there seem to be more seasonal "specials" than regular shows on TV. But this Thursday (7:30 p.m., E.S.T.), CBS will carry a special that really is special. For one thing, the program is unpretentious; for another, it is unprolonged (30 minutes). Finally, it represents the overdue TV debut of the comic strip Peanuts.

A Charlie Brown Christmas stars all the familiar Charles Schulz cartoon characters, faithfully animated by ex-Disney

Artist Bill Melendez. The parable, too, is pure Schulz. Christmas is coming, but "good ol' wishy-washy" Charlie Brown doesn't "feel the way I'm supposed to feel." "Look, Charlie Brown, let's face it," explains Lucy. "We all know that Christmas is a big commercial racket. It's run by a big Eastern syndicate, you know." Even Snoopy knows. He has entered a "home lighting and display contest," which, its advertisement promises, will help him "find the true meaning of Christmas."

Snoopy, who upstages the rest of the company every time he is onscreen, wins first prize with his doghouse decorations. Nice Guy Charlie Brown naturally finishes last—he can't even find a decent Christmas tree. "You've been dumb before, Charlie Brown," snorts Lucy, "but this time you really did it." Then Linus saves Charlie's day by narrating the story of the first Christmas and by telling him: "It's not a bad little tree, really. It just needs love." So Linus props it up with his security blanket, and Lucy and the rest of the kids provide Charlie with ornaments—and a little one-day-a-year love. The voices of the characters, dubbed by real rather than stage kids, are occasionally amateurish but contribute to the refreshingly low-key tone. In any case, listeners will grow accustomed to the voices. Three more Peanuts programs are on the drawing boards, and A Charlie Brown Christmas is one children's special this season that bears repeating.

Mendelson was elated by what he had just read. "To my total surprise and relief, it was a great, positive preview!" Mendelson later recalled.[33] He raced home to call both Schulz and Melendez and read them the *Time* article. Mendelson's partners were as thrilled, and relieved, as he was.

Burgheim's review is notable in several respects. First, he made absolutely no mention of the music accompanying the special. Whether Vince Guaraldi's compositions made no impression on the *Time* magazine editor, favorably or unfavorably, or whether Burgheim's review may have been edited for space constraints, will never be known. Second, the review handled Linus's lengthy recitation of Scripture only in the most oblique way: "Then Linus saves Charlie's day by narrating the story of the first Christmas and by telling him: 'It's not a bad little tree, really. It just needs love.'" No reader of Burgheim's review would be prepared for Linus's minute-long, spotlit soliloquy from the Gospel of Luke. Burgheim also noted that "three more *Peanuts* programs are in the works." (He was clearly unaware that a CBS executive had bluntly informed Lee Mendelson that the network would never buy another *Peanuts* special.)

Because Burgheim had been granted an exclusive sneak preview of the special, he may have been inclined to write something positive in order to maintain good relations with the network. But then again, a reviewer's reputation and career would not be enhanced by writing a glowing review of a program that would be ridiculed by the viewing audience or other critics. And Burgheim had, just three months earlier, written a searing takedown of the three television networks' fall lineups. Burgheim was frank with his readers by noting that the non-professional voice talent in *A Charlie Brown Christmas* is "occasionally amateurish," but he softened his criticism by adding that this actually contributes to the program's "refreshingly low-key tone...In any case, listeners will grow accustomed to the voices." He makes no note of the rough animation and in fact lauds "ex-Disney Artist Bill Melendez" who has "faithfully animated" Charles Schulz's cartoon characters.

Why Burgheim's reaction was so positive, contrasted with that of the CBS executives, is impossible to judge. Perhaps it was the writer's own Midwestern values; Burgheim's own childhood in St. Louis, although certainly more privileged than Charles Schulz's upbringing as a barber's son in Minneapolis, would in many ways have been similar. Also, *Time* magazine in 1965 was still under the stewardship of Henry R. Luce, its conservative founder, who remained the weekly publication's editorial chairman. Under Luce's management the magazine would hardly bristle at a program that resonated with American values and a Christian theme.

Time exerted a powerful influence on shaping the public's view of events in the 1960s, and the magazine practiced the type of point-of-view journalism that would be recognizable to viewers of MSNBC and Fox News today. In 1965 *Time* distributed 3.2 million copies a week, as many as *Newsweek* (1.8 million) and *U.S. News & World Report* (1.4 million) combined. *Time* was also received by two-thirds of the members of Congress and was the third most popular magazine among media executives.[34] A savage review in America's leading weekly publication could have poisoned the public's perception of *A Charlie Brown Christmas* just prior to broadcast, dissuading millions of viewers from tuning in as well as shaping the opinion of those who did.[35] (One can imagine this scene in countless households across America: "Daddy, we want to watch *A Charlie Brown Christmas* tonight." "Oh gosh, kids, *Time* magazine says it's horrible. Let's just watch *Rudolph* again when they show that.")

Whether Burgheim's glowing review in *Time* was met with guffaws or relief at CBS is unknown, but the two executives who screened *A Charlie Brown Christmas* with Lee Mendelson were concerned enough about the program's quality to expose it to more senior executives. They sought to make others aware of their concerns—if only to protect their own careers if the show inevitably crashed and burned. They very well may have debated or discussed the idea of not broadcasting the program at all. In fact, Frank Stanton, the president of CBS since 1946 and the right-hand man of CBS chairman and founder William Paley, would hear of the mounting worries over the quality of the Charlie Brown special and would screen it himself. Stanton disagreed with his colleagues' negative perception of the program. In an interview years later with David Michaelis, a biographer of Charles Schulz, Stanton claimed that after watching the special he "had a difficult job selling [it] to some of my associates. They thought I had really flipped." As Michaelis noted: "[Stanton] claimed no special instinct for what would go over on the air, but a doctorate in psychology from Ohio State plus ten years in CBS's research department taught him that respectability and cleanliness were essential values of the American television audience of that time."[36]

Stanton didn't reference the biblical issue directly in his interview with Michaelis, but he did mention his CBS colleagues' objection to *Peanuts*' lack of "class." As Stanton noted, *Peanuts* "didn't have the class that some of my associates were looking for, and of course, that was just one of the reasons that it was so great." He also referenced their objections to the show's low-budget look. "Charlie Brown didn't have any fancy sets, and the specials at that time were real Hollywood productions—simplicity wasn't known to them— you just had to have an idea."[37]

If CBS had seriously considered exercising the nuclear option and not broadcasting the *Peanuts* holiday special at all, certainly Burgheim's uplifting review would have given the network's executives enough reason to pause and reconsider their decision, as well as providing them with sufficient political cover to justify televising the show despite their serious misgivings. It would have been unusual but certainly not unprecedented for a network in 1965 (or now) to pull a television show before it was aired, even one that had already been heavily promoted. In 1960 NBC had canceled a prime-time game show called *Head of the Class* that had already been listed in *TV Guide*.[38] In 1963 NBC also dropped *The Robert Taylor Show* from its Thursday-night schedule after four episodes had been shot but shortly before the first episode was to be aired.[39]

One has to appreciate the delightful irony that it was a Jewish television critic who may quite possibly have ensured the broadcast of Charles Schulz's holiday special, which had as its central theme the true meaning of Christmas. Yet, as Lee Mendelson knew, while Richard Burgheim's positive review in *Time* magazine was a great relief and had tremendously buoyed the spirits of the producer, Charles Schulz, and Bill Melendez, in just four days the ultimate critic would decide the fate of *A Charlie Brown Christmas*—the American viewing audience.

THE AUDIENCE

✦

A t 4:43 p.m. Eastern time, on Thursday, December 9, 1965, less than three hours before the broadcast of *A Charlie Brown Christmas*, an explosive fireball was observed in the skies by the residents of states stretching from Michigan to Pennsylvania and was reported by two dozen pilots. Whether it was a meteor entering the atmosphere, an errant missile test, the burning up of a Soviet satellite as its orbit decayed into the atmosphere, or the crash of a UFO remains debated by astronomers, NASA, and conspiracy theorists. The incident has become known as "the Pennsylvania Roswell" or the Kecksburg incident (an object reportedly landed in the woods near the town of Kecksburg, near Pittsburgh). Whatever its cause, the event seems like a cosmic harbinger for the premiere broadcast of the *Peanuts* special—but was it auspicious or ominous?

At seven thirty p.m. Eastern Time, CBS preempted an episode of *The Munsters* to broadcast *A Charlie Brown Christmas*. *The Munsters* was a popular sitcom about a family of friendly monsters starring Fred Gwynne as Herman Munster, a clumsy, comical

Frankenstein-like creation. The special's broadcast followed the *CBS Evening News* with Walter Cronkite and was a lead-in for *Gilligan's Island*, a comedic sitcom about seven quirky castaways surviving on a deserted island.

Just nine days earlier, on November 30, CBS had broadcast a starkly different special, a CBS News special report detailing the battle of Ia Drang Valley, the first major engagement between American troops and the North Vietnamese Army. The intense, close-quarters battle, which had taken place two weeks earlier, resulted in the highest casualties that US forces had suffered in the war thus far: 240 dead and 470 wounded.*

At the same time CBS aired the *Peanuts* holiday special, ABC was broadcasting the US Driving Championship competition *Road America 500*, and NBC was airing *Daniel Boone*, a fictionalized series on the life of the frontiersman starring Fess Parker.

Millions of American families sat down in eager anticipation to watch perhaps only the second televised Christmas special they had ever seen. With children sprawled out on the carpet, their noses only inches from the screen, and their parents seated on chairs or perhaps a plastic-covered couch close behind, they faced their family television set—Philco, General Electric, Zenith, Admiral, RCA Victor. The televisions were black and white for most; fewer than 10 percent of households had a color unit. It may have been a small, battleship gray portable set, carried by a lift handle on top from the bedroom to a living room and propped up on a small table or perhaps a chair. Or for a privileged few, it may have been a massive midcentury modern piece of furniture, with cherry wood veneer, and sliding

---

* The battle was memorialized in the book *We Were Soldiers Once...and Young*, by Lieutenant General Harold G. Moore and Joseph L. Galloway. The book would be adapted into a movie starring Mel Gibson as then Lt. Col. Moore.

doors revealing the curved television lens flanked by stereo speakers. The sets were turned on, rabbit ear antennae were extended, volume and tuning knobs were adjusted, and an array of transistors and tubes slowly warmed up sending a flickering image to the thick, green-tinted glass screen.

The cold open of *A Charlie Brown Christmas* is a classic winter scene that Charles Schulz had suggested when he drafted the original one-page outline of the show for Coca-Cola—snow gently falls on some of the *Peanuts* characters, including Snoopy, skating on a frozen pond. (Snoopy, always the scene stealer, glides effortlessly across the ice without the aid of any skates.) Linus and his friend Charlie Brown, who already looks crestfallen, carry their skates over their shoulders and head toward their friends. The two boys pause at a brick wall, where Charlie Brown confesses, "I think there must be something wrong with me, Linus. Christmas is coming but I'm not happy. I don't feel the way I'm supposed to feel…I always end up feeling depressed." It's a vulnerable admission of a personal crisis amid the joy of the holiday season. Underscored by Vince Guaraldi's melancholic tune "Christmas Time Is Here" in the background, the scene sets the tone for the program and establishes immediately that it will be a dramatically different type of Christmas special than the prior year's offering of *Rudolph the Red-Nosed Reindeer*.

Out on the ice Snoopy plays "crack the whip" with a long conga line of skaters, scattering them like billiard balls to the pond's edges. When Charlie Brown and Linus enter the ice, Snoopy reprises his antics, snatching Linus's blanket in his teeth and wrapping up the two newcomers in the process. The beagle first flings Charlie Brown into a tree, and the impact shakes the accumulated snow loose from the tree's branches, revealing a garish title card spelling out "A

CHARLIE BROWN Christmas"—"A" is in cardinal red and alone on the first line of the title; "CHARLIE BROWN" is in all capitals and in blue, but difficult to read, obscured by the tree limbs behind the lettering; "Christmas" is in red, occupies the final third line, is equal in size to the two other lines combined, but is a completely different font of lowercase letters than the rest of the title card, and the initial letter *C* is illuminated in an elaborate script like a medieval Bible. Below the title are two sprigs of holly, capping off a title card that is simultaneously cliché, clashing, and challenging to read. Snoopy next sends Linus on a collision course with a sign, which shakes so violently that at first the viewer can't make out the sign's writing, but then the camera zooms in, and in the closeup we clearly see "BROUGHT TO YOU BY THE PEOPLE IN YOUR TOWN WHO BOTTLE COCA-COLA."*

In the next scene Charlie Brown is disappointed to discover he has not received a single Christmas card in his mailbox. He makes his way over to Lucy's psychiatric booth, where he tells her, "I am in sad shape." Before he can unload his anxieties, Lucy interrupts him and demands payment. The sound of her patient's nickel plinking against the inside of her can spurs Lucy to wax poetic about the "beautiful sound of cold, hard cash." Charlie Brown then confesses, "I feel depressed. I know I should be happy, but I'm not." Lucy rifles through a list of phobias, in an attempt to isolate Charlie Brown's fear, before her patient offers, "Actually, Lucy, my trouble is Christmas. I just don't understand it. Instead of feeling happy, I feel sort of let down." Lucy helpfully advises that Charlie Brown needs involvement and suggests that he direct the upcoming Christmas play. She also offers that she can relate to her patient's feeling of depression during the holiday season, explaining that the source of

* The Coca-Cola sign would eventually be excised and no longer appears in the current version of the special on Apple TV+.

her despondency is that she never receives what she really wants for Christmas—real estate!

Lucy's revelation to Charlie Brown of her crass interest in "cold, hard cash" and real estate is followed up by his encounters with two more characters who are similarly greedily disposed: Snoopy has "gone commercial" by entering a neighborhood Christmas lights contest which offers a money reward, and Sally dictates a letter to her older brother for Santa Claus, asking him to "Just send money. How about tens and twenties?" When Charlie Brown expresses his dismay, his little sister protests, "All I want is my fair share!"

Charlie Brown then proceeds to rehearsal for the school Christmas play, where the new director unsuccessfully attempts to corral the attention of his actors and stage assistants. Schroeder bangs out the tune "Linus and Lucy" on his piano, accompanied by Snoopy on a guitar and Pig-Pen on a double bass, while the entire crew of kids break out in frenzied dance moves. Lucy intercedes on the director's behalf, but she is mercilessly mocked by Snoopy's comedic mimicry. When she threatens to slug the misbehaving beagle, he delivers the ultimate indignity—a sloppy dog kiss. Lucy also physically threatens Linus—giving him "five good reasons" to memorize his lines, while she makes a fist, closing one finger at a time.* Charlie Brown attempts once again to take charge, but his plans are disrupted by his young actors who refuse to follow his instructions. Escorted by Linus, the frustrated director decides to head off to find a proper Christmas tree to set the mood for the play.

The two boys arrive at a Christmas tree lot that abounds with wonderful, colorful trees—all apparently made of aluminum. Charlie Brown spots what is apparently the lot's sole real tree, a tiny sapling sprouting only three branches with sparse needles, and mounted

---

* This scene would be revised in a subsequent version by showing a closeup of Lucy's hand as she makes a fist.

onto an oversized wooden stand. Without a hint of irony Linus asks rhetorically, "Gee, do they still make wooden Christmas trees?" Charlie Brown is drawn to the tiny conifer with the tenderness of a cat lover rescuing a scrawny kitten at an animal shelter. He disregards Linus's cautionary reminder that Lucy wanted a "modern" tree (she had instructed the director to "Get the biggest aluminum tree you can find"). Charlie Brown is not dissuaded. "I don't care. We'll decorate it and it will be just right for our play. Besides, I think it needs me."

When Charlie Brown returns to the stage, he places his tree on top of Schroeder's piano. The actors immediately express their contempt for the sad sapling as well as for the director himself before walking away with mocking laughter. A crushed Charlie Brown then expresses his remorse for picking the tree. "Everything I do turns into a disaster. I guess I really don't know what Christmas is all about," he says, before throwing his head back and his arms wide and shouting to the theater's empty seats, "Isn't there anyone who knows what Christmas is all about?" Without hesitating, a thumb-sucking Linus withdraws his finger from his mouth and confidently responds, "Sure, Charlie Brown. I can tell you what Christmas is all about." He walks to center stage, clutching his blanket, and asks, "Lights, please?" A spotlight then illuminates the small figure of Linus Van Pelt, who is now seen from the distant balcony of the theater, and he begins to speak while the camera slowly draws closer. For the next sixty seconds, Linus speaks softly, but clearly, unaccompanied by any musical soundtrack and unadorned by any special effects:

And there were in the same country, shepherds abiding in the fields, keeping watch over their flock by night. And lo, the angel of the Lord came upon them, and the glory of the Lord shown round about them, and they were sore afraid. And the angel *said unto them, "Fear not, for behold I bring you good tidings of great joy, which shall be to all people. For unto you is born this day in the city of David, a Savior, which is Christ the Lord. And this shall be a sign unto you—ye shall find a babe wrapped in swaddling clothes, lying in a manger." And suddenly there was with the angel, a multitude of the heavenly host praising God, and saying, "Glory to God in the highest, and on Earth peace, good will toward men."**

Linus retrieves his blanket, exits stage left, and approaches Charlie Brown. "That's what Christmas is all about, Charlie Brown," says Linus.

A now fortified Charlie Brown picks up his forlorn tree and walks home underneath a canopy of twinkling stars with Linus's spotlit soliloquy of Scripture echoing in his head. He stops at Snoopy's doghouse, which now displays a first place ribbon, the beagle having secured top honors in the neighborhood holiday decorating contest. Charlie Brown removes a round red ornament from the dazzling doghouse and hangs it from a branch of the small tree, but the weak sapling buckles under the weight of the decoration. "Oh, everything I touch gets ruined!" exclaims the completely dejected protagonist, who abandons the tree and slinks away. The *Peanuts* gang of kids then surprisingly appears. They surround the tree, as an attentive Linus straightens the drooping branch and wraps the tree stand with his beloved blanket. With a flurry of arm movements, the children remove Snoopy's doghouse decorations and transfer them to the small tree. Charlie Brown returns and is surprised to see that the tree that he thought he had ruined has now been stunningly transformed into a lush, vibrant fir tree, now radiant with Christmas decorations.

---

*   Luke 2:8–14, King James Version of the Bible.

The children shout, "Merry Christmas, Charlie Brown!" and they break out in song, singing "Hark! The Herald Angels Sing."

The credits roll in white lettering, but the background is ivory snow and falling snowflakes, rendering many names completely illegible. After the credits, the original broadcast included a brief clip of Charles Schulz sitting at his studio desk, thanking Coca-Cola and its bottlers for sponsoring the program. It was the only personal endorsement Charles Schulz ever made throughout his career.

The morning after the special's broadcast, Lee Mendelson walked into the neighborhood coffee shop that he frequented. There were about twenty people inside, and as he began to visit with the friendly faces, he discovered that everyone had watched the special. It was his first inkling that perhaps the show may have done well, but the producer cautioned himself against reading too much into their reaction. After all, the producer thought, these people knew him, and perhaps they were merely being polite.

Then a call came from CBS. It was one of the same executives Mendelson had met with in New York who had shredded the show after the screening at Black Rock. The executive was upbeat. The show had performed well. Extremely well. A 45 market share, meaning almost half of the country had tuned in—15.5 million viewers![1] "We are going to order four more," the executive said. Before hanging up, however, apparently feeling a need to justify his earlier skepticism at the special's screening, the executive interjected, "Well, my aunt in New Jersey hated it, too."[2]

The unbelieving "aunt in New Jersey" was a distinct minority as positive reviews, telegrams, and letters flowed in. "All heaven broke loose" is how McCann executive John Allen described the overwhelmingly positive reception. A reviewer for the *Washington Post* wrote that "good old Charlie Brown, a natural born loser... finally turned up a winner." CBS president Frank Stanton personally called Charles Schulz to congratulate him. A few days later, Mike Dann, the network's vice president for programming, admitted what was now obvious: "We had the most amazing reaction to this show, it was far more than we expected. We not only got letters, but schools sent long petitions asking us to repeat the show." Coca-Cola's president, J. Paul Austin, called McCann-Erickson to ensure that the program would be repeated the following year.[3]

Four months after the special's broadcast, *A Charlie Brown Christmas* received the prestigious George Foster Peabody Award, given for the most powerful, enlightening, and invigorating stories in television and radio. The special was also nominated for an Emmy in the category of Outstanding Children's Program. The special was competing against CBS's *Captain Kangaroo* series, a production of *The World of Stuart Little* on NBC Children's Theatre, and a three-part film titled *The Adventures of Gallegher*, which was broadcast on *Walt Disney's Wonderful World of Color*. The creators of *A Charlie Brown Christmas* assumed they had no chance of winning against such professional competition. Melendez had to feel a twinge of anxiety going up against his former employer Walt Disney, whom he had gone out on strike against twenty-five years earlier.

The Emmy ceremony was held on May 22, 1966, and was a bicoastal event with awards being presented both in New York City and in Los Angeles (at the Hollywood Palladium). The nominees for the category the Charlie Brown special was nominated in were announced in New York, while Charles Schulz, Lee Mendelson, and Bill Melendez were in Hollywood. Schulz's father, Carl, was also in attendance. (Vince Guaraldi arrived late to the event, but tardy attendees were barred at the door, so the pianist returned to his hotel to watch the awards.) The presenters in New York were the two puppets and comedienne behind the entertainment show *Kukla, Fran and Ollie*. In Los Angeles, the presenter was Danny Kaye, a high-energy, fast-talking comedic actor who hosted his own show at the time, *The Danny Kaye Show*.

The winner was announced by a puppet, Ollie the Dragon, in New York City. "And the winner, in Hollywood, is *A Charlie Brown Christmas*." There was a moment of hesitation at the table of Schulz, Melendez, and Mendelson before Lee and Bill rose from their seats. Mendelson urged Schulz to also stand up, but the cartoonist only smiled awkwardly and motioned for his colleagues to go to the stage to accept the award. Once up on stage Mendelson accepted the award from Danny Kaye, and then spoke graciously at the podium. "It is our great pleasure to introduce to you the man who's brought so much happiness to so many people—Mr. Charles Schulz!" The cartoonist then appeared at the podium, while Lee pressed the Emmy award into Melendez's hands, who then passed it to Schulz. The cartoonist spoke only one sentence, a commentary on his round-headed creation: "Charlie Brown is not used to winning, so we thank you."[4]

One week later, on May 28, Schulz would be awakened by screams and come rushing to the guest suite, where his father was staying. Carl was passed out on the floor, dead of a heart attack. He was sixty-nine years old. He had retired only two years earlier. For almost five decades he had worked at his corner barber shop, where he was embedded in the fabric of the neighborhood. Schulz's relationship with his father contained some noticeable strain, yet the son remained as proud of his father as the father must have been of the son. It is possible that as a boy, the sensitive young cartoonist was wounded by the lack of demonstrative affection or verbalization of his father's love, a common attribute of father-son relationships of that era. Years later, Schulz would express regret that he had failed to tell his father how proud he was of his service as an usher at his church. *Peanuts* would make Charles Schulz one of the most admired creators in the world, and yet, two decades after the passing of his father, Charles Schulz would divulge to an interviewer that his greatest ambition, besides being remembered as the greatest cartoonist that ever lived, was to be as well liked as his father.[5]

The Charlie Brown Christmas special continued to run every holiday season on CBS until 2000, when it debuted on ABC. The show would remain on ABC until the broadcast/streaming rights to the special were acquired by Apple Inc. from Peanuts Worldwide LLC (a subsidiary of WildBrain, Ltd.) and Lee Mendelson Film Productions. Apple had bought the rights for the tech giant's streaming service, Apple TV+. A public outcry ensued from viewers upset that the special would no longer be available on free broadcast television. It was a testament to the special's hold on popular culture that to many fans the program seemed to have entered the realm of a public good. To assuage angry fans, a month after Apple's announcement, the company made a deal with PBS to show the program ad-free on the network for one night before Christmas.[6] That arrangement was terminated in 2022, but Apple did make the special available for free viewing from December 22 to December 25 on Apple TV+.

As the final credits begin to roll on our own journey through the making of *A Charlie Brown Christmas*, the important question still remains to be answered: What is it that makes the special, despite all its technical shortcomings, an enduring classic? Why did it succeed in captivating an audience in spite of the skepticism of the television network executives? Why did it triumph despite the misgivings of Melendez and Mendelson? Both of the special's co-creators were also doubting Thomases (the biblical metaphor being perhaps particularly apt here given their concerns of the overt religiosity in the special). I will attempt to offer my own judgment.

First, Vince Guaraldi's musical compositions are so faultless that they wrap the rushed animation and the slow-paced story in a kind of protective acoustical cocoon, like a musical invisibility cloak.* "Christmas Time Is Here" sets the perfect melancholic tone for the program in the special's opening skating scene. "Linus and Lucy" injects a caffeinated jolt of whimsy and joy into the special's otherwise plodding pace at precisely the right moment. From the song's first immediately recognizable notes until its conclusion, it provides the serotonin uplift that the program desperately needs. The frenzied dancing of the *Peanuts* characters to the tune is one of the special's most iconic moments, rivaling the powerful solemnity of Linus's monologue shortly thereafter. In a clever juxtaposition, the two sharply contrasting scenes occurring on the same stage—a madcap jumble of cartoon characters in an animated rave set to lively jazz music followed by a solitary figure's soliloquy without a soundtrack— brilliantly accentuate each other.

Second, the special's animation and art, while certainly uneven, is at times enchanting. The director's framing of scenes is simple but meaningful and never distracting. The artwork of the star-populated night sky and of the Christmas tree lot looks like Impressionist art. Perhaps the biggest issue is that the look and feel of the artwork is not consistent, reflecting the various styles of the animators who prepared it, a concession necessitated by the production's deadline.

---

* Vince Guaraldi's soundtrack for *A Charlie Brown Christmas* is certified Triple Platinum and has sold over three million copies. It was voted into the Grammy Hall of Fame in 2007 and was added to the Library of Congress's National Recording Registry's list of "culturally, historically, or aesthetically important" American recordings.

However, viewers seemed to brush aside any of these shortcomings, if they even noticed them at all. (Even the best resolution television of that day would have provided a gauze-like filter of any broadcast compared to today's screens.) Indeed the rushed look of the limited animation feels consistent with the childlike innocence of the program in a way that a Disney production, with its striving for realism, would have seemed contrived and pretentious. In a sense the look of the special mirrors an elementary school's play, just like one of the key scenes of the show itself. The animation seemed to charm viewers, and any continuity issues were an unnoticed blemish. Similarly the voice talent was perfectly cast, as evidenced by how completely the audience embraced the voice actors as the actual voices of the characters. No one seemed to register any dissonance between the voices they may have assigned the *Peanuts* characters in their own heads while reading the comic strip and what they heard in the special.

Also, the theme of alienation and sadness expressed by Charlie Brown is one that powerfully resonates with many. Charlie Brown was the postwar Everyman, a childhood precursor to a Willy Loman (the stage play *Death of a Salesman* premiered on Broadway in 1949, the year before *Peanuts* was first published) or, in the contemporary era, a pre–*Breaking Bad* Walter White, struggling against the crushing cruelties and indignities of the world. He's a misfit, who is estranged from his own cohort of friends, as well as from his own dog, which howls in protest when its owner is introduced as the Christmas play's director,* prompting Charlie Brown to mutter, "Man's best friend," in resigned sarcasm.

The protagonist as noble misfit is one that is so common as to be a trope, found in movies from *Superman*'s Clark Kent to *Dirty*

---

* Snoopy's howl has a more haunting sound in the original version of the Christmas special. It was toned down in the revised version.

Harry's Harry Callahan to Marvel superheroes. Yet scratch the surface, and the misfit's peculiarities are merely a thin varnish underneath which lies a superhuman savior.

Even Rudolph was an athletically gifted reindeer who took to the skies on his first try with ease. His misfit status reflected his herd's lack of acceptance of his ruby-red nose, not from any meaningful character flaw. (The gifts discarded on the Island of Misfit Toys were more seriously damaged, yet they are a mere sideshow in the program and are even abandoned in the original version of the special—an outcome that disturbed so many viewers that the program was subsequently altered for a happier ending for the defective toys.)

Yet Charlie Brown's affliction doesn't disguise a superhero. His misfit status isn't merely the zigzag pattern of his shirt; it's his inability to succeed at life. He's a misfit to the core of his being. His superpower, to the extent he has one, is that despite suffering continuous defeats, he is never defeated. While he certainly never overcomes his misfortunes, nor is there any hint of an expectation that he ever will, he is never permanently beaten. This is the essential formula that fueled the *Peanuts* cartoon strip for five decades.

But that doesn't explain why our round-headed protagonist's alienation captivated audiences so powerfully in *A Charlie Brown Christmas*. There are many *Peanuts* television specials, yet none stuck the landing so profoundly and so permanently in the hearts and minds of viewers, and in the landscape of American pop culture, as the Christmas program. In *A Charlie Brown Christmas*, the protagonist's feeling of disconnectedness is compounded by seasonal factors. It is fueled by the commercialism and consumerism that have commandeered the Christmas season. And it is this sense of seasonal alienation that I believe the adult audience identifies with the most.

In doing research for my book, I would frequently speak to friends, to acquaintances, as well as to complete strangers about my project, to test their reaction to the *Peanuts* special, in an effort to see how (and why) the program resonates with people today. The most common reaction for those adults who are fans of the special is a spontaneous gleeful exuberance at the special's undiluted religious content. These fans cheer at Schulz, like he is their spiritual Spartacus, embracing his moral courage in tackling the real meaning of Christmas in the face of secular skepticism.

What Charles Schulz, and his co-creators, Lee Mendelson, Bill Melendez, and Vince Guaraldi, had done was, in a word, subversive, and in a way very appropriate to the 1960s counterculture. Animating from the Bible, putting jazz music in a Christmas special, proclaiming an overtly religious message—none of this had been done before. It could even be argued that *A Charlie Brown Christmas* both augured the Jesus movement of the 1960s and 1970s, as well as helped to usher it in.

Linus's recitation from the Gospel of Luke arrives like a thunderbolt of clarity, without a hint of foreshadowing and with only a one-sentence introduction—a veritable Linus ex machina. It clears away the confusion about the true meaning of Christmas with the force of a pressure washer, answering Charlie Brown's persistent question—"Isn't there anyone who can tell me what Christmas is all about?"—with a stunning Scriptural simplicity. His speech demolishes the paywall of commerce surrounding Christmas and rescues the true meaning of the holiday, and in doing so, he rescues the audience as well. The special's reception demonstrated that the viewing public, while preoccupied by holiday shopping, was actually starving for spiritual meaning, like a malnourished child gorging on junk food while starving for nutrients.

Linus's soliloquy of Scripture is the special's climactic moment, an event that is so powerful that it reaches back and scrambles the beginning. Every time I have watched the program, I'm struck by how dark and depressing it is at the outset. Linus's redemptive speech seems to rework the memory of the entire special into a program composed only of joy and holiday cheer, editing its earlier scenes of casual cruelties. The sight of the once frail sapling first rescued and then "killed" by Charlie Brown, later transformed into an adorned Christmas tree by the frenzied hands of his friends, erases Charlie Brown's depression. It is like the pain of childbirth wiped away by the vision of one's beautiful newborn.

In Charles Schulz's own Bible, across from the Gospel of Matthew's* account of Christ's birth, the cartoonist had written:

> *Christmas is primarily a children's day, for it takes the innocent faith of a child to appreciate it.*
>
> *The Christmas story is filled with characters who have the same perfect faith.*
>
> *Joseph and Mary, the 3 wise men.*
>
> *The Christmas story is a story of purity and can be appreciated only by the pure mind.*
>
> *Our Lord is a Holy God and if we are to approach Him, we must be holy and pure, and filled with the same faith as the wise men.*[7]

Linus occupied a special place in Schulz's heart. In the pantheon of all the *Peanuts* characters, the cartoonist considered Linus the most fun to work with, and the most innocent. "Linus will grow out of his problems and grow up and be the most successful of all

---

* Christ's birth is recounted in two of the Gospels, Matthew and Luke.

the children," Schulz noted. When the blanket-carrying character speaks, he does so with both the innocent lisp of a child and the moral clarity of a martyr. Linus answers Charlie Brown's question with the candor of a child completely oblivious to the protocols of politeness that may prohibit the discussion of an embarrassing truth. While Linus spoke, millions of Americans sat before their television sets in stunned amazement, cheerfully shocked that, yes, the *Peanuts* special was...going...*there!* In the flurry of letters that flooded CBS, Coca-Cola, and Charles Schulz's studio, many, if not most, of the viewers explained that they were motivated to write in to express their appreciation that the special had fearlessly addressed the real meaning of Christmas.

Charles Schulz had known his audience better than the CBS network executives and even better than his creative partners. The cartoonist had once told Lee Mendelson, "There will always be a market for innocence in this country."[8] And on December 9, 1965, the audience had proven him correct.

EPILOGUE

◆

J. PAUL AUSTIN, the president of Coca-Cola who had likely kicked off his company's search for a Christmas special, would go on to take the mantle of CEO and chairman of the board of the company the year after the broadcast of *A Charlie Brown Christmas*. His reign at the soft drink company would see its transition into a professionally managed global operation, including opening up markets in China and the Soviet Union. Austin and McCann-Erickson would have another marketing undertaking that would make a lasting impression on pop culture. In 1971 the agency gathered two hundred young people of various nationalities and ethnic backgrounds on a hillside in Italy and had them lip-sync the words to an idealistic tune—"I'd Like to Buy the World a Coke." Austin found the words and sentimentality of the tune cloying and contrived and almost killed the ad, but he relented and deferred to his advertising team. The song became a pop hit. When he ascended to the presidency of Coca-Cola, the company had sales of $567 million. When he retired in 1981, Coca-Cola's sales were ten times larger, at $5.9 billion. Austin died in Atlanta on December 26, 1985, after succumbing to Parkinson's and Alzheimer's disease. He was seventy years old.[1]

NEIL REAGAN would help manage his brother's two successful gubernatorial campaigns while continuing to head the Los Angeles office of McCann-Erickson. He retired after a forty-year career in advertising, twenty-five years of which were spent at the ad agency. When his younger brother was first elected president in 1980, Neil and his wife, Bess, joined his brother and Nancy Reagan before the inauguration in Washington, DC. Ronald invited his brother and sister-in-law to stay at Blair House* along with him and the soon to be first lady. But the former governor designated that his younger brother be given the much grander quarters typically reserved for the president-elect. Neil recognized that it was a meaningful gesture in recognition for the deep but unspoken affection that the two brothers had for each other.

RONALD REAGAN, in his first campaign for governor, aided by the advice of his brother and McCann-Erickson, soundly trounced Edmund "Pat" Brown, the two-term incumbent, on November 8, 1966, winning by a million-vote margin. Five months after being sworn into office, Reagan declared May 24, 1967, to be Charles M. Schulz Day and he personally presented Schulz with a proclamation that in part teasingly stated, "Happiness is having Charles Schulz as a California resident—all those bucks rolling in."[2] In 1969 Reagan honored Schulz again with the state's Creative Citizenship Award. The two men would begin a correspondence that would continue into Reagan's presidency. At one point, Schulz was considering ending his perennial drama involving Lucy pulling the football away

---

*   Blair House is the president's official guesthouse and is located diagonally across from the White House. It typically houses visiting chiefs of states and heads of government. It is actually four connected 19th century townhomes with more than 120 rooms. It was inside Blair House on April 18, 1861, that Francis Blair, at the direction of President Lincoln, offered Colonel Robert E. Lee command of the Union Army. See *Blair House: The President's Guest House* by William Seale (White House Historical Association).

from Charlie Brown. It had become the longest running annual gag in comic strip history (appearing in *Peanuts* every year from 1951 until 1999, with only a handful of exceptions). The cartoonist himself had grown somewhat weary of finding a new comical twist to the narrative every year and had considered ending it. Upon learning that the setup was a favorite of Reagan's, however, Schulz continued the gag for the remainder of his life.* Once elected president, Ronald and Nancy Reagan always celebrated Christmas in Washington, DC, so their Secret Service protection detail could spend the holiday with their families.[3] When Reagan was shot in 1981, Schulz extended get-well wishes from Snoopy. Reagan drew his own cartoon in reply, one of a cowboy, which Schulz hung on his office wall. Almost six years after leaving the presidency, on November 5, 1994, in a touching letter addressed to "My Fellow Americans," Reagan disclosed that he had been diagnosed with Alzheimer's disease. He died at his home in Los Angeles on June 5, 2004.

MARION HARPER JR., the brilliant adman who became president of McCann-Erickson at thirty-two and went on to revolutionize the advertising industry, would be fired by the board of directors of the company that he had built into the world's largest ad agency. On November 9, 1967, six of Harper's hand-picked directors voted to remove him from his position as CEO after the company was threatened by its bankers, who notified the company that it was in default on its debt covenants. Harper's manic buying spree had finally run out of cash. The ad agency had to turn to some of its biggest clients to advance billings to keep the company liquid and be able to pay its employees. Paul Austin agreed that Coca-Cola would lend its support to save the advertising firm.[4] Harper attempted to resuscitate his career in 1970 when he formed a new agency with two

---

* Charles M. Schulz, *My Life with Charlie Brown* (University Press of Mississippi, 2010), 153.

other partners. His return to advertising was short-lived, however, and he resigned from the agency six months after its formation.[5] He spent the rest of his life in Oklahoma, in isolation from his prior life on Madison Avenue, and refusing calls from reporters. Harper died on October 25, 1989, of a heart attack at his home in Oklahoma City. He was seventy-three years old, the same age as his father when he had passed away.[6]

NEAL GILLIATT, the McCann executive who was best friends with J. Paul Austin and helped land the Coca-Cola account at the ad agency because of his relationship with an Indiana bottler, would spend thirty-seven years with McCann-Erickson and its parent company, Interpublic. He wrote articles promoting the idea of a chief marketing officer sitting in executive offices alongside the chief executive officer, chief operating officer, and chief financial officer. He also served on the Grace Commission, formally known as the President's Private Sector Survey on Cost Control. He died on September 23, 2000, at the age of eighty-two after suffering a stroke on a business trip. He was survived by his wife of fifty-seven years, Mary; a son, David; and two granddaughters.[7]

FRANK STANTON, the president of CBS, became good friends with Charles Schulz following the broadcast of the Charlie Brown Christmas special. Whenever the cartoonist learned that a *Peanuts* comic strip struck Stanton as particularly funny, Schulz would retrieve the original artwork from the syndicate, personalize it with a note, autograph it, and send it to his friend. Despite the promises of William Paley to promote Stanton to the position of CEO in 1966, when Paley turned sixty-five, the CBS chairman denied Stanton the job. Stanton continued as president of the broadcasting company until 1971, when he left his executive post, serving as vice chairman for two years until his retirement in 1973. Before stepping down as president, Stanton faced his biggest confrontation with the government in 1971 after CBS broadcast a documentary titled *The Selling of the Pentagon*. When the House Commerce Committee subpoenaed CBS's outtakes and scripts from the program, Stanton refused the request and the committee threatened him with jail. The confrontation prompted Schulz to send a note of support to his friend, writing, "Please don't worry about congress. They are no match for you." Stanton died asleep at his home in Boston on December 24, 2006, at the age of ninety-eight.

RICHARD BURGHEIM, the *Time* critic whose review of *A Charlie Brown Christmas* perhaps saved the show from being canceled, would continue as an entertainment critic for the magazine. He later became one of the founding editors of the highly successful *People* magazine. His next venture, *TV-Cable Week*, would not be nearly as successful. Undertaken to compete with the popular *TV Guide*, the new Time, Inc. offering was perhaps the most complex publishing undertaking ever. *TV-Cable Week* listed all programming, broadcast and cable, by channel, by market in the United States. After spending $47 million on the venture, the management at Time's executive offices shut the new publication down after only four months. As Burgheim, always a man of devastating humor, had trenchantly noted at the magazine's launch party, "To paraphrase what Winston Churchill once said under somewhat different circumstances, when it comes to *TV-Cable Week* and Time, Inc.'s shareholders, never will so many have owed so much to so few."[8] He lives in New York City.

PETER ROBBINS, the actor who first put a voice to Charles Schulz's character Charlie Brown, went on to reprise his role in *It's the Great Pumpkin, Charlie Brown* and in the animated movie *A Boy Named Charlie Brown*. Robbins retired from acting before attending college and worked as a real estate agent in San Diego. He struggled with mental health issues and drug addiction and was diagnosed with bipolar disorder. In 2015 he was sentenced to five years in prison for making threats to the manager of a mobile home park and to a San Diego sheriff. When he was released from prison he remarked, "Charlie Brown fans are the greatest fans in the world and everybody is willing, I hope, to give me a second chance." He died by suicide in Oceanside, California, on January 18, 2022, at the age of sixty-five.[9]

CHRISTOPHER SHEA, who voiced Linus in *A Charlie Brown Christmas*, would go on to reprise the role in four more *Peanuts* television specials. He also appeared in other television series during the 1960s and 1970s. On August 19, 2010, he died of natural causes at the age of fifty-two in Honeydew, Humboldt County, California. He was survived by his wife and two daughters.

DONNA JOHNSON WOLD, the red-haired woman who had broken Charles Schulz's heart, would remain happily married to Al Wold for the rest of her life. She would always keep the small white cat toy that Schulz had given her to return to him to accept his offer of marriage. She became a mother to four children and a foster mother to scores more. Her spouse was promoted to district fire chief and by all accounts was a devoted husband. Donna read the *Peanuts* comic strip daily, and when the little red-haired girl first appeared in its panels she instantly recognized the inside jokes or experiences she and the cartoonist had shared. She carefully cut out and saved the romantic correspondence disguised as cartoons, reveling in the coded messages that only she and one other person would truly understand. On a trip through California with her husband, she stopped by the ice arena in Santa Rosa that Schulz and his wife had constructed, which the cartoonist was known to frequent. While her husband patiently waited in the car outside, Donna went inside the arena in hopes of seeing her suitor from so many years ago, but he wasn't there. Donna Wold never had any regrets about her life, though. "I think I'm the luckiest person in the world," she said.

"I've had a good life. A very happy life." She died on August 9, 2016, of heart failure and complications from diabetes.

VINCE GUARALDI sued Fantasy Records, his recording label, in 1966 and was released from his contract. He then signed a three-record deal with Warner Bros.–Seven Arts in 1968. His inaugural album was a compilation of popular *Peanuts* compositions and became a hit. The next two albums were not well received, however, either by consumers or by critics, who described Guaraldi's compositions as overindulgent and unfocused. The record label chose not to retain the artist at the end of their deal. Guaraldi declined lucrative offers to perform all over the country and, instead of cashing in on his *Peanuts* fame, chose to perform exclusively at San Francisco–area jazz clubs. On the evening of February 6, 1976, after recording the soundtrack for another *Peanuts* special, *It's Arbor Day, Charlie Brown*, Guaraldi performed at Butterfield's Nightclub in Menlo Park. After finishing his first set, his interpretation of the Beatles' "Eleanor Rigby," Guaraldi collapsed and died of a massive heart attack. He was only forty-seven years old.

CHARLES M. "SPARKY" SCHULZ's comic strip characters went on to leave an indelible mark on global popular culture. The cartoonist continued to gently tackle relevant social topics, including race relations, with his quirky, anxiety-ridden characters. In 1968, three months after the assassination of Martin Luther King Jr., Schulz introduced a new *Peanuts* character, a young African American boy named Franklin. In 1969 the Apollo 10 command module was named *Charlie Brown* and the lunar module was named *Snoopy*. In 1997 someone asked Schulz what award he was most proud of, and it suddenly occurred to the cartoonist that what he was proudest of was not the unprecedented two Reuben awards for cartooning, or the Emmy or Peabody awards, or the countless other honors bestowed upon him as the creator of *Peanuts*. To the US Army veteran, the greatest honor he had received was the combat infantryman's badge he had earned, some fifty-three years earlier, as a young staff sergeant during World War II. The military decoration was displayed in a frame on a wall in the cartoonist's studio.[10] Schulz and his first wife, Joyce, divorced in 1971, and the following year he married Jean Forsyth Clyde, whom he met at his hockey rink. The pair remained together for the rest of the cartoonist's life. Schulz died of colon cancer in 2000 at the age of seventy-seven, just hours before his last cartoon ran in the Sunday newspapers. His grave marker notes his dates of birth and passing, his service in the US Army during World War II, and his rank of staff sergeant. It makes no mention of his role as the creator of the most popular comic strip in history.

BILL MELENDEZ, the former Disney animator, was the only person Charles Schulz ever entrusted with animating his comic strip characters. Melendez and his studio worked on every single *Peanuts* television special, with Melendez directing most of them. Late in his life, when asked if he had any regrets, Melendez only expressed one: that he had never expressed his appreciation to Walt Disney for the training and classes that he had received at his studio. He died at the age of ninety-one in 2008, but his recorded voice would live on as the voice of Snoopy in movies released after the animator's death.

LEE MENDELSON, the unproven producer who in 1963 had boldly reached out to Charles Schulz with an idea about making a *Peanuts* documentary, would go on to produce over a hundred film and television productions. To this day his unsold documentary on Charles Schulz has never been broadcast. Mendelson won twelve Emmys and four Peabodys. He was the last of the four principals behind the making of *A Charlie Brown Christmas* to pass away. Mendelson died in 2019 at the age of eighty-six—on Christmas Day.

AUTHOR'S NOTE
ON EARTH PEACE

◆

Later in his life, Charles Schulz would become more comfortable openly discussing his battle with depression, but in 1965, the year of the making of *A Charlie Brown Christmas*, the stigma was perhaps too great, and maybe Schulz was struggling too much to be able to properly address the issue. Yet some of the symptoms he exhibited were truly frightening. Without specifying the period of his life involved, in a book published in 1975 Schulz stated: "A couple of years ago, some events in my life saddened me to such a degree that I could no longer listen to the car radio. I did not want to risk becoming depressed while riding alone in the car, and I found that almost everything I listened to on the car radio would send me into a deep depression."[1] He added: "I went through one strange phase in my life when I became quite disturbed by dreams, which occurred to me irregularly over a period of several weeks. I would find in my dreams that I was crying uncontrollably, and when I awakened, I was extremely depressed."[2] He confessed to a biographer that "When I'm in a hotel room alone, I worry about getting so depressed I might jump out of a window."[3]

Schulz's first wife, Joyce, became increasingly exasperated by her husband's melancholy and anxiety. She had done her best to create a wonderful home environment at Coffee Grounds, but she could not comprehend how her very successful husband, who had achieved such incredible success and financial security, could be depressed. Joyce encouraged her husband to see a psychiatrist, but he refused, explaining that he was afraid that if he were somehow cured of his condition, his talent for cartooning might also somehow evaporate. Later in life the cartoonist wrote: "Generally speaking, it seems more good cartoon ideas have come out of a mood of sadness than a feeling of well-being."[4]

"I don't understand why you're depressed. I'd be ecstatic," his wife told him. "My mother and the war" was her husband's terse reply, his words as sparse as they were truthful. As Schulz would later write, "I place the source of many of my problems on those three years in the army. The lack of any timetable or any idea as to when any of us would get out was almost unbearable...we were completely convinced that we were going to be in for the rest of our lives. The war seemed to have no end in sight."[5]

Why, though, had Schulz's always present anxiety suddenly worsened in 1965? My personal theory is that Schulz's response to his wife was an insightful self-diagnosis of the ultimate source of his issues. I believe that it is most likely that Schulz suffered from undiagnosed post-traumatic stress disorder from his World War II combat experience, compounded by the traumatic loss of his mother as he departed for basic training at Camp Campbell. PTSD was a little understood condition at the time. The likely reason that it suddenly worsened into physical manifestations and panic attacks the same year as he undertook the making of the Christmas special was most probably the escalating war in Vietnam.

Televised images of the war, including combat footage of violent encounters between American troops and their Vietcong and North Vietnamese adversaries, were being broadcast into American living rooms in 1965. For example, on August 5, 1965, CBS News broadcast footage of US Marines in Vietnam using flamethrowers and Zippo lighters to burn down a village of thatched huts while villagers fled. The news report shocked the American public. If Schulz had seen these images, as is likely, it had to trigger his vivid memory of when his own US Army unit had burned down a German village from which it had received gunfire. Years later Schulz could recall the image of a "hysterical woman standing in her front yard while her house was on fire and all the cows were walking around."[6] While working in his studio, Schulz's concentration would sometimes be broken by the overhead roar of fighter jets from nearby Hamilton Air Force Base that were training in the skies above his Sebastopol home.

To support my theory I examined all of the *Peanuts* comic strips for 1965, fairly certain that if Schulz were feeling war-related anxiety, consciously or even subconsciously, the cartoonist would almost certainly work it out in the one area of his life where he felt most in control. Schulz's safe space was his work studio, and he worked through many, if not all, of his issues within the small confines of the panels of his cartoons. As Gary Groth noted, *Peanuts* was "a comic strip about the interior crises of the cartoonist himself."[7] Schulz himself wrote, "When everything seems hopeless and all of that, I know I can come to the studio and think: Here's where I'm at home. This is where I belong—in this room, drawing pictures."[8] I was not surprised to discover that the cartoonist introduced two new and notable storylines that related to war and military service during the same turbulent year American soldiers went off to war in Vietnam.

The first storyline was a recurring series revolving around camping, and it first appeared in a cartoon on June 5, 1965.[9] In the concluding panel of that day's strip, Charlie Brown is riding the bus and looks out the window with anxious despair and says, "I feel like I'm being drafted." The central recurring theme of the camping comics is loneliness, and in those cartoons the characters mimic the terrible loneliness Schulz felt both as a boy in summer camp and as a young soldier at Camp Campbell, Kentucky. As Schulz himself wrote, "All of the summer-camp ideas that I have drawn are a result of my having absolutely no desire as a child to be sent away to summer camp. To me, that was the equivalent of being drafted. When World War II came along, I met it with the same lack of enthusiasm."[10] Notably, when Charlie Brown does eventually make a friend at camp, that boy's name is Roy, the same name as the soldier (Elmer Roy Hagemeyer) who befriended Schulz at boot camp. Since Schulz was typically inking his comic strip eleven weeks before its publication date, that meant Schulz would have drafted these cartoons around late March or early April of that year, the same time that a panic attack prevented him from flying to New York to attend the Reuben Award dinner. Notably the aerial bombardment of North Vietnam, known as Operation Rolling Thunder, commenced on March 2, 1965.

In the summer of 1965, Schulz also created another variation on a character that he would send off to war in his comic strip. Snoopy, Schulz's most surrealistic creation, was already challenging Charlie Brown for primacy as the strip's most popular character when Schulz saw his thirteen-year-old son Monte playing with a plastic model airplane he had constructed, a Fokker triplane.* Schulz's creative

---

* Monte always insisted that he had first suggested Snoopy as the World War I pilot. Schulz, who was always jealous about the originality of his creations, and loath to use the many suggestions offered to him for storylines by friends and strangers, frequently denied his son's claims. Near the end of his life, however, the cartoonist did allow that Monte had "inspired it" (Charles Schulz, *My Life with Charlie Brown* [University Press of Mississippi, 2010], 155).

impulses took flight, so to speak. He recalled two World War I movies from his childhood, Howard Hughes's epic film *Hell's Angels*, and
Howard Hawks's *The Dawn Patrol*. It occurred to Schulz to adorn
Snoopy with a silk scarf, leather pilot's cap, and goggles and place
him on top of his doghouse, where he could become a flying ace
engaged in aerial combat with none other than the Red Baron.

What better way for a combat veteran foot soldier from World
War II to process his wartime trauma than to romanticize it—first,
by placing it in an earlier war and thereby giving it an emotional
distance, and, second, by taking it from the ground to the air and
thereby removing it from the harsh infantry perspective that Schulz
had experienced (the air war is always romantic to grunts) and making it surreal, heroic, and comedic at the same time—in short, war
stripped of all its ugly harsh realities.

Notably, Snoopy, the World War I ace, when he is on the ground,
traverses some of the same French sites that US Army Staff Sergeant
Charles Schulz had two decades earlier, including the Chateau du
Mal Voisin (the Castle of the Bad Neighbor), where the greatest
danger our dashing flyboy beagle encounters is the possibility of a
broken heart as he pursues romance with French mademoiselles.*
The following year, Schulz introduced another military persona
for Snoopy, this time as a member of the French Foreign Legion.[11]
Clearly the topic of war was on the cartoonist's mind.

As the Vietnam War escalated, Schulz temporarily dropped
Snoopy as the Flying Ace. He felt that the association with war made

---

* In 1976 Schulz named the vicious cat that lives next door to Snoopy World
War Two. The cat, like its battles with the bulbous-nosed beagle, would not
visually appear in the strip, but their "off-screen" scrapes would produce
visible results like a scratched-up Snoopy and a destroyed doghouse. The
cat's owner described her as a "kitten." Snoopy would estimate that the feline
weighed up to two hundred pounds.

it inappropriate at the time.* "Well, because everybody was suddenly realizing that this was such a monstrous war. It just didn't seem funny. So, I just stopped doing it. Then going into bookstores and seeing the revival of war books, mostly World War II, Korea, World War I books, I thought, 'It's coming back again,' so I started doing some more. But I didn't do him fighting the Red Baron. Mostly it was just sitting in the French café flirting with the waitress."[12]

Schulz suffered from essentially every symptom listed for post-traumatic stress disorder found in the *Diagnostic and Statistical Manual of Mental Disorders* (better known as the *DSM*)—he had experienced a life-threatening event, had recurring nightmares, avoided leaving home, was easily startled, suffered from depression, felt panicked, and had strong feelings of guilt and shame. Although he would become open to discussing his battle with depression publicly, he would never seek proper psychiatric care, afraid that being cured would deprive him of the emotional pain that fueled his creativity.

The conscientious cartoonist almost never declined an interview request, however, and perhaps Schulz felt the probing questions of the reporter allowed him to unburden himself and discuss his life and his fears in the safe cocoon of his studio, kind of a journalistic therapy. Yet despite battling depression and anxiety, Schulz remained incredibly productive, for decades faithfully tackling his duties to

---

* Like many Americans, Schulz eventually turned against the Vietnam War. A Republican who had voted for Lyndon Johnson for president in 1964, Schulz came to regret his vote because of Johnson's Vietnam policies. After Democratic senator Robert F. Kennedy, running for his party's nomination for the presidency as an antiwar candidate, was assassinated in 1968, Schulz made ten drawings of *Peanuts* characters, one for each of Kennedy's children, and sent them to his widow. A month later Ethel Kennedy expressed her thanks to Schulz: "It is very cozy to have Snoopy and his pals on our walls, mixed up with photographs of the family, which we think of them as anyway."

produce his daily cartoon strip, and he never lost his creativity and his sense of humor.

When commentators focus on the religious message delivered by Linus in the climactic scene of *A Charlie Brown Christmas*, they focus exclusively on the heralding the birth of Jesus. If that were the only message that Schulz wished to convey, however, then he could have concluded the biblical recitation with the first four verses. In my opinion, the powerful message contained in the last verse is overlooked—"Glory to God in the highest, and on earth peace, good will toward men"—the message of peace on earth is also one that would have powerfully resonated with the emotionally scarred combat veteran of World War II, especially in the context of the escalating conflict in Vietnam.

APPENDIX
A Charlie Brown Christmas Credits[*]

Written by:

Charles M. Schulz

Directed by:

Bill Melendez

Executive Producer:

Lee Mendelson

Original score composed & conducted by:

Vince Guaraldi

Graphic Blandishment by:

Ed Levitt · Bernard Gruver · Ruth Kissane · Dean Spille ·
Beverly Robbins · Eleanor Warren · Frank Smith ·
Bob Carlson · Rudy Zamora · Bill Littlejohn ·
Alan Zaslove · Ruben Timmins[**] · Herman Cohen ·
Manuel Perez · Russ Von Neida · John Walker

---

[*] This is the original credit version. The current credit version lists these
voice talents: *Charlie Brown*—Peter Robbins, *Linus*—Christopher Shea,
Lucy—Tracy Stratford.

[**] Reuben Timmins's first name was apparently misspelled as "Ruben
Timmins" in the 1965 special and has never been corrected.

Editing:

Robert T. Gillis

Sound:

Producers' Sound Service

A Lee Mendelson-Bill Melendez Production

In co-operation with United Feature Syndicate Inc.

MERRY CHRISTMAS from the people who bottle...
Coca-Cola

ACKNOWLEDGMENTS

✦

MARC ROSS, founder of Caracal, a geopolitical business communications firm based in Washington, DC, was always available to read drafts and provide valuable insights and thoughts. Marc is an insightful thinker on business and global affairs, an occasional coauthor of mine, and also a good friend.

DUNCAN BOOTHBY, who taught me that nothing ruins a good war story like an eyewitness, was always available to share his thoughts on the book's narrative, no matter what time zone he might be in on the planet.

RICK GIBSON, senior vice chancellor of Pepperdine University, provided the initial encouragement that I needed when I discussed the book concept with him at the California Club. Unbeknownst to me at the time, but perhaps in a fitting coincidence, was the fact that Rick himself is a gifted cartoonist.

PETE PETERSON, dean of the Public Policy School of Pepperdine University, provided helpful validation of the book's concept, as well as its cover, and he had some excellent thoughts on the book's organization. Pete is a gifted leader and a good friend.

Former Secretary of Defense WILLIAM J. PERRY, who selected me for the National Security Education Program, deserves credit for launching me on the unpredictable path for this book, as do former US senator and governor of Oklahoma DAVID BOREN and retired admiral BOBBY RAY INMAN, my former professor at the University of Texas School of Law. I would also like to thank Generals DAVID PETRAEUS, STANLEY MCCHRYSTAL, and MICHAEL LINNINGTON and the troops of the US Army's 101st Airborne Division with whom I had the honor to spend time with in Iraq.

DOUGLAS BRINKLEY, presidential historian and professor, was a wonderful writing mentor to me during my time at the Norman Mailer Writers Colony, as was CHARLES B. STROZIER, noted Lincoln expert and psychotherapist.

NOEMIE GRAU helped immeasurably with all the various details of the book, but especially with reviewing and proofreading the first drafts and always providing encouragement and support.

TOM TRIGGS and BRIAN SULLIVAN provided the wonderful counsel of two incredibly capable attorneys whom I also consider among my closest friends. They were always available, despite the busy demands of their legal practice, to provide sound legal as well as general business advice. Their colleague and UCLA lecturer JEFF MODISETT was also a valuable sounding board for the book's concept. *Tu bonus amicus.*

All of my former colleagues at DIGITAL DOMAIN helped to shape my understanding of both the magic and technical details of filmmaking: JOHN TEXTOR, who overlooked my occasional mysterious absences; CLIFF PLUMER; ED LUNSFORD; JOE GABRIEL; CHARLES YU, a truly gifted writer; ED ULBRICH, who has always been available to discuss a story idea; and RUSS GLASGOW, who has graciously helped with a number of my projects.

MATT LATIMER, founder of Javelin, and DYLAN COLLIGAN, editorial director at Javelin, immediately responded to my inquiry regarding my thoughts for a book about the making of the Charlie Brown Christmas special, and they provided much more support than a typical agent in supporting the project. I'm lucky to have them representing me.

ALEX PAPPAS, editorial director of CENTER STREET, was incredibly supportive of the book and helped immeasurably in guiding its development, and I will always appreciate his encouraging words throughout the writing process. ABIGAIL SKINNER enthusiastically took on the thankless task of reviewing the first rough draft of the manuscript and provided invaluable comments and provided the encouragement I needed to undertake the book's preface. LORI PAXIMADIS provided a very detailed copy edit of the manuscript. CAROLYN LEVIN undertook a professional legal review of the book's contents.

SARAH BREAUX, archivist at the incredible Charles M. Schulz Museum and Research Center, was helpful for locating personal photos of Charles Schulz used in the book as well as confirming a number of details of the cartoonist's life and career.

ANDRE CHAMPAGNE's encouragement, positive energy, and experience with creative endeavors was both an inspiration and an invaluable resource.

KATHY SHOEMAKER, reference coordinator at the Stuart A. Rose Manuscript, Archives, and Rare Book Library, Robert Woodruff Library at Emory University, was helpful in directing me to the Coca-Cola archives located there as well as in navigating its contents.

DR. EDUARDO TINOCO, business librarian at USC Libraries and a wonderful friend, never failed to astonish me by being able to find any article, frequently late at night and on weekends. One would expect nothing less from a former US Army Ranger turned research librarian. Truly, *Rangers Lead the Way!*

Acknowledgments

JENNIFER NEWBY-SKAGGS, archivist at the Ronald Reagan Presidential Library & Museum, assisted with research on President Reagan's correspondence with his brother, Neil.

JOANNE DRAKE, chief administrative officer of the Ronald Reagan Presidential Foundation and Institute, was helpful in navigating information related to the lives of President Reagan and his brother, Neil.

ZOË COBLIN was incredibly helpful as a research assistant performing archival research at Emory University's library, where she helped to locate and review documents related to J. Paul Austin, the president of Coca-Cola, as well as doing the important work of transcribing interviews of key figures. She has a promising career ahead of her in her future endeavors.

DAVID WILLAT and CARY CEDARBLADE were both wonderful in sharing their recollections as members of the children's choir for the Charlie Brown Christmas special.

DERRICK BANG deserves credit for his notable biography on Vince Guaraldi, *Vince Guaraldi at the Piano*, as well as for his religious devotion to footnotes.

LUKE BOGGS, a former speechwriter for Coca-Cola, was helpful with introductions to archivists at the soft drink company.

JULIANA ARRIETTY was helpful in cheerfully discussing matters of concept and style.

JAMES SEGELSTEIN was kind enough to share recollections of his father, CBS executive Irwin Segelstein.

J. PAUL AUSTIN III was helpful in providing further understanding of his grandfather J. Paul Austin, the president of Coca-Cola.

BRUCE STOCKLER, editorial director of McCann Worldgroup, was helpful in locating archival newsletters from the 1960s discussing the making of the special.

Acknowledgments

MEREDITH SELF, assistant archivist at the New York Philharmonic, was very helpful in identifying archival material related to the philharmonic, including relevant material for Neal Gilliatt, the McCann executive who served on its board.

KELLY LOGAN of Original Joe's restaurant was able to confirm details about the restaurant's dates of operation and opening. The San Francisco eatery was a favorite of the founders of Fantasy Records and played a role in key turning points of our story.

SUSAN HORMUTH proved incredibly knowledgeable in navigating the Library of Congress, where Frank Stanton's papers are located.

NOTES

The Producer

1. "How Baseball Legends Mays and McCovey Helped Spark the Beloved 'Peanuts' Holiday Specials," *Washington Post*, November 3, 2018.
2. "Life After Snoopy," *Stanford Magazine*, November/December 1997.
3. "How Baseball Legends Mays and McCovey Helped Spark the Beloved 'Peanuts' Holiday Specials."
4. "A Charlie Brown Christmas Interview with Producer Lee Mendelson," *TV Time Machine*, n.d., https://soundcloud.com/user-12836139/a -charlie-brown-christmas-interview-with-producer-lee-mendelson.
5. Charles M. Schulz, *My Life with Charlie Brown* (University Press of Mississippi, 2010), 121.

The Sponsor

1. Descriptions of Coca-Cola office holiday decorations from this period come from the company's in-house publication, *The Refresher*: "It's Christmas at Our Home," November–December 1964, 12–15.
2. Frederick Allen, *Secret Formula: The Inside Story of How Coca-Cola Became the Best-Known Brand in the World* (HarperCollins, 1994), 313.
3. "The Night Atlanta Truly Became Too Busy to Hate," Coca-Cola website, January 4, 2016, https://www.coca-colacompany.com/news /martin-luther-king-nobel-peace-prize.
4. "Tribute to Doctor King Disputed in Atlanta," *New York Times*, December 29, 1964.
5. Frederick Allen, *Atlanta Rising: The Invention of an International City, 1946–1996* (Taylor Trade Publishing, 1996), 141.
6. Allen, *Atlanta Rising*, 143.
7. "Statement by Ivan Allen, Jr., Mayor of Atlanta, Ga., before Committee of Commerce regarding S. 1732, Bill to Eliminate Discrimination in

Public Accommodations Affecting Interstate Commerce," July 26, 1963, https://ivanallen.iac.gatech.edu/mayoral-records/traditional/files/show /7504.

8. Andrew Young, in his book *An Easy Burden*, maintains that the meeting was held at the Commerce Club's eighteenth-floor dining room and it was attended by J. Paul Austin and Mayor Allen. Coca-Cola's website says the meeting was at the Piedmont Driving Club. It is possible that there was more than one meeting with business leaders.

9. "The Night Atlanta Truly Became Too Busy to Hate."

10. "Tribute to Doctor King Disputed in Atlanta," *New York Times*, December 29, 1964.

11. The opening of the hotel can be found on the website of writer-photographer Pete Candler ("Next Door Is Closer Than You Remember," A Deeper South, May 28, 2019, https://www.adeepersouth .com/stories/2019/5/28/nextdoor), and the description of the hotel is from an advertisement for the hotel found in the *Atlanta Constitution* in June 1913.

12. "Next Door Is Closer Than You Remember."

13. Description of the hotel paintings is found on a hotel postcard, which can be retrieved at http://www.atlantatimemachine.com/downtown /ansley_02.htm.

14. "How Martin Luther King Jr.'s 1964 Nobel Peace Prize Challenged Atlanta's Tolerance," *Atlanta Journal-Constitution*, January 4, 2017, https://www.ajc.com/news/king-nobel-challenged-atlanta-tolerance /bExE4m07T4KCuOD88E3diK.

15. See Nobel Prize website for Ralph Bunche: https://www.nobelprize.org /prizes/peace/1950/bunche/biographical.

16. Brian Urquhart, *Ralph Bunche: An American Life* (W. W. Norton, 1993), 25.

17. Allen, *Secret Formula*, 310.

18. "The Time Coca-Cola Got White Elites in Atlanta to Honor Martin Luther King, Jr.," NPR, April 4, 2015, https://www.npr.org/sections /codeswitch/2015/04/04/397391510/when-corporations-take-the -lead-on-social-change.

19. Mark Pendergrast, *For God, Country, and Coca-Cola* (Basic Books, 1993), 260.

20. Pendergrast, *For God, Country, and Coca-Cola*, 268.
21. Allen, *Secret Formula*, 314.
22. Allen, *Secret Formula*, 233–34.
23. Allen, *Secret Formula*, 320–21.
24. "Andy Warhol, *Green Coca-Cola Bottles*," Whitney Museum of American Art, n.d., https://whitney.org/collection/works/3253; "What's the Story behind Andy Warhol's Coca-Cola Bottle Painting?" Coco-Cola Australia website, n.d., https://www.coca-colacompany.com/au/faqs/whats-the-history-behind-andy-warhols-coca-cola-bottle-painting.
25. Allen, *Secret Formula*, 314, 321.
26. Allen, *Secret Formula*, 313–14.

The Agency

1. "Coca-Cola to Quit D'Arcy Ad Agency," *New York Times*, October 14, 1955.
2. "Did Coca-Cola Invent Santa Claus?" Coca-Cola website, n.d., https://www.coca-colacompany.com/faqs/did-coca-cola-invent-santa.
3. Russ Johnston, *Marion Harper: An Unauthorized Biography* (Crain Books, 1982), 118–19.
4. Frederick Allen, *Secret Formula: The Inside Story of How Coca-Cola Became the Best-Known Brand in the World* (HarperCollins, 1994), 281.
5. "The Most Important Events in the History of the Coca-Cola Company in the Years 1950 through 1959," Coca-Cola Great Britain website, n.d., https://www.coca-cola.co.uk/our-business/history/1950s.
6. "Meet Mary Alexander, the first African American Woman to Appear in Coca-Cola Advertising: A Humble Trailblazer," Coca-Cola website, n.d., https://www.coca-colacompany.com/news/mary-alexander-the-first-african-american-woman-in-coke-ads.
7. Stewart Alter, *Truth Well Told: McCann-Erickson and the Pioneering of Global Advertising* (McCann-Erickson Worldwide Publishers, 1994), 143.
8. In his unauthorized biography of Marion Harper, Russ Johnston notes that the meeting was in August. His book provides a detailed account of Marion Harper's pre-meeting rituals as well as how he conducted himself in client meetings.

9. Johnston, *Marion Harper*, 116.
10. Johnston, *Marion Harper*, 120.
11. Alter, *Truth Well Told*, 148. See also Johnston, *Marion Harper*, 120.
12. Elisabeth Spurensuche, "What Do We Really Know about Herta Herzog?" Research Gate, January 2008, https://www.researchgate.net/publication/315431223_What_Do_We_Really_Know_About_Herta_Herzog_Eine_Spurensuche.
13. Spencer Klaw, "What Is Marion Harper Saying?" *Fortune*, January 1961, 132.
14. Alter, *Truth Well Told*, 150; Johnston, *Marion Harper*, 120.
15. "Coca-Cola to Quit D'Arcy Ad Agency," *New York Times*, October 14, 1955.
16. Klaw, "What Is Marion Harper Saying?" 134.
17. Klaw, "What Is Marion Harper Saying?" 134.
18. Johnston, *Marion Harper*, 4.
19. Johnston, *Marion Harper*, 5.
20. Klaw, "What Is Marion Harper Saying?" 134.
21. Johnston, *Marion Harper*, 6.
22. Johnston, *Marion Harper*, 16–17.
23. Johnston, *Marion Harper*, 17–20.
24. Johnston, *Marion Harper*, 33.
25. Johnston, *Marion Harper*, 23.
26. Alter, *Truth Well Told*, 16.
27. Johnston, *Marion Harper*, 215.
28. Johnston, *Marion Harper*, 215.
29. Johnston, *Marion Harper*, 123.
30. Johnston, *Marion Harper*, 123.
31. Johnston, *Marion Harper*, 113–14.
32. Johnston, *Marion Harper*, 83.
33. David Halberstam, *The Best and the Brightest* (Random House, 1972), 13.
34. Klaw, "What Is Marion Harper Saying?" 138.
35. "Advertising: Conflicts and Marion Harper," *New York Times*, December 6, 1982.
36. Johnston, *Marion Harper*, 156.
37. "Advertising: Training for Decision Is Urged by Marion Harper," *New York Times*, May 18, 1960.

38. Johnston, *Marion Harper*, 146–49.
39. "Marion Harper, 73, Advertising Man," *New York Times*, November 8, 1962.
40. "Advertising: To the Top at Last," *Time*, October 18, 1963.
41. Johnston, *Marion Harper*, 212.
42. Johnston, *Marion Harper*, x.
43. "The Coup d'Etat at Interpublic," *Fortune*, February 1968, 196.
44. "Marion Harper Jr. Marries Miss Valerie Feit in Miami," *New York Times*, November 17, 1963. Also, "Milestones," *Time*, June 24, 1966. See also "The Coup d'Etat at Interpublic," 196.
45. Johnston, *Marion Harper*, 43.
46. "The Coup d'Etat at Interpublic," 203.
47. Details on Neal Gilliatt's life can be found in the following: "Neal Gilliatt Advertising Executive, 82," *New York Times*, September 23, 2000; "Neal Gilliatt," Prabook, n.d., https://prabook.com/web/neal .gilliatt/492569; "Neal Gilliatt," Indiana University website, n.d., https: //honorsandawards.iu.edu/awards/honoree/2387.html.

The Network

1. David Halberstam, *The Powers That Be* (Knopf, 1979), 253.
2. Fred W. Friendly, *Due to Circumstances beyond Our Control* (Random House, 1967).
3. Friendly, *Due to Circumstances beyond Our Control*.
4. Halberstam, *The Powers That Be*, 328.
5. Halberstam, *The Powers That Be*, 339–40.
6. Sally Bedell Smith, *In All His Glory: The Life of William S. Paley, the Legendary Tycoon and His Brilliant Circle* (Simon and Schuster, 1990), 445–46.
7. Halberstam, *The Powers That Be*, 488.
8. Lewis J. Paper, *Empire: William S. Paley and the Making of CBS* (St. Martin's Press, 1987), 237–38.
9. Smith, *In All His Glory*, 432–33.
10. "Specials: Now a $50 Million Plum," *Broadcasting*, May 24, 1965, 31.
11. David Ogilvy, *Confessions of an Advertising Man* (Atheneum, 1963), 75.
12. "Specials: Now a $50 Million Plum," 33.
13. "Specials: Now a $50 Million Plum." See also Jared Bahir Browsh, *Hanna-Barbera: A History* (McFarland and Company, 2022), 72.

The Cartoonist

1. Charles M. Schulz, *My Life with Charlie Brown* (University Press of Mississippi, 2010), xi.
2. David Michaelis, *Schulz and Peanuts: A Biography* (HarperCollins, 2007), 316.
3. Michaelis, *Schulz and Peanuts*, 328–31.
4. Schulz, *My Life with Charlie Brown*, 97.
5. Michaelis, *Schulz and Peanuts*, 44.
6. Michaelis, *Schulz and Peanuts*, 432.
7. Conrad Groth, ed., *What Cartooning Really Is: The Major Interviews with Charles M. Schulz* (Fantagraphics Books, 2020), 106.
8. Michaelis, *Schulz and Peanuts*, 82–83.
9. Michaelis, *Schulz and Peanuts*, 148–49.
10. Groth, ed., *What Cartooning Really Is*, 106–7.
11. Michaelis, *Schulz and Peanuts*, 190.
12. "I was 23 at the time we began to write these letters, and he saved three or four of them. And Jeannie [Schulz's second wife] and I were both so impressed at the amount of ambition that I had showed up in those letters." Groth, ed., *What Cartooning Really Is*, 211.
13. Schulz, *My Life with Charlie Brown*, 17.
14. Michaelis, *Schulz and Peanuts*, 174–76.
15. Beverly Gherman, *Sparky: The Life and Art of Charles Schulz* (Chronicle Books, 2010), 58–59.
16. Johnson, *Good Grief: The Story of Charles M. Schulz*, 86.
17. "Comics: Good Grief," *Time*, April 9, 1965.
18. Charles M. Schulz, "I'll Be Back in Time for Lunch," *Los Angeles Times*, March 17, 1985.
19. Michaelis, *Schulz and Peanuts*, 482.
20. Michaelis, *Schulz and Peanuts*, 433–4.
21. Charles Schulz's commencement address at Saint Mary's College, delivered June 11, 1966. The cartoon was published on August 15, 1965, and can be found in Charles M. Schulz, *The Complete Peanuts: 1965 to 1966* (Fantagraphics, 2007), 98. While the strip appeared after Mendelson had finally received his call from McCann, Schulz would have come up with the idea for the prank at the same time that the producer was nervously awaiting the call. Schulz was required by his

contract with the syndicate to deliver his Sunday comics eleven weeks prior to their publication.

22. Lee Mendelson, *A Charlie Brown Christmas: The Making of a Tradition* (HarperCollins, 2000), 17–19.

The Director

1. "Lee Mendelson, Producer," interview by Karen Herman, June 11, 2003, Television Academy Foundation website, https://interviews .televisionacademy.com/interviews/lee-mendelson.
2. Mel Blanc and Philip Bashe, *That's Not All Folks* (Warner Books, 1988), 267.
3. Charles Solomon, *The Art and Making of Peanuts Animation: Celebrating Fifty Years of Television Specials* (Chronicle Books, 2012), 13.
4. David Michaelis, *Schulz and Peanuts: A Biography* (HarperCollins, 2007), 349.
5. Solomon, *The Art and Making of Peanuts Animation*, 11.
6. Stephen J. Lind, *A Charlie Brown Religion: Exploring the Spiritual Life and Work of Charles M. Schulz* (University Press of Mississippi, 2015), 66.
7. Neal Gabler, *Walt Disney: The Biography* (Aurum Press Ltd., 2007), 235–36.
8. George Drake letter to Michael Arens, November 4, 1937.
9. Blanc and Bashe, *That's Not All Folks*, 57.
10. Don Peri, *Working with Walt: Interviews with Disney Artists* (University Press of Mississippi, 2008), 8–9.
11. Blanc and Bashe, *That's Not All Folks*, 59.
12. Blanc and Bashe, *That's Not All Folks*, 58.
13. Blanc and Bashe, *That's Not All Folks*, 93.
14. Blanc and Bashe, *That's Not All Folks*, 60.
15. Blanc and Bashe, *That's Not All Folks*, 69, 131–32.
16. Blanc and Bashe, *That's Not All Folks*, 221.

The Adman

1. Jim Hilliker provides a very detailed history of KFWB in his online article "Celebrating KFWB's 90th Anniversary: Lost Radio History from the Warner Brothers Years 1925–1950," https://jeff560.tripod .com/kfwb.html. The site also contains links to recordings of Neil

Reagan, the arrival of movie stars for the Academy Awards on March 2, 1944, as well as a recording of a radio play starring Ronald Reagan from 1938.

2. Interview of Neil Reagan, June 25, 1981, UCLA Library, Center for Oral History. Betty Furness's Wikipedia page claims that the actress involved in this incident was not her but June Graham, who was substituting for her. It states that Furness made this claim more than two decades after the incident, on a 1981 TV special called *TV's Censored Bloopers*, but I could not find this show. Some sources claim that the reason the door would not open was because Westinghouse had switched the refrigerator on the set to a new "power door" model. On this new model, the door would not open if it was not plugged in unless someone knew a certain "trick." Apparently the stagehands had not plugged in the power refrigerator, and when Furness (or Graham) went to open the door, it wouldn't budge.

3. Interview of Neil Reagan.

4. Interview of Neil Reagan.

5. Anne Edwards, *Early Reagan: The Rise to Power* (Taylor Trade, 1987), 33.

6. Edwards, *Early Reagan*, 33–34.

7. Edwards, *Early Reagan*, 35. See also Interview of Neil Reagan.

8. Ronald Reagan, *Where's the Rest of Me? The Ronald Reagan Story* (Duell, Sloan and Pearce, 1965), 14.

9. Reagan, *Where's the Rest of Me?*, 7.

10. Edwards, *Early Reagan*, 25.

11. Reagan, *Where's the Rest of Me?*, 8.

12. Reagan, *Where's the Rest of Me?*, 8–9.

13. Reagan, *Where's the Rest of Me?*, 8–9.

14. Edwards, *Early Reagan*, 40.

15. Edwards, *Early Reagan*, 37.

16. Edwards, *Early Reagan*, 50.

17. Edwards, *Early Reagan*, 54.

18. Interview of Neil Reagan.

19. Edwards, *Early Reagan*, 58.

20. Edwards, *Early Reagan*, 105.

21. Edwards, *Early Reagan*, 67; Interview of Neil Reagan.

22. Edwards, *Early Reagan*, 68, 104.
23. Edwards, *Early Reagan*, 68.
24. Interview of Neil Reagan; Edwards, *Early Reagan*, 68.
25. Reagan, *Where's the Rest of Me?*, 31.
26. Interview of Neil Reagan.
27. Interview of Neil Reagan.
28. Interview of Neil Reagan.
29. Interview of Neil Reagan.
30. Edwards, *Early Reagan*, 143–44.
31. Interview of Neil Reagan.
32. Edwards, *Early Reagan*, 478.
33. Interview of Neil Reagan.
34. Ronald Reagan, *Reagan: A Life in Letters* (Free Press, 2004), 9.
35. Edwards, *Early Reagan*, 43.
36. Reagan, *Reagan: A Life in Letters*, 9.
37. Jennings Brown, "How *A Charlie Brown Christmas* Almost Wasn't," *New York* magazine, November 16, 2016. In video interviews available online, Lee Mendelson would say he was almost certain the visitor from McCann-Erickson was Neil Reagan, the older brother of the future president. Given Mendelson's recollection, the management role Reagan held as head of the McCann-Erickson Los Angeles office, and the importance of the special to McCann since it was being sponsored by a premiere client—that is, Coca-Cola—it is very reasonable to assume the visitor was Reagan.
38. Celeste Headlee and Sean Powers, "How Coca-Cola Saved 'A Charlie Brown Christmas,'" GPB, December 20, 2017, https://www.gpb.org/news/2017/12/20/how-coca-cola-saved-charlie-brown-christmas.

The Jazz Musician

1. Derrick Bang, *Vince Guaraldi at the Piano* (McFarland & Company, 2012), 161.
2. Vince Guaraldi, *The Easy Peanuts Illustrated Songbook* (Hal Leonard, 2015), 13.
3. Paul Zollo, "How the Vince Guaraldi Trio Tune 'Linus and Lucy' Became an American Standard," *American Songwriter*, December 21, 2020, https://americansongwriter.com/how-vince-guaraldis-jazz-became-a-standard-because-of-charlie-brown.

4. Bang, *Vince Guaraldi at the Piano*, 119.
5. Zollo, "How the Vince Guaraldi Trio Tune 'Linus and Lucy' Became an American Standard."
6. Bang, *Vince Guaraldi at the Piano*, 119.
7. Bang, *Vince Guaraldi at the Piano*, 142.
8. Bang, *Vince Guaraldi at the Piano*, 142.
9. Bang, *Vince Guaraldi at the Piano*, 143.
10. "Religion: Heretic or Prophet?" *Time*, November 11, 1966.
11. Bang, *Vince Guaraldi at the Piano*, 148.
12. Bang, *Vince Guaraldi at the Piano*, 149.
13. "Grace Cathedral Architecture," Grace Cathedral website, n.d., https://gracecathedral.org/architecture.
14. Will Kane, "Grace Cathedral Replica Doors a Doorway to Italy," SFGate, June 18, 2012, https://www.sfgate.com/bayarea/article/Grace-Cathedral-replica-doors-a-doorway-to-Italy-3640981.php.
15. "Vince Guaraldi," Unconservatory, February 10, 2006, http://www.unconservatory.org/celam/guaraldibio.html.
16. Bang, *Vince Guaraldi at the Piano*, 149.
17. Bang, *Vince Guaraldi at the Piano*, 153.
18. "Selma to Montgomery March," Martin Luther King, Jr. Research and Education Institute website, n.d., https://kinginstitute.stanford.edu/encyclopedia/selma-montgomery-march.
19. A video of Martin Luther King Jr.'s sermon at Grace Cathedral can be found on YouTube. Also see "Martin Luther King Jr. Remembered at San Francisco's Grace Cathedral," ABC7 News, April 4, 2018, https://abc7news.com/grace-cathedral-martin-luther-king-jr-san-francisco-history-mlk-sermon-events/3302070; Katie Dowd, "On MLK Day, Remembering Martin Luther King Jr.'s San Francisco Sermon at Grace Cathedral," SFGate, January 16, 2017, https://www.sfgate.com/bayarea/article/MLK-Day-Martin-Luther-King-Jr-San-Francisco-10860349.php.
20. Bang, *Vince Guaraldi at the Piano*, 175–76.
21. Guaraldi, *The Easy Peanuts Illustrated Songbook*, 14.
22. Bang, *Vince Guaraldi at the Piano*, 183–84.
23. Bang, *Vince Guaraldi at the Piano*, 176, 187–88.

The Animators and Actors

1. Charles Solomon, *The Art and Making of Peanuts Animation: Celebrating Fifty Years of Television Specials* (Chronicle Books, 2012), 7.
2. Solomon, *The Art and Making of Peanuts Animation*, 26.
3. David Michaelis, *Schulz and Peanuts: A Biography* (HarperCollins, 2007), 357.
4. Lee Mendelson, *A Charlie Brown Christmas: The Making of a Tradition* (Harper Collins, 2000), 20, 24, 59.
5. Stephen J. Lind, *A Charlie Brown Religion: Exploring the Spiritual Life and Work of Charles M. Schulz* (University Press of Mississippi, 2015), 59.
6. Solomon, *The Art and Making of Peanuts Animation*, 19.
7. Charles M. Schulz, *Conversations* (University Press of Mississippi, 2000), 124.
8. Mendelson, *A Charlie Brown Christmas*, 43.
9. Solomon, *The Art and Making of Peanuts Animation*, 20.
10. Solomon, *The Art and Making of Peanuts Animation*, 27.
11. Solomon, *The Art and Making of Peanuts Animation*, 27.
12. Melendez ASIA interview.
13. Solomon, *The Art and Making of Peanuts Animation*, 25.
14. Amid Amidi, *Cartoon Modern: Style and Design in 1950's Animation* (Chronicle Books, 2006), 70.
15. Mendelson, *A Charlie Brown Christmas*, 57.
16. Mendelson, *A Charlie Brown Christmas*, 59.
17. Schulz, *Conversations*, 121–22.
18. Solomon, *The Art and Making of Peanuts Animation*, 22.
19. Mendelson, *A Charlie Brown Christmas*, 57.
20. Schulz, *Conversations*, 124.
21. Tom Sito interview with Bill Littlejohn, August 24, 2007.
22. Solomon, *The Art and Making of Peanuts Animation*, 13.
23. Solomon, *The Art and Making of Peanuts Animation*, 11.
24. See Adam Wernick and Ben Manilla, "The Music of Vince Guaraldi Helped Make 'A Charlie Brown Christmas' a Cultural Icon," *The World*, December 27, 2014, https://theworld.org/stories/2014-12-27/music-vince -guaraldi-helped-make-charlie-brown-christmas-cultural-icon.

25. See "Lee Mendelson, Producer," interview by Karen Herman, June 11, 2003, Television Academy Foundation website, https://interviews .televisionacademy.com/interviews/lee-mendelson.
26. Mendelson, *A Charlie Brown Christmas*, 23–24.

The Television Critic

1. Ronald A. Bergman, "Age Discrimination in Employment: Air Carriers," *Journal of Air Law and Commerce* 36, no. 1 (1970): 3–29.
2. "'Boeing Boeing' Opens," *New York Times*, December 24, 1965, 24.
3. American Airlines advertisement in *Fortune*, June 1965, 97.
4. Thomas E. Pierson, "American Airlines In-Flight Entertainment System," Paper 381 (October 1965), Audio Engineering Society.
5. "American Airlines Vol. 11 November 1965 Reel to Reel Tape," Archive .org, https://archive.org/details/AmericanAirlinesVol11November1965.
6. Robert Metz, *CBS: Reflections in a Bloodshot Eye* (Playboy Press, 1975), 243.
7. William S. Paley, *As It Happened: A Memoir by William S. Paley* (Doubleday, 1979), 342–43.
8. Lewis J. Paper, *Empire: William S. Paley and the Making of CBS* (St. Martin's Press, 1987), 248.
9. Paper, *Empire*, 248–49.
10. I identified Michael Dann and Irwin Segelstein as the likely executives in the meeting with Mendelson after reviewing the CBS Annual Report for 1965 (printed three months after Mendelson's meeting) which lists the top executives in all CBS departments, including the top twenty officers at the CBS Television Network, and then by eliminating all the officers who were in non-programming roles such as sales, public information, information services, etc. I was able to determine each executive's job function by cross-referencing another contemporaneous list found in *TV Factbook No. 37*, an industry reference book, which lists all CBS Television Network executives by job title and department. Dann and Segelstein would appear to be the top two programming executives that Mendelson referred to as being present.
11. Lee Mendelson, *A Charlie Brown Christmas: The Making of a Tradition* (HarperCollins, 2000), 27. Also see David Michaelis, *Schulz and Peanuts: A Biography*, 358.

12. Michaelis, *Schulz and Peanuts*, 358; Lee Mendelson, *Charlie Brown and Charlie Schulz* (World Publishing, 1970), 156.
13. Mendelson, *A Charlie Brown Christmas*, 29.
14. Mendelson, *Charlie Brown and Charlie Schulz*, 157.
15. *Washington University Magazine and Alumni News*, Summer 1996, 44.
16. Discussions of Mary Burgheim's life are from her obituary. See "Mary Burgheim; Was Teacher," *St. Louis Post-Dispatch*, January 18, 1996, 8.
17. Harvard Yearbook, 1955. The yearbook notes Burgheim's address as 6 Jaccord Lane, which is a typo; it should say 6 Jaccard Lane. Zillow provides information on the size of the home's lot. The 1940 census provides information on Burgheim's father's profession and the fact that a servant lived at the home.
18. Details on Nathan Burgheim's life are from his obituary in the *St. Louis Post-Dispatch*, "N.H. Burgheim; Executive and Civic Leader," November 8, 1965.
19. "Mary Institute and St. Louis Country Day School," Wikipedia, https://en.wikipedia.org/wiki/Mary_Institute_and_St._Louis_Country_Day_School.
20. Information on Burgheim's high school years is sourced from the St. Louis Country Day School yearbook, Codasco, 1951.
21. Harvard Yearbook, 1955.
22. Christopher Byron, *The Fanciest Dive: What Happened When the Media Empire of Time/Life Leaped without Looking into the Age of High-Tech* (W. W. Norton, 1986), 266.
23. "Nona Macdonald Wed to Richard Burgheim," *New York Times*, February 16, 1965, 32.
24. "Down the Tube: Fisco at Time, Inc.," *Washington Post*, February 23, 1986.
25. "Cinema: The New Pictures, Jan. 6, 1958," *Time*, January 6, 1958, 74.
26. Byron, *The Fanciest Dive*, 36.
27. See "Television: The Overstuffed Tube," *Time*, September 24, 1965.
28. James Landers, *The Weekly War: Newsmagazines and Vietnam* (University of Missouri Press, 2004), 55.
29. Lee Mendelson, *A Charlie Brown Christmas*, 29.
30. See *Time*, December 10, 1965.

31. "David Gahr, Photographer of Musicians, Dies at 85," *New York Times*, May 29, 2008.

32. Evan Andrews, "The Day Dylan Went Electric," History.com, July 24, 2015 (updated August 26, 2018), https://www.history.com/news/the-day-dylan-went-electric.

33. Mendelson, *A Charlie Brown Christmas*, 29.

34. Landers, *The Weekly War*, 15.

35. Landers, *The Weekly War*, 12.

36. David Michaelis, *Schulz and Peanuts: A Biography* (HarperCollins, 2007), 358.

37. Michaelis, *Schulz and Peanuts*, 359.

38. "Head of the Class," Game Show Pilot Light, n.d., http://www.usgameshows.net/x.php?show=HeadOfTheClass.

39. Richard F. Shepard, "N.B.C.-TV Cancels Series of Dramas," *New York Times*, July 18, 1963, 55.

The Audience

1. Stephen J. Lind, *A Charlie Brown Religion: Exploring the Spiritual Life and Work of Charles M. Schulz* (University Press of Mississippi, 2015), 73.

2. Charles Solomon, *The Art and Making of Peanuts Animation: Celebrating Fifty Years of Television Specials* (Chronicle Books, 2012), 11.

3. Lind, *A Charlie Brown Religion*, 76.

4. David Michaelis, *Schulz and Peanuts: A Biography* (HarperCollins, 2007), 360.

5. Conrad Groth, ed., *What Cartooning Really Is: The Major Interviews with Charles M. Schulz* (Fantagraphics Books, 2020), 213.

6. Daniel Victor, "Apple, After Outcry, Makes 'Peanuts' Holiday Specials Available on PBS," *New York Times*, November 19, 2020.

7. Lind, *A Charlie Brown Religion*, 70.

8. "Bay Area Producer Reflects on 'A Charlie Brown Christmas' 50th Anniversary," ABC 7 News, November 28, 2015, https://abc7news.com/lee-mendelson-a-charlie-brown-christmas-50th-anniversary-peanuts-charles-schulz/1102111.

Epilogue

1. "J.P. Austin Dead; Coca-Cola Leader," *New York Times*, December 27, 1985.

2. David Michaelis, *Schulz and Peanuts: A Biography* (HarperCollins, 2007), 377.

3. Nancy Reagan, *I Love You, Ronnie: The Letters of Ronald Reagan to Nancy Reagan* (Random House, 2001), 139.

4. "The Coup d'Etat at Interpublic," *Fortune*, February 1968.

5. "Advertising: Harper Out at Rosenfeld Post," *New York Times*, July 16, 1970.

6. "Marion Harper Jr., 73, a Leader in the Advertising Industry, Dies," *New York Times*, October 26, 1989.

7. "Neal Gilliatt Advertising Executive, 82," *New York Times*, September 23, 2000. See also "The Chief Marketing Officer: A Maverick Whose Time Has Come," *Business Horizons*, January–February 1986.

8. Christopher Byron, *The Fanciest Dive: What Happened When the Media Empire of Time/Life Leaped without Looking into the Age of High-Tech* (W. W. Norton, 1986), 205–6.

9. Brie Stimson, "'Charlie Brown' Voice Actor from 1965 Christmas Special Dead at 65," Fox News, January 26, 2022, https://www.foxnews.com/entertainment/charlie-brown-voice-actor-from-1965-christmas-special-dead-at-65.

10. Charles M. Schulz, *Conversations* (University Press of Mississippi, 2000), 186.

Author's Note

1. Charles M. Schulz, *Conversations* (University Press of Mississippi, 2000), 156.

2. Charles M. Schulz, *My Life with Charlie Brown* (University Press of Mississippi, 2010), 163.

3. Rheta Grimsley Johnson, *Good Grief: The Story of Charles M. Schulz* (Pharos Books, 1989), 39.

4. Schulz, *My Life with Charlie Brown*, 156.

5. Schulz, *My Life with Charlie Brown*, 13.

6. David Michaelis, *Schulz and Peanuts: A Biography* (HarperCollins, 2007), 146.
7. Charles M. Schulz, *The Complete Peanuts: 1965 to 1966* (Fantagraphics Books, 2007), 314.
8. Schulz, *My Life with Charlie Brown*, 66.
9. Schulz, *The Complete Peanuts: 1965 to 1966*, 67.
10. Schulz, *My Life with Charlie Brown*, 13.
11. French legionnaire Snoopy was introduced on August 22, 1965.
12. Conrad Groth, ed., *What Cartooning Really Is: The Major Interviews with Charles M. Schulz* (Fantagraphics Books, 2020), 37–38.

ABOUT THE AUTHOR

Michael Keane is an adjunct professor at Pepperdine University's School of Public Policy and a former professor at the University of Southern California. He is the author of the illustrated children's Christmas book *The Night Santa Got Lost* and is a former executive with Digital Domain, a leading visual effects and digital film studio in Hollywood. Keane has also worked in military affairs and was selected as a fellow for the Department of Defense's highly competitive National Security Education Program.